THE WORLD'S CLASSICS

535

PLAYS & PLAYERS

Oxford University Press, Amen House, London E.C.4

GLASGOW NEW YORK TORONTO MELBOURNE WELLINGTON
BOMBAY CALCUTTA MADRAS KARACHI LAHORE DACCA
CAPE TOWN SALISBURY NAIROBI IBADAN ACCRA
KUALA LUMPUR HONG KONG

BERNARD SHAW

PLAYS & PLAYERS

ESSAYS ON THE THEATRE

Selected
with an Introduction by
A. C. WARD

LONDON
OXFORD UNIVERSITY PRESS

BERNARD SHAW

Born: Dublin 26 July 1856
Died: Ayot St. Lawrence, Hertfordshire
2 November 1950

Bernard Shaw was dramatic critic to The Saturday Review *from* 5 *January* 1895 *to* 21 *May* 1898. *His writings in that capacity were collected in three volumes, as* Our Theatres in the Nineties, *in* 1931. *The present selection for* The World's Classics *was first published in* 1952 *and reprinted in* 1955, 1958, *and* 1963

PRINTED IN GREAT BRITAIN

Contents

CONTENTS

Introduction

'It is the capacity for making good or bad art a personal matter that makes a man a critic. . . . When people do less than their best, and do that less at once badly and self-complacently, I hate them, loathe them, detest them, long to tear them limb from limb and strew them in gobbets about the stage or platform. . . . In the same way, really fine artists inspire me with the warmest personal regard. . . . When my critical mood is at its height, personal feeling is not the word: it is passion: the passion for artistic perfection—for the noblest beauty of sound, sight, and action—that rages in me.'—Bernard Shaw in *The World*, 3 September 1890 (reprinted in *Music in London 1890–94*, vol. i, p. 54, 1931).

THERE is much of Shaw himself in the John Tanner of *Man and Superman*, particularly in the speech telling of the birth in him of 'moral passion'. Tanner speaks also of the passion of the artist and the passion of the thinker, and in these three passions—moral passion, aesthetic passion, intellectual passion—are the roots of Shaw's uniqueness as a critic. In all his writings he was, consistently and persistently, a critic: a critic of art, a critic of life. Art in any form was to him a function of life, and as a creator, in his plays, he employed the shaping hand of the artist upon the raw material of experience.

It is less controversial and therefore less time-wasting to speak of Shaw's uniqueness among dramatic critics, than of his pre-eminence. There is no infallible criterion of judgement to determine whether he is better or less good than Hazlitt, Leigh Hunt, Lamb, or any other of the notable writers on plays and acting; but it is beyond question that no one else has written dramatic criticism *like* Shaw's, though not for want of trying. Those who have attempted to imitate him have failed through the false assumption that Shaw's renown as a critic depended upon the exploitation of his own personality: that egoism and impudence, with a saucing of epigram and paradox, constituted his stock-in-trade, and would therefore be equipment enough for any youngster setting up as a critic.

If Shaw appeared to exploit his own personality it was not only because his personality was unique in essence. It was, not less importantly, a personality sustained by knowledge, integrity, passion for the good and hatred of the bad, coupled with the ability to weigh and consider justly the bad as well as the good. He was attentive and courteous to lesser wits, observing well before he judged; and when he crusaded —as he did in the direction of Henry Irving—he chose an opponent well armed and armoured.

What Shaw saw and heard in the theatre on any occasion might seem to him absurd; nevertheless the absurdity had to be analysed and reasons given coolly for the verdict pronounced. Thus, in the article headed 'Satan Saved at Last' (see below, p. 161) he examines the stage version of Marie Corelli's *The Sorrows of Satan* with as much attention and care as he gave on other occasions to Ibsen and to Henry James. Indeed, it is probable that Shaw was the only first-rate critic who ever took Marie Corelli seriously. From her great host of admirers she received adulation, from her detractors scorn; but the adulation and the scorn were alike uncritical. Though Shaw judged *The Sorrows of Satan* to be unreal, impossible, philosophically incoherent, and morally absurd, these were quite other than hasty impressions. 'Let me not', he says, 'dismiss The Sorrows of Satan too cavalierly; for I take Miss Marie Corelli to be one of the most sincere and independent writers at present before the public.' This is characteristic of the invariable intellectual courtesy with which Shaw approached his duties as a critic. He might reach the conclusion that an author or an actor was an incompetent or a nincompoop or a numskull. If he did, he would express the opinion with energy, but not without producing the evidence or assigning reasons to support the conclusion. Courtesy of this kind—rooted in the conviction that every piece of work has an inalienable right to fair and informed judgement—can only be exercised by a critic with an outward-reaching mind which gathers knowledge from every quarter. Anyone coming to Shaw's dramatic essays without preparation or prejudice cannot but be impressed both by the range and depth of his knowledge and by his genuine *interest* in the things about which he was knowledgeable: not only 'important' things such as the poetry of Shakespeare, the searching intellect of Ibsen, and thence onward to God's purposes with His creatures, but also so 'unimportant' a thing as skirt-dancing. Behind it all was Shaw's certainty that whatever Man does should be done, in effect, to the glory of God. In other words, human duty and honour demand from every individual a stretching towards perfection in the thing attempted. A skirt-dancer's function is to be a 'good' (i.e. technically perfect) skirt-dancer. So, having sat out a musical farce in which there was inefficient skirt-dancing, Shaw discourses instructively on that art, first presenting, as it were, his credentials:

The formula for criticizing a dancer is simple enough. At the two extremes of the art are the step-dancer who dances with the feet alone, with spine rigid, shoulders pushed up to the top of it and nailed hard there, fists clinched, neck stiff as iron, and head held convulsively as if only the most violent effort of continence on the dancer's part could keep it from exploding. At the other you have the perfect dancer along whose limbs the rhythmic stream flows unbroken to the very tips of the fingers and roots of the hair, whose head moves beautifully, whose nape and wrists make the music visible, who can flex the spine at each vertebra more certainly than an ordinary person can flex his finger at each joint, and who is the personification of skill, grace, strength, and health.[1]

Irving's production of Comyns Carr's *King Arthur* at the Lyceum in January 1895 led Shaw to discourse on the new realistic fashion of staging and costuming in terms which show that his knowledge ranged as easily among the works of early and later Italian painters and architects as among the performances of dancers. But having praised the mounting and dressing of *King Arthur*, in that third week of his career as a dramatic critic he presented what was to be the burden of his case against Irving in the years ahead:

. . . my own art, the art of literature, is left shabby and ashamed amid the triumph of the arts of the painter and the actor. I sometimes wonder where Mr Irving will go when he dies—whether he will dare to claim, as a master artist, to walk where he may any day meet Shakespear whom he has mutilated, Goethe whom he has travestied [in an adaptation of *Faust* by W. G. Wills], and the nameless creator of the hero-king [Arthur] out of whose mouth he has uttered jobbing verses.

In view of the often repeated assertion that Shaw persistently belittled Irving, it is worth noting that in this passage he concedes him the rank of a master artist, while in the following lines he goes on to speak of him as rising 'to the height of his art' and as

[1] 'A Musical Farce' (*A Man About Town*, by Huan Mee and Alfred Carpenter. Avenue Theatre, London, 2 January 1897): *The Saturday Review*, 9 January 1897; *Our Theatres in the Nineties*, vol. iii, pp. 8 ff.

impersonating King Arthur 'with the noblest feeling, and the most sensitive refinement of execution'.

Shaw was constantly aware of Irving's greatness and never dissembled his awareness. Indeed, he declared it by casting Irving for the part Shaw thought most important in the theatre of that time: the part of the saviour of dramatic literature—through Shakespeare and Ibsen. The greatest living actor, he claimed, should *serve* the greatest playwright of the sixteenth century and the greatest playwright of the nineteenth century. Irving, on the other hand, looked upon playwrights as servants of the actor, and upon their works as stuff to be pressed into the mould of the actor's personality. If in the pressing the work became distorted, no matter. Though Irving was the most prolific and the most important producer of Shakespeare through several decades, he had no practical respect for the plays as Shakespeare wrote them. He cut and patched to suit his own taste, his own abilities, his own idiosyncrasies, his own limitations. The public approved and applauded; Shaw objected.

Shaw was passionately convinced that Shakespeare's genius lay in mastery of word music, in the magic of poetry. Why, Shaw asks,

> ... why should we, the heirs of so many greater ages, with the dramatic poems of Goethe and Ibsen in our hands, and the music of a great dynasty of musicians, from Bach to Wagner, in our ears—why should we waste our time on the rank and file of the Elizabethans, or encourage foolish modern persons to imitate them, or talk about Shakespear as if his moral platitudes, his jingo claptraps, his tavern pleasantries, his bombast and drivel, and his incapacity for following up the scraps of philosophy he stole so aptly, were as admirable as the mastery of poetic speech, the feeling for nature, and the knack of character-drawing,

fun, and heart wisdom which he was ready, like a true son of the theatre, to prostitute to any subject, any occasion, and any theatrical employment?[1]

To those whose attachment to Shakespeare is strongly emotional this attitude may still appear outrageous; and insufficient heed will still be given to Shaw's praise of the poetry, of the feeling for nature, of the character-drawing, fun, and heart wisdom—no small allowance of grace. It has to be appreciated that on the stage in the eighteen-nineties Shakespeare the poet was subordinated to Shakespeare-the-anything-and-everything-else that suited the actor-managers' quirks. Again and again Shaw drew attention to Shakespeare's virtues: 'his gift of telling a story . . . his enormous power over language . . . his humor; his sense of idiosyncratic character; and his prodigious fund of . . . vital energy';[2] 'as far as sonority, imagery, wit, humor, energy of imagination, power over language, and a whimsically keen eye for idiosyncrasies can make a dramatist, Shakespear was the king of dramatists'.[3] Shaw's quarrel with the current literary interpreters rested upon his refusal to accept Shakespeare as 'a man of ideas' serviceable to the nineteenth–twentieth century. The contemporary stage, in Shaw's judgement, was an intellectual vacuum; and, as he saw it, actors and managers with a vested interest in the vacuum were holding off the one contemporary playwright, Ibsen, whose ideas could fill it. When, occasionally, some non-commercial organization staged an Ibsen play, Shaw's determination to encourage the enterprise could incite him to welcome the players as the 'revealers to London of a much greater dramatist

[1] See below, p. 108–9.
[2] p. 116.
[3] p. 292.

than Shakespear'[1]—greater, that is to say, as a man of ideas valid and fruitful in contemporary life.

In retrospect the battle between Shaw and Irving (a battle in which Irving was for the most part a passive resister) can be seen as a comedy of misconceptions in which both were equally at fault, both equally right. Shaw was right in principle in asking for Shakespeare unIrvingized; he was right in wishing to link the greatest living playwright, Ibsen, with the greatest living English actor, Irving. But Shaw was wrong in so far as he singled out for his purposes an inappropriate human instrument. Irving was nobody's instrument but his own. To do Shakespeare as Shaw wanted Shakespeare done, or to do Ibsen at all, Irving would have needed to sink his own personality in theirs. And Irving, like Shaw, was unsinkable. If Irving had been interested enough and had had the necessary impudent wit, he would have counter-attacked by asking that Shaw should write plays according to the Irving formula. It would have been no more unreasonable, however highly undesirable, to invite Shaw to subject himself to Irving's acting needs than to expect Irving to conform to Shaw's literary and sociological ideals.

Irving did what he could do and did it superbly, however great a misfortune it might have been that the higher reaches of poetry and moral and social zeal were beyond his interests and powers, and that romantic gimcrackery served his abilities and satisfied his ambitions.

There are two ways at least of selecting effectively from Bernard Shaw's *Our Theatres in the Nineties*. One is to pick, like stones from their setting, all the

[1] See p. 234.

brilliant passages, all the epigrams and paradoxes, all the comic asides—in short, all the scintillation and all the fun. The other way is to take each of the weekly articles that Shaw wrote for *The Saturday Review* from 5 January 1895 to 21 May 1898 as a unit not to be fractured, and to select only whole units, even when portions treat of plays and players now obscure or forgotten. The second way has been taken here. It is thus possible to offer a fairly representative cross-section of English theatre history in the eighteen-nineties, and also to demonstrate Shaw's gift of writing intelligently and illuminatingly—often on larger matters branching from trifles—even when the subject imposed on him by the week's plays was neither intelligent nor luminous. The material in the present book does in fact bear upon the major figures, alive or dead, whose work sustained the London theatres in the last years of the nineteenth century: Shakespeare, Ibsen, Oscar Wilde, Pinero, Henry Arthur Jones; Irving, Ellen Terry, Mrs. Patrick Campbell, Forbes Robertson, Beerbohm Tree, George Alexander, Lewis Waller, Janet Achurch, Elizabeth Robins, Irene Vanbrugh, Julia Neilson; with Duse and Bernhardt as distinguished visitors.

No doubt it is inevitable that, being written by men of letters, dramatic criticism should often show a disproportionate leaning towards the play and an insufficient concern with the players. 'Unlike most critics', said Shaw, 'I am fond of acting', and the enjoyment provided by his theatre criticisms comes largely from that fondness, supported by the ability to distinguish between good acting and bad and to analyse the characteristics of both. Though he was never a professional actor, experienced professionals have made it known that at rehearsals of his own plays Shaw could always supply a masterly illustrative performance of any effect or interpretation he desired of an actor—or of an actress. In the essays that follow, his enthusiasm is matched by his knowledge of the art and craft of acting: he could teach when teaching was to the point; he could admire with a just and touching generosity when fine personal art enchanted him, as the art of the Terrys did. Among the actresses of his day it was to Ellen Terry that his heart opened widest, though at a distance safe to both. It was on her account that he named Irving 'our national theatrical Minotaur' (p. 182), without convincing Ellen Terry that she was the sacrifice, yet also without diminishing her admiration and warm regard for Shaw himself. On her list of friends found after Ellen Terry's death in 1928 Shaw's name stood second, preceded only by that of Charles Reade.

March 1952 A. C. WARD

This selection from Bernard Shaw's theatre essays has been compiled by permission of the Public Trustee and the Society of Authors.

Two New Plays

GUY DOMVILLE. *A play in three acts. By* Henry James. *St James's Theatre, 5 January* 1895.

AN IDEAL HUSBAND. *A new and original play of modern life. By* Oscar Wilde. *Haymarket Theatre, 3 January* 1895.

[12 *January* 1895][1]

THE truth about Mr James's play is no worse than that it is out of fashion. Any dramatically disposed young gentleman who, cultivating sentiment on a little alcohol, and gaining an insight to the mysteries of the eternal feminine by a couple of squalid intrigues, meanwhile keeps well aloof from art and philosophy, and thus preserves his innocence of the higher life of the senses and of the intellect, can patch up a play tomorrow which will pass as real drama with the gentlemen who deny that distinction to the works of Mr Henry James. No doubt, if the literary world were as completely dominated by the admirers of Mr Rider Haggard as the dramatic world is by their first cousins, we should be told that Mr James cannot write a novel. That is not criticism: it is a mere begging of the question. There is no reason why life as we find it in Mr James's novels—life, that is, in which passion is subordinate to intellect and to fastidious artistic taste—should not be represented on the stage. If it is real to Mr James, it must be real to others; and why should not these others have their drama instead of being banished from the theatre (to the theatre's great loss) by the monotony and

[1] Date of publication in the *Saturday Review.*

vulgarity of drama in which passion is everything, intellect nothing, and art only brought in by the incidental outrages upon it. As it happens, I am not myself in Mr James's camp: in all the life that has energy enough to be interesting to me, subjective volition, passion, will, make intellect the merest tool. But there is in the centre of that cyclone a certain calm spot where cultivated ladies and gentlemen live on independent incomes or by pleasant artistic occupations. It is there that Mr James's art touches life, selecting whatever is graceful, exquisite, or dignified in its serenity. It is not life as imagined by the pit or gallery, or even by the stalls: it is, let us say, the ideal of the balcony; but that is no reason why the pit and gallery should excommunicate it on the ground that it has no blood and entrails in it, and have its sentence formulated for it by the fiercely ambitious and wilful professional man in the stalls. The whole case against its adequacy really rests on its violation of the cardinal stage convention that love is the most irresistible of all the passions. Since most people go to the theatre to escape from reality, this convention is naturally dear to a world in which love, all powerful in the secret, unreal, day-dreaming life of the imagination, is in the real active life the abject slave of every trifling habit, prejudice, and cowardice, easily stifled by shyness, class feeling, and pecuniary prudence, or diverted from what is theatrically assumed to be its hurricane course by such obstacles as a thick ankle, a cockney accent, or an unfashionable hat. In the face of this, is it good sense to accuse Mr Henry James of a want of grip on the realities of life because he gives us a hero who sacrifices his love to a strong and noble vocation for the Church? And yet when some unmannerly playgoer, untouched by either love or religion, chooses to send a derisive howl from the gallery at such a situation, we are to sorrowfully admit, if you please, that Mr James is no dramatist, on the general ground that 'the drama's laws the drama's patrons give.' Pray, which of its patrons?—the cultivated majority who, like myself and all the ablest of my colleagues, applauded Mr James on Saturday, or the handful of rowdies who brawled at him? It is the business of the dramatic critic to educate these dunces, not to echo them.

Admitting, then, that Mr James's dramatic authorship is valid, and that his plays are *du théâtre* when the right people are in the theatre, what are the qualities and faults of Guy Domville? First among the qualities, a rare charm of speech. Line after line comes with such a delicate turn and fall that I unhesitatingly challenge any of our popular dramatists to write a scene in verse with half the beauty of Mr James's prose. I am not now speaking of the verbal fitness, which is a matter of careful workmanship merely. I am speaking of the delicate inflexions of feeling conveyed by the cadences of the line, inflexions and cadences which, after so long a course of the ordinary theatrical splashes and daubs of passion and emphasis, are as grateful to my ear as the music of Mozart's Entführung aus dem Serail would be after a year of Ernani and Il Trovatore. Second, Guy Domville is a story, and not a mere situation hung out on a gallows of plot. And it is a story of fine sentiment and delicate manners, with an entirely worthy and touching ending. Third, it relies on the performers, not for the brute force of their personalities and popularities, but for their finest accomplishments in grace of manner, delicacy of diction, and dignity of style. It is pleasant to be able to add that this reliance, rash as it undeniably is in these days, was not disappointed. Mr Alexander, having been treated little better than a tailor's dummy by Mr Wilde, Mr Pinero, and Mr Henry Arthur Jones successively, found himself treated as an artist by Mr James, and repaid the compliment, not only, as his manager, by charming eighteenth-century stage setting of the piece, but, as actor, by his fine execution of the principal part, which he touched with great skill and judgment. Miss Marion Terry, as Mrs Peveril, was altogether charming, every movement, every tone, harmonized perfectly with the dainty grace and feeling of her lines. In fact, had the second act been equal to the first and third, and the acting as fine throughout as in the scenes between Mr Alexander and Miss Terry (in which, by the way, they were well supported by Mr Waring), the result would have been less doubtful. It will be a deplorable misfortune if Guy Domville does not hold the stage long enough to justify Mr Alexander's enterprise in producing it.

Unfortunately, the second act dissolved the charm rather badly; and what was more, the actors felt it. The Falstaffian make-up of Mrs Saker, and the senseless drunken scene, which Mr Alexander played with the sobriety of desperation, made fuss instead of drama; and the dialogue, except for a brief and very pretty episode in which Miss Millard and Mr Esmond took part, fell off into mere rococo. Little of this act can be remembered with pleasure except Miss Millard's 'Forgive me a little,' and a few cognate scraps of dialogue. It had better have been left out, and the wanderings of the prodigal taken for granted. And, to weight it still further, it contained a great deal of the gentleman who played Lord Devenish, and played him just as he might have played an elderly marquis in a comic opera, grimacing over a snuff-box, and withering all sense and music out of Mr James's lines with a diction which I forbear to describe. He was very largely responsible for the irritation which subsequently vented itself on the author; and I am far from sure that I ought not to borrow a weapon from the Speaker of the House of Commons, and go to the extreme length of naming him.

Guy Domville is preceded by a farce (called in the bill a comedy) by Julian Field, entitled Too Happy by Half. It is deftly turned out from old and seasoned materials, and is capital fun for the audience and for Mr Esmond and Miss Millard. Miss Millard is not yet quite experienced enough to do very easy work quite well: she is the least bit crude occasionally.

Mr Oscar Wilde's new play at the Haymarket is a dangerous subject, because he has the property of making his critics dull. They laugh angrily at his epigrams, like a child who is coaxed into being amused in the very act of setting up a yell of rage and agony. They protest that the trick is obvious, and that such epigrams can be turned out by the score by any one lightminded enough to condescend to such frivolity. As far as I can ascertain, I am the only person in London who cannot sit down and write an Oscar Wilde play at will. The fact that his plays, though apparently lucrative, remain unique under these circumstances, says much for the self-denial of our scribes. In a certain sense Mr Wilde is to me our only thorough playwright. He plays with everything: with wit, with philosophy, with drama, with actors and audience, with the whole theatre. Such a feat scandalizes the Englishman, who can no more play with wit and philosophy than he can with a football or a cricket bat. He works at both, and has the consolation, if he cannot make people laugh, of being the best cricketer and footballer in the world. Now it is the mark of the artist that he will not work. Just as people with social ambitions will practise the meanest economies in order to live expensively; so the artist will starve his way through incredible toil and discouragement sooner than go and earn a week's honest wages. Mr Wilde, an arch-artist, is so colossally lazy that he trifles even with the work by which an artist escapes work. He distils the very quintessence, and gets as product plays which are so unapproachably playful that they are the delight of every playgoer with twopenn'orth of brains. The English critic, always protesting that the drama should not be didactic, and yet always complaining if the dramatist does not find sermons in stones and good in everything, will be conscious of a subtle and pervading levity in An Ideal Husband. All the literary dignity of the play, all the imperturbable good sense and good manners with which Mr Wilde makes his wit pleasant to his comparatively stupid audience, cannot quite overcome the fact that Ireland is of all countries the most foreign to England, and that to the Irishman (and Mr Wilde is almost as acutely Irish an Irishman as the Iron Duke of Wellington) there is nothing in the world quite so exquisitely comic as an Englishman's seriousness. It becomes tragic, perhaps, when the Englishman acts on it; but that occurs too seldom to be taken into account, a fact which intensifies the humor of the situation, the total result being the Englishman utterly unconscious of his real self, Mr Wilde keenly observant of it and playing on the self-unconsciousness with irresistible humor, and finally, of course, the Englishman annoyed with himself for being amused at his own expense, and for being unable to convict Mr Wilde of what seems an obvious misunderstanding of human nature. He is shocked, too, at the danger to the foundations of society when seriousness is publicly laughed at. And to complete the oddity of the situation, Mr Wilde, touching what he himself reverences, is absolutely the most sentimental dramatist of the day.

It is useless to describe a play which has no thesis: which is, in the purest integrity, a play and nothing less. The six worst epigrams are mere alms handed with a kind smile to the average suburban playgoer; the three best remain secrets between Mr Wilde and a few choice spirits. The modern note is struck in Sir Robert Chiltern's assertion of the individuality and courage of his wrongdoing as against the mechanical idealism of his stupidly good wife, and in his bitter criticism of a love that is only the reward of merit. It is from the philosophy on which this scene is based that the most pregnant epigrams in the play have been condensed. Indeed, this is the only philosophy that ever has produced epigrams. In contriving the stage expedients by which the action of the piece is kept going, Mr Wilde has been once or twice a little too careless of stage illusion: for example, why on earth should Mrs Cheveley, hiding in Lord Goring's room, knock down a chair? That is my sole criticism.

The performance is very amusing. The audience laughs conscientiously: each person comes to the theatre prepared, like a special artist, with the background of a laugh ready sketched in on his or her features. Some of the performers labor intensely at being epigrammatic. I am sure Miss Vane Featherstone and Miss Forsyth could play Lady Macbeth and Medea with less effort than Lady Basildon and Mrs Marchmont, who have nothing to do but sit on a sofa and be politely silly for ten minutes. There is no doubt that these glimpses of expensive receptions in Park Lane, with the servants announcing titles *ad libitum*, are enormously attractive to social outsiders (say ninety-nine hundredths of us); but the stage reproduction is not convincing: everybody has an outrageous air of being at a party; of not being used to it; and, worst of all, of enjoying themselves immensely. Mr Charles Hawtrey has the best of the fun among the principals. As everyone's guide, philosopher, and friend, he has moments in which he is, I think, intended to be deep, strong, and tender. These moments, to say the least, do not quite come off; but his lighter serious episodes are excellent, and his drollery conquers without effort. When Miss Neilson sits still and lets her gifts of beauty and grace be eloquent for her, she is highly satisfying; but I cannot say the same for the passages in which she has to take the stage herself and try to act. She becomes merely artificial and superficially imitative. Miss Fanny Brough makes Lady Markby, an eminently possible person, quite impossible; and Miss Maude Millet, playing very well indeed as Mabel Chiltern, nevertheless occasionally spoils a word by certain vowel sounds which are only permissible to actresses of the second rank. As an adventuress who, like the real and unlike the stage adventuress, is not in love with any one, and is simply selfish, dishonest, and third rate, Miss Florence West is kinetoscopically realistic. The portrait is true to nature; but it has no artistic character: Miss West has not the art of being agreeably disagreeable. Mr Brookfield, a great artist in small things, makes the valet in the third act one of the heroes of the performance. And Mr Waller is handsome and dignified as the ideal husband, a part easily within his means. His management could not have been more auspiciously inaugurated.

Poor Shakespear!

ALL'S WELL THAT ENDS WELL. *Performance by the Irving Dramatic Club at St George's Hall,* 22 *and* 24 *January* 1895.

[2 *February* 1895]

WHAT a pity it is that the people who love the sound of Shakespear so seldom go on the stage! The ear is the sure clue to him: only a musician can understand the play of feeling which is the real rarity in his early plays. In a deaf nation these plays would have died long ago. The moral attitude in them is conventional and secondhand: the borrowed ideas, however finely expressed, have not the overpowering human interest of those original criticisms of life which supply the rhetorical element in his later works. Even the individualization which produces that old-established British speciality, the Shakespearean 'delineation of character,' owes all its magic to the turn of the line, which lets you into the secret of its utterer's mood and temperament, not by its commonplace meaning, but by some subtle exaltation, or stultification, or slyness, or delicacy, or hesitancy, or what not in the sound of it. In short, it is the score and not the libretto that keeps the work alive and fresh; and this is why only musical critics should be allowed to meddle with Shakespear—especially early Shakespear. Unhappily, though the nation still retains its ears, the players and playgoers of this generation are for the most part deaf as adders. Their appreciation of Shakespear is sheer hypocrisy, the proof being that where an early play of his is revived, they take the utmost pains to suppress as much of it as possible, and disguise the rest past recognition, relying for success on extraordinary scenic attractions; on very popular performers, including, if possible, a famously beautiful actress in the leading part; and, above all, on Shakespear's reputation and the consequent submission of the British public to be mercilessly bored by each of his plays once in their lives, for the sake of being able to say they have seen it. And not a soul has the hardihood to yawn in the face of the imposture. The manager is praised; the bard is praised; the beautiful actress is praised; and the free list comes early and comes often, not without a distinct sense of conferring a handsome compliment on the acting manager. And it certainly is hard to face such a disappointment without being paid for it. For the more enchanting the play is at home by the fireside in winter, or out on the heather of a summer evening—the more the manager, in his efforts to realize this enchantment by reckless expenditure on incidental music, colored lights, dances, dresses, and elaborate rearrangements and dislocations of the play—the more, in fact, he departs from the old platform with its curtains and its placards inscribed 'A street in Mantua,' and so forth, the more hopelessly and vulgarly does he miss his mark. Such crown jewels of dramatic poetry as Twelfth Night and A Midsummer Night's Dream, fade into shabby colored glass in his purse; and sincere people who do not know what the matter is, begin to babble insufferably about plays that are meant for the study and not for the stage.

Yet once in a blue moon or so there wanders on to the stage some happy fair whose eyes are lodestars and whose tongue's sweet air's more tunable than lark to shepherd's ear. And the moment she strikes up the true Shakespearean music, and feels her way to her part altogether by her sense of that music, the play returns to life and all the magic is there. She may make nonsense of the verses by wrong conjunctions and misplaced commas, which shew that she has never worked out the logical construction of a single sentence in her part; but if her heart is in the song, the protesting commentator-critic may save his breath to cool his porridge: the soul of the play is there, no matter where the sense of it may be. We have all heard Miss Rehan perform this miracle with Twelfth Night, and turn it, in spite of the impossible Mr Daly, from a hopelessly ineffective actress show into something like the exquisite poem its author left it. All I can remember of the last performance I witnessed of A Midsummer Night's Dream is that Miss Kate Rorke got on the stage somehow and began to make some music with Helena's lines, with the result that Shakespear, who had up to that moment lain without sense or motion, immediately began to stir uneasily and shew signs of quickening, which lasted until the others took up the word and struck him dead.

Powerful among the enemies of Shakespear are the commentator and the elocutionist: the commentator because, not knowing Shakespear's language, he sharpens his reasoning faculty to examine propositions advanced by an eminent lecturer from the Midlands, instead of sensitizing his artistic faculty to receive the impression of moods and inflexions of feeling conveyed by word-music; the elocutionist because he is a born fool, in which capacity, observing with pain that poets have a weakness for imparting to their dramatic dialogue a quality which he describes and deplores as 'sing-song,' he devotes his life to the art of breaking up verse in such a way as to make it sound like insanely pompous prose. The effect of this on Shakespear's earlier verse, which is full of the naïve delight of pure oscillation, to be enjoyed as an Italian enjoys a barcarolle, or a child a swing, or a baby a rocking-cradle, is destructively stupid. In the later plays, where the barcarolle measure has evolved into much more varied and complex rhythms, it does not matter so much, since the work is no longer simple enough for a fool to pick to pieces. But in every play from Love's Labour 's Lost to Henry V, the elocutionist meddles simply as a murderer, and ought to be dealt with as such without benefit of clergy. To our young people studying for the stage I say, with all solemnity, learn how to pronounce the English alphabet clearly and beautifully from some person who is at once an artist and a phonetic expert. And then leave blank verse patiently alone until you have experienced emotion deep enough to crave for poetic expression, at which point verse will seem an absolutely natural and real form of speech to you. Meanwhile, if any pedant, with an uncultivated heart and a theoretic ear, proposes to teach you to recite, send instantly for the police.

Among Shakespear's earlier plays, All 's Well that Ends Well stands out artistically by the sovereign charm of the young Helena and the old Countess of Rousillon, and intellectually by the experiment, repeated nearly three hundred years later in A Doll's House, of making the hero a perfectly ordinary young man, whose unimaginative prejudices and selfish conventionality make him cut a very fine mean figure in the atmosphere created by the nobler nature of his wife. That is what gives a certain plausibility to the otherwise doubtful tradition that Shakespear did not succeed in getting his play produced (founded on the absence of any record of a performance of it during his lifetime). It certainly explains why Phelps, the only modern actor-manager tempted by it, was attracted by the part of Parolles, a capital study of the adventurous yarn-spinning society-struck coward, who also crops up again in modern fiction as the hero of Charles Lever's underrated novel, A Day's Ride: a Life's Romance. When I saw All's Well announced for performance by the Irving Dramatic Club, I was highly interested, especially as the performers were free, for once, to play Shakespear for Shakespear's sake. Alas! at this amateur performance, at which there need have been none of the miserable commercialization compulsory at the regular theatres, I suffered all the vulgarity and absurdity of that commercialism without its efficiency. We all know the stock objection of the Brixton Family Shakespear to All's Well—that the heroine is a lady doctor, and that no lady of any delicacy could possibly adopt a profession which involves the possibility of her having to attend cases such as that of the king in this play, who suffers from a fistula. How any sensible and humane person can have ever read this sort of thing without a deep sense of its insult to every charitable woman's humanity and every sick man's suffering is, fortunately, getting harder to understand nowadays than it once was. Nevertheless All's Well was minced with strict deference to it for the members of the Irving Dramatic Club. The rule for expurgation was to omit everything that the most pestiferously prurient person could find improper. For example, when the non-commissioned officer, with quite becoming earnestness and force, says to the disgraced Parolles: 'If you could find out a country where but women were that had received so much shame, you might begin an impudent nation,' the speech was suppressed as if it were on all fours with the obsolete Elizabethan badinage which is and should be cut out as a matter of course. And to save Helena from anything so shocking as a reference to her virginity, she was robbed of that rapturous outburst beginning

> There shall your master have a thousand loves—
> A mother and a mistress and a friend, etc.

But perhaps this was sacrificed in deference to the opinion of the editor of those pretty and handy little books called the Temple Shakespear, who compares the passage to 'the nonsense of some foolish conceited player'—a criticism which only a commentator could hope to live down.

The play was, of course, pulled to pieces in order that some bad scenery, totally unconnected with Florence or Rousillon, might destroy all the illusion which the simple stage directions in the book create, and which they would equally have created had they been printed on a placard and hung up on a curtain. The passage of the Florentine army beneath the walls of the city was managed in the manner of the end of the first act of Robertson's Ours, the widow and the girls looking out of their sitting-room window, whilst a few of the band gave a precarious selection from the orchestral parts of Berlioz's version of the Rackoczy March. The dresses were the usual fancy ball odds and ends, Helena especially distinguishing herself by playing the first scene partly in the costume of Hamlet and partly in that of a waitress in an Aerated Bread shop, set off by a monstrous auburn wig which could by no stretch of imagination be taken for her own hair. Briefly, the whole play was vivisected, and the fragments mutilated, for the sake of accessories which were in every particular silly and ridiculous. If they were meant to heighten the illusion, they were worse than failures, since they rendered illusion almost impossible. If they were intended as illustrations of place and period, they were ignorant impostures. I have seen poetic plays performed without costumes before a pair of curtains by ladies and gentlemen in evening dress with twenty times the effect: nay, I will pledge my reputation that if the members of the Irving Dramatic Club will take their books in their hands, sit in a Christy Minstrel semicircle, and read the play decently as it was written, the result will be a vast improvement on this St George's Hall travesty.

Perhaps it would not be altogether kind to leave these misguided but no doubt well-intentioned ladies and gentlemen without a word of appreciation from their own point of view. Only, there is not much to be said for them even from that point of view. Few living actresses could throw themselves into the sustained transport of exquisite tenderness and impulsive courage which makes poetry the natural speech of Helena. The cool young woman, with a superior understanding, excellent manners, and a habit of reciting Shakespear, presented before us by Miss Olive Kennett, could not conceivably have been even Helena's thirty-second cousin. Miss Lena Heinekey, with the most beautiful old woman's part ever written in her hands, discovered none of its wonderfully pleasant good sense, humanity, and originality: she grieved stagily all through in the manner of the

Duchess of York in Cibber's Richard III. Mr Lewin-Mannering did not for any instant make it possible to believe that Parolles was a real person to him. They all insisted on calling him *parole*, instead of Parolles, in three syllables, with the *s* sounded at the end, as Shakespear intended: consequently, when he came to the couplet which cannot be negotiated on any other terms:

> Rust, sword; cool, blushes; and, Parolles, thrive;
> Theres place and means for every man alive,

he made a desperate effort to get even with it by saying:

> Rust, rapier; cool, blushes; and, *parole*, thrive,

and seemed quite disconcerted when he found that it would not do. Lafeu is hardly a part that can be acted: it comes right if the right man is available: if not, no acting can conceal the makeshift. Mr Herbert Everitt was not the right man; but he made the best of it. The clown was evidently willing to relish his own humor if only he could have seen it; but there are few actors who would not have gone that far. Bertram (Mr Patrick Munro), if not the most intelligent of Bertrams, played the love scene with Diana with some passion. The rest of the parts, not being character studies, are tolerably straightforward and easy of execution; and they were creditably played, the king (Mr Ernest Meads) carrying off the honors, and Diana (Mrs Herbert Morris) acquitting herself with comparative distinction. But I should not like to see another such performance of All 's Well or any other play that is equally rooted in my deeper affections.

An Old New Play and a New Old One

THE IMPORTANCE OF BEING EARNEST. *A trivial comedy for serious people. By* Oscar Wilde. *St James's Theatre,* 14 *February* 1895.

? *A play in* ? *acts. By* ?. *Opera Comique,* 16 *February* 1895.

THE SECOND MRS TANQUERAY. *A play in four acts. By* Arthur W. Pinero. *London: W. Heinemann.* 1895.

[23 *February* 1895]

IT is somewhat surprising to find Mr Oscar Wilde, who does not usually model himself on Mr Henry Arthur Jones, giving his latest play a five-chambered title like The Case of Rebellious Susan. So I suggest with some confidence that The Importance of Being Earnest dates from a period long anterior to Susan. However it may have been retouched immediately before its production, it must certainly have been written before Lady Windermere's Fan. I do not suppose it to be Mr Wilde's first play: he is too susceptible to fine art to have begun otherwise than with a strenuous imitation of a great dramatic poem, Greek or Shakespearean; but it was perhaps the first which he designed for practical commercial use at the West End theatres. The evidence of this is abundant. The play has a plot—a gross anachronism; there is a scene between the two girls in the second act quite in the literary style of Mr Gilbert, and almost inhuman enough to have been conceived by him; the humor is adulterated by stock mechanical fun to an extent that absolutely scandalizes one in a play with such an author's name to it; and the punning title and several of the more farcical passages recall the epoch of the late H. J. Byron. The whole has been varnished, and here and there veneered, by the author of A Woman of no Importance; but the general effect is that of a farcical comedy dating from the seventies, unplayed during that period because it was too clever and too decent, and brought up to date as far as possible by Mr Wilde in his now completely formed style. Such is the impression left by the play on me. But I find other critics, equally entitled to respect, declaring that The Importance of Being Earnest is a strained effort of Mr Wilde's at ultra-modernity, and that it could never have been written but for the opening up of entirely new paths in drama last year by Arms and the Man. At which I confess to a chuckle.

I cannot say that I greatly cared for The Importance of Being Earnest. It amused me, of course; but unless comedy touches me as well as amuses me, it leaves me with a sense of having wasted my evening. I go to the theatre to be moved to laughter, not to be tickled or bustled into it; and that is why, though I laugh as much as anybody at a farcical comedy, I am out of spirits before the end of the second act, and out of temper before the end of the third, my miserable mechanical laughter intensifying these symptoms at every outburst. If the public ever becomes intelligent enough to know when it is really enjoying itself and when it is not, there will be an end of farcical comedy. Now in The Importance of Being Earnest there is plenty of this rib-tickling: for instance, the lies, the deceptions, the cross purposes, the sham mourning, the christening of the two grown-up men, the muffin eating, and so forth. These could only have been raised from the farcical plane by making them occur to characters who had, like Don Quixote, convinced us of their reality and obtained some hold on our sympathy. But that unfortunate moment of Gilbertism breaks our belief in the humanity of the play. Thus we are thrown back on the force and daintiness of its wit, brought home by an exquisitely grave, natural, and unconscious execution on the part of the actors. Alas! the latter is not forthcoming. Mr Kinsey Peile as a man-servant, and Miss Irene Vanbrugh as Gwendolen Fairfax, alone escaped from a devastating consciousness of Mr Wilde's reputation, which more or less preoccupied all the rest, except perhaps Miss Millard, with whom all comedy is a preoccupation, since she is essentially a sentimental actress. In such passages as the Gilbertian quarrel with Gwendolen, her charm rebuked the scene instead of enhancing it. The older ladies were, if they will excuse my saying so, quite maddening. The violence of their affectation, the insufferable low comedy soars and swoops of the voice, the rigid shivers of elbows, shoulder, and neck, which are supposed on the stage to characterize the behavior of ladies after the age of forty, played havoc with the piece. In Miss Rose Leclerq a good deal of this sort of thing is only the mannerism of a genuine if somewhat impossible style; but Miss Leclerq was absent through indisposition on the night of my visit; so that I had not her style to console me. Mr Aynesworth's easy-going Our Boys style of play suited his part rather happily; and Mr Alexander's graver and more refined manner made the right contrast with it. But Mr Alexander, after playing with very nearly if not quite perfect conviction in the first two acts, suddenly lost confidence in the third, and began to spur up for a rattling finish. From the moment that began, the play was done with. The speech in which Worthing forgives his supposed mother, and the business of searching the army lists, which should have been conducted with subdued earnestness, was bustled through to the destruction of all verisimilitude and consequently all interest. That is the worst of having anyone who is not an inveterate and hardened comedian in a leading comedy part. His faith, patience, and relish begin to give out after a time; and he finally commits the unpardonable sin against the author of giving the signal that the play is over ten minutes before the fall of the curtain, instead of speaking the last line as if the whole evening were still before the audience. Mr Alexander does not throw himself genuinely into comedy: he condescends to amuse himself with it; and in the end he finds that he cannot condescend enough. On the whole I must decline to accept The Importance of Being Earnest as a day less than ten years old; and I am altogether unable to perceive any uncommon excellence in its presentation.

I am in a somewhat foolish position concerning a play at the Opera Comique, whither I was bidden this day week. For some reason I was not supplied with a program; so that I never learnt the name of the play. I believed I recognized some of the members of the company—generally a very difficult thing to do in a country where, with a few talented exceptions, every actor is just like every other actor—but they have now faded from my memory. At the end of the second act the play had advanced about as far as an ordinary dramatist would have brought it five minutes after the first rising of the curtain; or, say, as far as Ibsen would have brought it ten years before that event. Taking advantage of the second interval to stroll out into the Strand for a little exercise, I unfortunately forgot all about my business, and actually reached home before it occurred to me that I had not seen the end of the play. Under these circumstances it would ill become me to dogmatize on the merits of the work or its performance. I can only offer the management my apologies.

I am indebted to Mr Heinemann for a copy of The Second Mrs Tanqueray, which he has just published in a five-shilling volume, with an excellent photographic portrait of the author by Mr Hollyer. Those who did not see the play at the St James's Theatre can now examine the literary basis of the work that so immoderately fascinated playgoing London in 1893. But they must not expect the play to be as imposing in the library as it was on the stage. Its merit there was relative to the culture of the playgoing public. Paula Tanqueray is an astonishingly well-drawn figure as stage figures go nowadays, even allowing for the fact that there is no cheaper subject for the character draughtsman than the ill-tempered sensual woman seen from the point of view of the conventional man. But off the stage her distinction vanishes. The novels of Anthony Trollope, Charles Lever, Bulwer Lytton, Charles Reade, and many other novelists, whom nobody praised thirty years ago in the terms in which Mr Pinero is praised now, are full of feats of character-drawing in no way inferior—to say the least—to Mr Pinero's. The theatre was not ready for that class of work then: it is now; and accordingly Mr Pinero, who in literature is a humble and somewhat belated follower of the novelists of the middle of the nineteenth century, and who has never written a line from which it could be guessed that he is a contemporary of Ibsen, Tolstoi, Meredith, or

Sarah Grand, finds himself at the dawn of the twentieth hailed as a man of new ideas, of daring originality, of supreme literary distinction, and even—which is perhaps oddest—of consummate stage craft. Stage craft, after all, is very narrowly limited by the physical conditions of stage representation; but when one turns over the pages of The Second Mrs Tanqueray, and notes the naïve machinery of the exposition in the first act, in which two whole actors are wasted on sham parts, and the hero, at his own dinner party, is compelled to get up and go ignominiously into the next room 'to write some letters' when something has to be said behind his back; when one follows Cayley Drummle, the confidant to whom both Paula and her husband explain themselves for the benefit of the audience; when one counts the number of doors which Mr Pinero needs to get his characters on and off the stage, and how they have finally to be supplemented by the inevitable 'French windows' (two of them); and when the activity of the postman is taken into consideration, it is impossible to avoid the conclusion that what most of our critics mean by mastery of stage craft is recklessness in the substitution of dead machinery and lay figures for vital action and real characters. I do not deny that an author may be driven by his own limitations to ingenuities which Shakespear has no occasion to cultivate, just as a painter without hands or feet learns to surpass Michael Angelo in the art of drawing with the brush held in the mouth; but I regard such ingenuity as an extremity to be deplored, not as an art to be admired. In the Second Mrs Tanqueray I find little except a scaffold for the situation of a step-daughter and step-mother finding themselves in the positions respectively of affianced wife and discarded mistress to the same man. Obviously, the only necessary conditions of this situation are that the persons concerned shall be respectable enough to be shocked by it, and that the step-mother shall be an improper person. Mr Pinero has not got above this minimum. He is, of course, sufficiently skilled in fiction to give Ellean, Mrs. Cortelyon, Ardale, Tanqueray, and Cayley Drummle a passable air of being human beings. He has even touched up Cayley into a Thackerayan *flâneur* in order to secure toleration of his intrusiveness. But who will pretend that any of these figures are more than the barest accessories to the main situation? To compare them with the characters in Robertson's Caste would be almost as ridiculous as to compare Caste with A Doll's House. The two vulgar characters produce the requisite jar—a pitilessly disagreeable jar—and that is all. Still, all the seven seem good as far as they go; and that very little way may suggest that Mr Pinero might have done good creative work if he had carried them further. Unfortunately for this surmise, he has carried Paula further; and with what result? The moment the point is reached at which that comparatively common gift of 'an eye for character' has to be supplemented by the higher dramatic gift of sympathy with character—of the power of seeing the world from the point of view of others instead of merely describing or judging them from one's own point of view in terms of the conventional systems of morals, Mr Pinero breaks down. I remember that when I saw the play acted I sat up very attentively when Tanqueray said to Paula 'I know what you were at Ellean's age. You hadnt a thought that wasnt a wholesome one; you hadnt an impulse that didnt tend towards good; you never harbored a notion you couldnt have gossiped about to a parcel of children. And this was a very few years back, etc. etc.' On the reply to that fatuous but not unnatural speech depended the whole question of Mr Pinero's rank as a dramatist. One can imagine how, in a play by a master-hand, Paula's reply would have opened Tanqueray's foolish eyes to the fact that a woman of that sort is already the same at three as she is at thirty-three, and that however she may have found by experience that her nature is in conflict with the ideals of differently constituted people, she remains perfectly valid to herself, and despises herself, if she sincerely does so at all, for the hypocrisy that the world forces on her instead of for being what she is. What reply does Mr Pinero put into her mouth? Here it is, with the stage directions: 'A few—years ago! (*She walks slowly towards the door, then suddenly drops upon the ottoman in a paroxysm of weeping.*) O God! A few years ago!' That is to say, she makes her reply from the Tanqueray-Ellean-Pinero point of view, and thus betrays the fact that she is a work of prejudiced observation instead of comprehension, and that the other characters only owe their faint humanity to the fact that they are projections of Mr Pinero's own personal amiabilities and beliefs and conventions. Mr Pinero, then, is no interpreter of character, but simply an adroit describer of people as the ordinary man sees and judges them. Add to this a clear head, a love of the stage, and a fair talent for fiction, all highly cultivated by hard and honorable work as a writer of effective stage plays for the modern commercial theatre; and you have him on his real level. On that level he is entitled to all the praise The Second Mrs Tanqueray has won him; and I very heartily regret that the glamor which Mrs Patrick Campbell cast round the play has forced me to examine pretensions which Mr Pinero himself never put forward rather than to acknowledge the merits with which his work is so concisely packed.

Mr Pinero's New Play

THE NOTORIOUS MRS EBBSMITH. *An original play in four acts. By* A. W. Pinero. *Garrick Theatre,* 13 *March* 1895.

[16 *March* 1895]

MR PINERO's new play is an attempt to reproduce that peculiar stage effect of intellectual drama, of social problem, of subtle psychological study of character, in short, of a great play, with which he was so successful in The Profligate and The Second Mrs Tanqueray. In the two earlier plays, it will be remembered, he was careful to support this stage effect with a substantial basis of ordinary dramatic material, consisting of a well worked-up and well worn situation which would have secured the success of a conventional Adelphi piece. In this way he conquered the public by the exquisite flattery of giving them plays that they really liked, whilst persuading them that such appreciation was only possible from persons of great culture and intellectual acuteness. The vogue of The Second Mrs Tanqueray was due to the fact that the commonplace playgoer, as he admired Mrs Patrick Campbell, and was moved for the twentieth time by the conventional wicked woman with a past, consumed with remorse at the recollection of her innocent girlhood, and unable to look her pure stepdaughter (from a convent) in the face, believed that he was one of the select few for whom 'the literary drama' exists, and thus combined the delights of an evening at a play which would not have puzzled

Madame Celeste with a sense of being immensely in the modern movement. Mr Pinero, in effect, invented a new sort of play by taking the ordinary article and giving it an air of novel, profound, and original thought. This he was able to do because he was an inveterate 'character actor' (a technical term denoting a clever stage performer who cannot act, and therefore makes an elaborate study of the disguises and stage tricks by which acting can be grotesquely simulated) as well as a competent dramatist on customary lines. His performance as a thinker and social philosopher is simply character acting in the domain of authorship, and can impose only on those who are taken in by character acting on the stage. It is only the make-up of an actor who does not understand his part, but who knows—because he shares—the popular notion of its externals. As such, it can never be the governing factor in his success, which must always depend on the commonplace but real substratum of ordinary drama in his works. Thus his power to provide Mrs Tanqueray with equally popular successors depends on his freedom from the illusion he has himself created as to his real strength lying in his acuteness as a critic of life. Given a good play, the stage effect of philosophy will pass with those who are no better philosophers than he; but when the play is bad, the air of philosophy can only add to its insufferableness. In the case of The Notorious Mrs Ebbsmith, the play is bad. But one of its defects: to wit, the unreality of the chief female character, who is fully as artificial as Mrs Tanqueray herself, has the lucky effect of setting Mrs Patrick Campbell free to do as she pleases in it, the result being an irresistible projection of that lady's personal genius, a projection which sweeps the play aside and imperiously becomes the play itself. Mrs Patrick Campbell, in fact, pulls her author through by playing him clean off the stage. She creates all sorts of illusions, and gives one all sorts of searching sensations. It is impossible not to feel that those haunting eyes are brooding on a momentous past, and the parted lips anticipating a thrilling imminent future, whilst some enigmatic present must no less surely be working underneath all that subtle play of limb and stealthy intensity of tone. Clearly there must be a great tragedy somewhere in the immediate neighborhood; and most of my colleagues will no doubt tell us that this imaginary masterpiece is Mr Pinero's Notorious Mrs Ebbsmith. But Mr Pinero has hardly anything to do with it. When the curtain comes down, you are compelled to admit that, after all, nothing has come of it except your conviction that Mrs Patrick Campbell is a wonderful woman. Let us put her out of the question for a moment and take a look at Mrs Ebbsmith.

To begin with, she is what has been called 'a platform woman.' She is the daughter of a secularist agitator—say a minor Bradlaugh. After eight years of married life, during which she was for one year her husband's sultana, and for the other seven his housekeeper, she has emerged into widowhood and an active career as an agitator, speaking from the platforms formerly occupied by her father. Although educated, well conducted, beautiful, and a sufficiently powerful speaker to produce a great effect in Trafalgar Square, she loses her voice from starvation, and has to fall back on nursing—a piece of fiction which shews that Mr Pinero has not the faintest idea of what such a woman's career is in reality. He may take my word for it that a lady with such qualifications would be very much better off than a nurse; and that the plinth of the Nelson column, the 'pitch' in the park, and the little meeting halls in poor parishes, all of which he speaks of with such an exquisitely suburban sense of their being the dark places of the earth, enter nowadays very largely into the political education of almost all publicly active men and women; so that the Duke of St Olpherts, when he went to that iron building in St Luke's, and saw 'Mad Agnes' on the platform, might much more probably have found there a future Cabinet Minister, a lady of his own ducal family, or even a dramatic critic. However, the mistakes into which Mr Pinero has been led by his want of practical acquaintance with the business of political agitation are of no great dramatic moment. We may forgive a modern British dramatist for supposing that Mrs Besant, for example, was an outcast on the brink of starvation in the days when she graduated on the platform, although we should certainly not tolerate such nonsense from any intellectually responsible person. But Mr Pinero has made a deeper mistake. He has fallen into the common error of supposing that the woman who speaks in public and takes an interest in wider concerns than those of her own household is a special variety of the human species; that she 'Trafalgar Squares' aristocratic visitors in her drawing room; and that there is something dramatic in her discovery that she has the common passions of humanity.

Mrs Ebbsmith, in the course of her nursing, finds a patient who falls in love with her. He is married to a shrew; and he proposes to spend the rest of his life with his nurse, preaching the horrors of marriage. Off the stage it is not customary for a man and woman to assume that they cannot co-operate in bringing about social reform without living together as man and wife: on the stage, this is considered inevitable. Mrs Ebbsmith rebels against the stage so far as to propose that they shall prove their disinterestedness by making the partnership a friendly business one only. She then finds out that he does not really care a rap about her ideas, and that his attachment to her is simply sexual. Here we start with a dramatic theme capable of interesting development. Mr Pinero, unable to develop it, lets it slip through his fingers after one feeble clutch at it, and proceeds to degrade his drama below the ordinary level by making the woman declare that her discovery of the nature of the man's feeling puts within her reach 'the only one hour in a woman's life,' in pursuance of which detestable view she puts on an indecent dress and utterly abandons herself to him. A clergyman appears at this crisis, and offers her a Bible. She promptly pitches it into the stove; and a thrill of horror runs through the audience as they see, in imagination, the whole Christian Church tottering before their eyes. Suddenly, with a wild scream, she plunges her hand into the glowing stove and pulls out the Bible again. The Church is saved; and the curtain descends amid thunders of applause. In that applause I hope I need not say I did not join. A less sensible and less courageous stage effect I have never witnessed. If Mr Pinero had created for us a woman whose childhood had been made miserable by the gloomy terrorism which vulgar, fanatical parents extract from the Bible, then he might fitly have given some of the public a very wholesome lesson by making the woman thrust the Bible into the stove and leave it there. Many of the most devoted clergymen of the Church of England would, I can assure him, have publicly thanked him for such a lesson. But to introduce a woman as to whom we are carefully assured that she was educated as a secularist, and whose one misfortune—her unhappy marriage—can hardly by any stretch of casuistry be laid to the charge of St. Paul's teaching; to make this woman senselessly say that all her misfortunes are due to the Bible; to make her throw it into the stove, and then injure herself horribly in pulling it out again: this, I submit, is a piece of claptrap so gross that it absolves me from all obligation to treat Mr Pinero's art as anything higher than the barest art of theatrical sensation. As in The Profligate, as in The Second Mrs Tanqueray, he has had no idea beyond that of doing something daring and bringing down the house by running away from the consequences.

I must confess that I have no criticism for all this stuff. Mr Pinero is quite right to try his hand at the higher drama; only he will never succeed on his present method of trusting to his imagination, which seems to me to have been fed originally on the novels and American humor of forty years ago, and of late to have been entirely starved. I strongly recommend him to air his ideas a little in Hyde Park or 'the Iron Hall, St Luke's,' before he writes his next play. I shall be happy to take the chair for him.

I should, by the way, like to know the truth about the great stage effect at the end of the second act, where Mrs Patrick Campbell enters with her plain and very becoming dress changed for a horrifying confection apparently made of Japanese bronze wallpaper with a bold pattern of stamped gold. Lest the maker should take an action against me and obtain ruinous damages, I hasten to say that the garment was well made, the skirt and train perfectly hung, and the bodice, or rather waistband, fitting flawlessly.

But, as I know nothing of the fashion in evening dresses, it was cut rather lower in the pectoral region than I expected; and it was, to my taste, appallingly ugly. So I fully believed that the effect intended was a terrible rebuke to the man's complaint that Mrs Ebbsmith's previous dress was only fit for 'a dowdy demagogue.' Conceive my feelings when everyone on the stage went into ecstasies of admiration. Can Mr Pinero have shared that admiration? As the hero of a recent play observes, 'That is the question that torments me.'

A great deal of the performance is extremely tedious. The first twenty minutes, with its intolerable, unnecessary, and unintelligible explanations about the relationships of the characters, should be ruthlessly cut out. Half the stage business is only Mr Pinero's old 'character actor' nonsense; and much of the other half might be executed during the dialogue, and not between the sentences. The company need to be reminded that the Garrick is a theatre in which very distinct utterance is desirable. The worrying from time to time about the stove should be dropped, as it does not in the least fulfil its purpose of making the Bible incident—which is badly stage managed—seem more natural when it comes.

Mr Hare, in the stalest of parts, gives us a perfect piece of acting, not only executed with extraordinary fineness, but conceived so as to produce a strong illusion that there is a real character there, whereas there is really nothing but that hackneyed simulacrum of a cynical and epigrammatic old libertine who has helped to carry on so many plots. Mr Forbes Robertson lent himself to the hero, and so enabled him to become interesting on credit. Miss Jeffreys, miraculously ill fitted with her part, was pleasant for the first five minutes, during which she was suggesting a perfectly different sort of person to that which she afterwards vainly pretended to become. The other characters were the merest stock figures, convincing us that Mr Pinero either never meets anybody now, or else that he has lost the power of observation. Many passages in the play, of course, have all the qualities which have gained Mr Pinero his position as a dramatist; but I shall not dwell on them, as, to tell the truth, I disliked the play so much that nothing would induce me to say anything good of it. And here let me warn the reader to carefully discount my opinion in view of the fact that I write plays myself, and that my school is in violent reaction against that of Mr Pinero. But my criticism has not, I hope, any other fault than the inevitable one of extreme unfairness.

I must change the subject here to say that Mr Clement Scott has been kind enough to let me know that he did not write the obituary notice which I ascribed to him throughout my recent utterance on the subject of the Censorship in these columns. Not that Mr Scott has at all changed his views on that subject. The continuity of his policy was strictly maintained by the actual writer of the article; so that the argument between us on that point remains, I am sorry to say, where it was. But as I have incidentally made it appear that Mr Scott wrote an anonymous obituary notice of his late friend, and made it the occasion for a defence of him against certain strictures of mine, I am bound not only to comply with Mr Scott's request to make it known that he did not write the article, but to express my sense of the very considerate terms in which he has pointed out my mistake, and to beg him to excuse it.

Duse and Bernhardt

[15 *June* 1895]

MR WILLIAM ARCHER's defence of the dramatic critics against Mr Street's indictment of them for their indifference to acting appears to be falling through. Mr Archer pleads that whereas Hazlitt and Leigh Hunt had frequent opportunities of comparing ambitious actors in famous parts, the modern dramatic critic spends his life in contemplating 'good acting plays' without any real people in them, and performers who do not create or interpret characters, but simply lend their pretty or popular persons, for a consideration, to fill up the parts. Mr Archer might have added another reason which applies to nearly all modern works: to wit, the operation of our copyright laws, whereby actors and actresses acquire the right not only to perform new plays but to prevent anyone else from performing them. Nevertheless we critics can now at last outdo Hazlitt and Leigh Hunt if we have a mind to; for we have just had two Mrs Ebbsmiths to compare, besides a fourth Fedora, and Duse and Sarah Bernhardt playing La Dame aux Camélias and Sudermann's Heimat against one another at Daly's Theatre and at Drury Lane. Clearly now or never is the time for a triumphant refutation of the grievance of the English actor against the English Press: namely, that hardly any critic knows enough about acting to be able to distinguish between an effective part and a well played one, or between the bag of tricks which every old hand carries and the stock of ideas and sense of character which distinguish the master-actor from the mere handy man.

This week began with the relapse of Sarah Bernhardt into her old profession of serious actress. She played Magda in Sudermann's Heimat, and was promptly challenged by Duse in the same part at Drury Lane on Wednesday. The contrast between the two Magdas is as extreme as any contrast could possibly be between artists who have finished their twenty years apprenticeship to the same profession under closely similar conditions. Madame Bernhardt has the charm of a jolly maturity, rather spoilt and petulant, perhaps, but always ready with a sunshine-through-the-clouds smile if only she is made much of. Her dresses and diamonds, if not exactly splendid, are at least splendacious; her figure, far too scantily upholstered in the old days, is at its best; and her complexion shews that she has not studied modern art in vain. Those charming roseate effects which French painters produce by giving flesh the pretty color of strawberries and cream, and painting the shadows pink and crimson, are cunningly reproduced by Madame Bernhardt in the living picture. She paints her ears crimson and allows them to peep enchantingly through a few loose braids of her auburn hair. Every dimple has its dab of pink; and her fingertips are so delicately incarnadined that you fancy they are transparent like her ears, and that the light is shining through their delicate blood-vessels. Her lips are like a newly-painted pillar box; her cheeks, right up to the languid lashes, have the bloom and surface of a peach; she is beautiful with the beauty of her school, and entirely inhuman and incredible. But the incredibility is pardonable, because, though it is all the greatest nonsense, nobody believing in it, the actress herself least of all, it is so artful, so clever, so well recognized a part of the business, and carried off with such a genial air, that it is impossible not to accept it with good-humor. One feels, when the heroine bursts on the scene, a dazzling vision of beauty, that instead of imposing on you, she adds to her own piquancy by looking you straight in the face, and saying, in effect: 'Now who would ever suppose that I am a grandmother?' That, of course, is irresistible; and one is not sorry to have been coaxed to relax one's notions of the dignity of art when she gets to serious business and shews how ably she does her work. The coaxing suits well with the childishly egotistical character of her acting, which is not the art of making you think more highly or feel more deeply, but the art of making you admire her, pity her, champion her, weep with her, laugh at her jokes, follow her fortunes breathlessly, and applaud her wildly when the curtain falls. It is the art of finding out all your weaknesses and practising on them—cajoling you, harrowing you, exciting you—on the whole, fooling you. And it is always Sarah Bernhardt in her own capacity who does this to you. The dress, the title of the play, the order of the words may vary; but the woman is always the same. She does not enter into the leading character: she substitutes herself for it.

All this is precisely what does not happen in the case of Duse, whose every part is a separate creation. When she comes on the stage, you are quite welcome to take your opera-glass and count whatever lines time and care have so far traced on her. They are the credentials of her humanity; and she knows better than to obliterate that significant handwriting beneath a layer of peach-bloom from the chemist's. The shadows on her face are grey, not crimson; her lips are sometimes nearly grey also; there are neither dabs nor dimples; her charm could never be imitated by a barmaid with unlimited pin money and a row of footlights before her instead of the handles of a beer-engine. The result is not so discouraging as the patrons of the bar might suppose. Wilkes, who squinted atrociously, boasted that he was only quarter of an hour behind the handsomest man in Europe: Duse is not in action five minutes before she is quarter of a century ahead of the handsomest woman in the world. I grant that Sarah's elaborate Monna Lisa smile, with the conscious droop of the eyelashes and the long carmined lips coyly disclosing the brilliant row of teeth, is effective of its kind—that it not only appeals to your susceptibilities, but positively jogs them. And it lasts quite a minute, sometimes longer. But Duse, with a tremor of the lip which you feel rather than see, and which lasts half an instant, touches you straight on the very heart; and there is not a line in the face, or a cold tone in the grey shadow that does not give poignancy to that tremor. As to youth and age, who can associate purity and delicacy of emotion, and simplicity of expression, with the sordid craft that repels us in age; or voluptuous appeal and egotistical self-insistence with the candor and generosity that attract us in youth? Who ever thinks of Potiphar's wife as a young woman, or St Elizabeth of Hungary as an old one? These associations are horribly unjust to age, and undeserved by youth: they belong of right to differences of character, not of years; but they rule our imaginations; and the great artist profits by them to appear eternally young. However, it would be a critical blunder as well as a personal folly on my part to suggest that Duse, any more than Sarah Bernhardt, neglects any art that could heighten the effect of her acting when she is impersonating young and pretty women. The truth is that in the art of being beautiful, Madame Bernhardt is a child beside her. The French artist's stock of attitudes and facial effects could be catalogued as easily as her stock of dramatic ideas: the counting would hardly go beyond the fingers of both hands. Duse produces the illusion of being infinite in variety of beautiful pose and motion. Every idea, every shade of thought and mood, expresses itself delicately but vividly to the eye; and yet, in an apparent million of changes and inflexions, it is impossible to catch any line at an awkward angle, or any strain interfering with the perfect abandonment of all the limbs to what appears to be their natural gravitation towards the finest grace. She is ambidextrous and supple, like a gymnast or a panther; only the multitude of ideas which find physical expression in her movements are all of that high quality which marks off humanity from the animals, and, I fear I must add, from a good many gymnasts. When it is remembered that the majority of tragic actors excel only in explosions of those passions which are common to man and brute, there will be no difficulty in understanding the indescribable distinction which Duse's acting acquires from the fact that behind every stroke of it is a distinctively human idea. In nothing is this more apparent than in the vigilance in her of that high human instinct which seeks to awaken the deepest responsive feeling without giving pain. In La Dame aux Camélias, for instance, it is easy for an intense actress to harrow us with her sorrows and paroxysms of phthisis, leaving us with a liberal pennyworth of sensation, not fundamentally distinguishable from that offered by a public execution, or any other evil in which we still take a hideous delight. As different from this as light from darkness is the method of the actress who shews us how human sorrow can express itself only in its appeal for the sympathy it needs, whilst striving by strong endurance to shield others from the infection of its torment. That is the charm of Duse's interpretation of the stage poem of Marguerite Gauthier. It is unspeakably touching because it is exquisitely considerate: that is, exquisitely sympathetic. No physical charm is noble as well as beautiful unless it is the expression of a moral charm; and it is because Duse's range includes these moral high notes, if I may so express myself, that her compass, extending from the depths of a mere predatory creature like Claude's wife up to Marguerite Gauthier at her kindest or Magda at her bravest, so immeasurably dwarfs the poor little octave and a half on which Sarah Bernhardt plays such pretty canzonets and stirring marches.

Obvious as the disparity of the two famous artists has been to many of us since we first saw Duse, I doubt whether any of us realized, after Madame Bernhardt's very clever performance as Magda on Monday night, that there was room in the nature of things for its annihilation within forty-eight hours by so comparatively quiet a talent as Duse's. And yet annihilation is the only word for it. Sarah was very charming, very jolly when the sun shone, very petulant when the clouds covered it, and positively angry when they wanted to take her child away from her. And she did not trouble us with any fuss about the main theme of Sudermann's play, the revolt of the modern woman against that ideal of home which exacts the sacrifice of her whole life to its care, not by her grace, and as its own sole help and refuge, but as a right which it has to the services of all females as abject slaves. In fact, there is not the slightest reason to suspect Madame Bernhardt of having discovered any such theme in the play; though Duse, with one look at Schwartze, the father, nailed it to the stage as the subject of the impending dramatic struggle before she had been five minutes on the scene. Before long, there came a stroke of acting which will probably never be forgotten by those who saw it, and which explained at once why those artifices of the dressing-table which help Madame Bernhardt would hinder Duse almost as much as a screen placed in front of her. I should explain, first, that the real name of the play is not Magda but Home. Magda is a daughter who has been turned out of doors for defying her father, one of those outrageous persons who mistake their desire to have everything their own way in the house for a sacred principle of home life. She has a hard time of it, but at last makes a success as an opera singer, though not until her lonely struggles have thrown her for sympathy on a fellow student, who in due time goes his way, and leaves her to face motherhood as best she can. In the fullness of her fame she returns to her native town, and in an attack of homesickness makes advances to her father, who consents to receive her again. No sooner is she installed in the house than she finds that one of the most intimate friends of the family is the father of her child. In the third act of the play she is on the stage when he is announced as a visitor. It must be admitted that Sarah Bernhardt played this scene very lightly and pleasantly: there was genuine good fellowship in the way in which she reassured the embarrassed gallant and made him understand that she was not going to play off the sorrows of Gretchen on him after all those years, and that she felt that she owed him the priceless experience of maternity, even if she did not particularly respect him for it. Her self-possession at this point was immense: the peach-bloom never altered by a shade. Not so with Duse. The moment she read the card handed her by the servant, you realized what it was to have to face a meeting with the man. It was interesting to watch how she got through it when he came in, and how, on the whole, she got through it pretty well. He paid his compliments and offered his flowers; they sat down; and she evidently felt that she had got it safely over and might allow herself to think at her ease, and to look at him to see how much he had altered. Then a terrible thing happened to her. She began to blush; and in another moment she was conscious of it, and the blush was slowly spreading and deepening until, after a few vain efforts to avert her face or to obstruct his view of it without seeming to do so, she gave up and hid the blush in her hands. After that feat of acting I did not need to be told why Duse does not paint an inch thick. I could detect no trick in it: it seemed to me a perfectly genuine effect of the dramatic imagination. In the third act of La Dame aux Camélias, where she produces a touching effect by throwing herself down, and presently rises with her face changed and flushed with weeping, the flush is secured by the preliminary plunge to a stooping attitude, imagination or no imagination; but Magda's blush did not admit of that explanation; and I must confess to an intense professional curiosity as to whether it always comes spontaneously.

I shall make no attempt to describe the rest of that unforgettable act. To say that it left the house not only frantically applauding, but actually roaring, is to say nothing; for had we not applauded Sarah as Gismonda and roared at Mrs Patrick Campbell as Fedora? But there really was something to roar at this time. There was a real play, and an actress who understood the author and was a greater artist than he. And for me, at least, there was a confirmation of my sometimes flagging faith that a dramatic critic is really the servant of a high art, and not a mere advertiser of entertainments of questionable respectability of motive.

Romeo and Juliet

ROMEO AND JULIET. *Lyceum Theatre,* 21 *September* 1895.

[28 *September* 1895]

How we lavish our money and our worship on Shakespear without in the least knowing why! From time to time we ripen for a new act of homage. Great preparations are made; high hopes are raised; everyone concerned, from the humblest *persona muta* on the stage to the sworn first-nighter in the gallery, is full of earnest belief that the splendor of the Swan will be revealed at last, like the Holy Grail. And yet the point of the whole thing is missed every time with ludicrous ineptitude; and often a ruined actor-manager spends the rest of his life, like the Ancient Mariner, in telling the tale of what it cost, and how So-and-So got his (or her) first chance in it, and how such and such other eminent people declared that nothing like it had ever been done before, and so on and so forth. Still, there is nothing for it but to try and try and try again. Every revival helps to exhaust the number of possible ways of altering Shakespear's plays unsuccessfully, and so hastens the day when the mere desire for novelty will lead to the experiment of leaving them unaltered. Let us see what there is to learn from Mr Forbes Robertson's revival of Romeo and Juliet, before that goes the way of all the other revivals. I hardly like to call Mr Forbes Robertson an artist, because he is notoriously a gentleman with a taste for painting, and the two things are usually incompatible. Your Englishman always conceives that to be romantic and to have a susceptible imagination is to be potentially a painter. His eye for form may be that of a carpenter, his sense of color that of a haberdasher's window-dresser in the Old Kent Road: no matter, he can still imagine historical scenes—'King James receiving the news of the landing of William of Orange' or the like—and draw them and color them, and he can dress up his wife as Zenobia or Dante's Beatrice or Dolly Varden, according to her style, and copy her. I do not level these disparaging observations at Mr Forbes Robertson: I only wish to make it clear that I approach his latest enterprise completely free from the common assumption that he is likely to stage Romeo and Juliet better than anyone else because he paints pictures and sends them to the exhibitions occasionally. To be quite frank, I am rather prejudiced against him by that fact, since I learnt in the days when I criticized pictures that his sense of color is essentially and Britannically an imaginative and moral one: that is, he associates low tones ('quiet colors' they call them in Marshall & Snellgrove's) with dignity and decency, and white linen with cleanliness and respectability. I am therefore not surprised to find the dresses at the Lyceum, though handsome and expensive, chastened by the taste of a British gentleman; so that the stalls can contemplate the fourteenth century and yet feel at home there—a remarkable result, and a very desirable one for those who like it. 'Mrs Patrick Campbell's dresses,' says the program, 'have been carried out by Mrs Mason, of New Burlington Street.' I can only say that I wish they had been carried out and buried. They belong to Mrs Mason, and are her triumph, instead of to Mrs Campbell. I know how to value an actress who is an artist in dressing fashionably, like Miss Gertrude Kingston; and I delight in one who is an artist in dressing originally, like Miss Ellen Terry; but a lady who is dressed by somebody else, according to somebody else's ideas, like any dressmaker-made woman of fashion, is artistically quite out of the question; and I can only excuse the Lyceum Juliet costumes on the supposition that Mrs Campbell deliberately aimed at suggesting by them the tutelage of a girl of fourteen who is not yet allowed to choose her own dresses.

The scenery is excellent. Mr William Harford's 'public place in Verona' has only one defect, and that a very English one. The sky is too cold, and the cypresses too pale: better have painted them with dabs of warm brown on an actually gold sky in the beautiful old fashion, than have risked that Constablesque suggestion, faint as it is, of English raininess and chill. But for the rest, it is easy to imagine that the flood of the Adige is really hurrying along behind that embankment as Mercutio leans idly over it. Friar Laurence's cell, too, is good: one can feel the shadowed cloisters outside, with the sunlight and the well in the middle of the quadrangle; and though I do not believe that a simple friar's cell often ran to the luxury of a couple of frescoes by Giotto, yet the touch is suggestive and pardonable. Mr Ryan's corner of Mantua in the last act would be perfect if the light could only be forced to Italian pitch: in fact it surpasses the real thing in respect of its freedom from the atrocious Mantuan stenches and huge mosquitoes from the marshes. Mr Harker has only one scene, that of Capulet's ball, a beautiful fourteenth-century loggia; whilst Mr Harford, having to do another scene in Capulet's house, has jumped forward to genteelly elegant Renascence work in carved white marble, in the manner of the Miracoli at Venice. It will be inferred, and rightly inferred, that the scenery is enormously in advance of that to which Mr Augustin Daly treated us for The Two Gentlemen of Verona. No doubt Mr Daly paid as much as Mr Forbes Robertson; but Mr Daly's scene-painters copied bad work, and Mr Forbes Robertson's have copied good. That makes all the difference.

Of course, in criticizing the general effect, the play and the acting cannot be altogether left out of account, though it would be unfair to lay too much stress on them. Perhaps the most difficult character in the play as far as finesse of execution goes is Mercutio. We see Mercutio in his first scene as a wit and fantasist of the most delicate order. In his next, apparently without any shock to the Elizabethan sense of congruity, he is a detestable and intolerable cad, the exact prototype of our modern 'Arry. The change gives such another glimpse into the manners of that time as you get in Much Ado from the astonishment which Benedick creates by taking to washing his face every day. By stage tradition, Mercutio is as much a leading part as Romeo, if not more so. Therefore, when the manager chooses Romeo, he should be particularly careful to choose a good Mercutio, lest he should appear to have that part purposely underplayed. Perhaps this was why

Mr Forbes Robertson went so far out of his way as to cast Mr Coghlan for the part. If so, he overreached himself; for he could not possibly have made a worse choice. I really cannot express myself politely on the subject of Mr Coghlan's performance. He lounges, he mumbles, he delivers the Queen Mab speech in a raffish patter which takes, and is apparently deliberately meant to take, all beauty of tone and grace of measure out of it. It may be that Mr Coghlan has studied the part carefully, and come to the conclusion that since the visit of the Montagues to Capulet's ball is a young blood's escapade, Mercutio should be represented as coming half drunk and lolling on the stone seat outside to repeat a tipsy rigmarole about nothing. In that case I must express my entire disagreement with Mr Coghlan's reading. Shakespear never leaves me in any doubt as to when he means an actor to play Sir Toby Belch and when to play Mercutio, or when he means an actor to speak measured verse and when slipshod colloquial prose.

Far better than Mr Coghlan's Mercutio, and yet quite the worst impersonation I have ever seen of a not very difficult old woman's part, was Miss Dolores Drummond's Nurse. Tybalt's is such an unmercifully bad part that one can hardly demand anything from its representative except that he should brush his hair when he comes to his uncle's ball (a condition which he invariably repudiates) and that he should be so consummate a swordsman as to make it safe for Romeo to fall on him with absolute abandonment, and annihilate him as Jean de Reszke used to annihilate Montariol. This is one of the great sensations of the play: unless an actor is capable of a really terrible explosion of rage, he had better let Romeo alone. Unfortunately, the 'fire-eyed fury' before which

Tybalt falls lies outside the gentlemanly limits of Mr Forbes Robertson's stage instinct; and it may be that his skill as an actor is not equal to the task of working-up the audience to the point at which they will imagine an explosion which cannot, of course, be real. At all events the duel scene has none of the murderous excitement which is the whole dramatic point of it: it is tamed down to a mere formal pretext for the banishment of Romeo. Mr Forbes Robertson has evidently no sympathy with Shakespear's love of a shindy: you see his love of law and order coming out in his stage management of the fighting scenes. Nobody is allowed to enjoy the scrimmage: Capulet and Montague are silenced; and the spectators of the duel are women—I should say ladies—who look intensely shocked to see gentlemen of position so grossly forgetting themselves. Mr Forbes Robertson himself fights with unconcealed repugnance: he makes you feel that to do it in that disorderly way, without seconds, without a doctor, shewing temper about it, and actually calling his adversary names, jars unspeakably on him. Far otherwise have we seen him as Orlando wrestling with Charles. But there the contest was in the presence of a court, with measured ground and due formality—under Queensberry rules, so to speak. For the rest, Mr Forbes Robertson is very handsome, very well dressed, very perfectly behaved. His assortment of tones, of gestures, of facial expressions, of attitudes, are limited to half a dozen apiece; but they are carefully selected and all of the best. The arrangements in the last scene are exceedingly nice: the tomb of the Capulets is beautifully kept, well lighted, and conveniently accessible by a couple of broad steps—quite like a new cathedral chapel. Indeed, when Romeo, contemplating the bier of Juliet (which reflected the utmost credit on the undertaker), said:

> I still will stay with thee,
> And never from this palace of dim night
> Depart again,

I felt that the sacrifice he was making in doing without a proper funeral was greatly softened. Romeo was a gentleman to the last. He laid out Paris after killing him as carefully as if he were folding up his best suit of clothes. One remembers Irving, a dim figure dragging a horrible burden down through the gloom 'into the rotten jaws of death,' and reflects on the differences of imaginative temperament that underlie the differences of acting and stage-managing.

As to Juliet, she danced like the daughter of Herodias. And she knew the measure of her lines to a hairsbreadth. Did I not say, long ago, that Mrs Tanqueray's piano-playing was worth all the rest of her? And yet I was taken in by Mrs Tanqueray—also by Mrs Ebbsmith, as we all were. Woman's great art is to lie low, and let the imagination of the male endow her with depths. How Mrs Patrick Campbell must have laughed at us whilst we were giving her all the credit—if credit it were—for our silly psychologizing over those Pinero parts! As Juliet she still fits herself into the hospitable manly heart without effort, simply because she is a wonderful person, not only in mere facial prettiness, in which respect she is perhaps not superior to the bevy of 'extra ladies' in the fashionable scenes in the new Drury Lane play, not even in her light, beautifully proportioned figure, but in the extraordinary swiftness and certainty of her physical self-command. I am convinced that Mrs Patrick Campbell could thread a needle with her toes at the first attempt as rapidly, as smoothly, as prettily, and with as much attention to spare for doing anything else at the same time as she can play an arpeggio. This physical talent, which is seldom consciously recognized except when it is professedly specialized in some particular direction (as in the case, for instance, of Miss Letty Lind), will, when accompanied by nimbleness of mind, quick observation, and lively theatrical instinct, carry any actress with a rush to the front of her profession, as it has carried Mrs Patrick Campbell. Her Juliet, nevertheless, is an immature performance at all the exceptional points which, please remember, are not very numerous, much of Juliet's business being of a kind that no 'leading lady' of ordinary ability could possibly fail in. All the conscious ideas gathered by her from the part and carried out in planned strokes of her own are commonplace. There is not a touch of tragedy, not a throb of love or fear, temper instead of passion: in short, a Juliet as unawakened as Richard III, one in whose death you dont believe, though you would not cry over it if you did believe. Nothing of it is memorable except the dance—the irresistible dance.

It should never be forgotten in judging an attempt to play Romeo and Juliet that the parts are made almost impossible, except to actors of positive genius, skilled to the last degree in metrical declamation, by the way in which the poetry, magnificent as it is, is interlarded by the miserable rhetoric and silly logical conceits which were the foible of the Elizabethans. When Juliet comes out on her balcony and, having propounded the question, 'What's in a name?' proceeds to argue it out like an amateur attorney in Christmas-card verse of the 'rose by any other name' order, no actress can make it appear natural to a century which has discovered the art of giving prolonged and intense dramatic expression to pure feeling alone, without any skeleton of argument or narrative, by means of music. Romeo has lines that tighten the heart or catch you up into the heights, alternately with heartless fustian and silly ingenuities that make you curse Shakespear's stagestruckness and his youthful inability to keep his brains quiet. It needs a great flowing tide of passion, an irresistibly impetuous march of music, to carry us over these pitfalls and stumbling-blocks, even when we are foolish enough to mistake the good for the bad, and to reverently accept Mr Coghlan as an authority on the subject of Mercutio. It would be folly to hold out any such hopes of rescue at the Lyceum. Of the whole company there is only one member who achieves artistic respectability as a Shakespearean player, and that is Mr Warde as Capulet. For the most part, one has to listen to the music of Shakespear—in which music, I repeat again and again, the whole worth and charm of these early plays of his lies—as one might listen to a symphony of Beethoven's with all the parts played on the bones, the big drum, and the Jew's harp. But the production is an unsparing effort, and therefore as honorable to Mr Forbes Robertson's management as the highest artistic success could make it. The more efforts of that kind we have, the sooner we shall have the artistic success.

The Old Acting and the New

THE COMEDY OF ERRORS. *Performance by the Elizabethan Stage Society in Gray's Inn Hall, 7 December 1895.*

[14 *December* 1895]

FOR a delightful, as distinguished from a commercially promising first night, the palm must be given this season to the Elizabethan Stage Society's performance of The Comedy of Errors in Gray's Inn Hall this day week. Usually I enjoy a first night as a surgeon enjoys an operation: this time I enjoyed it as a playgoer enjoys a pleasant performance. I have never, I hope, underrated the importance of the amateur; but I am now beginning to cling to him as the savior of theatrical art. He alone among the younger generation seems to have any experience of acting. Nothing is more appalling to the dramatic author than the discovery that professional actors of ten years standing have acquired nothing but a habit of brazening out their own incompetence. What is an actor nowadays, or an actress? In nine cases out of ten, simply a person who has been 'on tour' with half a dozen 'London successes,' playing parts that involve nothing but a little business thoughtlessly copied from the performances of their London 'creators,' with long intervals spent between each tour in the ranks of the unemployed. At the end of a lifetime so spent, the 'actor' will no doubt be a genuine expert at railway travelling, at taking lodgings, and at cajoling and bullying landladies; but a decent amateur of two years standing, and of the true irrepressible sort, will beat him hopelessly at his art. What a fate is that of these unhappy young professionals, sick to desperation of a provincial routine compared to which that of a commercial traveller is a dream of romance, longing for a chance which they have not skill enough to turn to account even if some accident thrust it upon them, and becoming less interesting and attractive year by year at a profession in which the steady increase of personal fascination should have no limit but positive senility and decrepitude! I remember, years ago, when the Playgoers' Club was in its infancy, hearing Mr Pinero, in the course of an address to that body, break into an enthusiastic eulogium on the actor of the past, produced by the old stock-company system, versatile, a singer, a dancer, a fencer, an elocutionist, ready to play any part at a day's notice, and equally expert in comedy, drama, melodrama, Christmas pantomime, and the 'legitimate.' There is some German novel in which a crowd of medieval warriors, fired by the eloquence of Peter the Hermit, burns with a Christian longing to rush to the Holy Land and charge in serried ranks on the Paynim hosts—all except one man, who is obviously not impressed. Indignant at his coldness, they demand what he means by it. 'Ive been there,' is his sufficient explanation. That is how I felt when I was listening to Mr Pinero. Having been brought up on the old stock-company actor, I knew that he was the least versatile of beings—that he was nailed helplessly to his own line of heavy or light, young or old, and played all the parts that fell to him as the representative of that line in exactly the same way. I knew that his power of hastily 'swallowing' the words of a part and disgorging them at short notice more or less inaccurately and quite unimprovably (three months rehearsal would have left him more at sea than three hours) was incompatible with his ever knowing his part in any serious sense at all. I remembered his one absurd 'combat' that passed for fencing, the paltry stepdance between the verses of his song in the pantomime that constituted him a dancer, the obnoxiousness of utterance which he called elocution and would impart to pupils for a consideration, the universal readiness which only meant that in his incorrigible remoteness from nature and art it mattered nothing what he did. Mr Pinero madly cited Sir Henry Irving as an example of the product of the stock-company training; but the fact is, when Sir Henry first attempted classical acting at the Lyceum, he did not know the A B C of it, and only succeeded by his original and sympathetic notions of the X Y Z. Nobody who is familiar with the best technical work of the Irving of today, its finish, dignity, and grace, and the exactitude of its expression of his thought and feeling, can (unless he remembers) form any idea of what our chief actor had to teach himself before he could carry veteran playgoers with him in his breach with the tradition of superhuman acting of which Barry Sullivan was, as far as I know, the last English exponent (need I say that the great Irish actor was born in Birmingham?). Barry Sullivan was a splendidly monstrous performer in his prime: there was hardly any part sufficiently heroic for him to be natural in it. He had deficiencies in his nature, or rather blanks, but no weaknesses, because he had what people call no heart. Being a fine man, as proud as Lucifer, and gifted with an intense energy which had enabled him to cultivate himself physically to a superb degree, he was the very incarnation of the old individualistic, tyrannical conception of a great actor. By magnifying that conception to sublimity, he reduced it to absurdity. There were just two serious parts which he could play—Hamlet and Richelieu—the two loveless parts in the grand repertory. I know that some people do not like to think of Hamlet as loveless, and that the Irving Hamlet has his heart in the right place, and almost breaks it in the scene with Ophelia; but this I take to be the actor's rebuke to Shakespear rather than an attempt to fulfil his intentions. Sir Henry Irving has never thought much of the immortal William, and has given him more than one notable lesson—for instance, in The Merchant of Venice, where he gave us, not 'the Jew that Shakespear drew,' but the one he ought to have drawn if he had been up to the Lyceum mark. Barry Sullivan, with his gift of lovelessness, *was* Hamlet, and consequently used to put his Ophelias out of countenance more than it is easy to describe. In Hamlet, as in Richelieu, it was right to create a figure whose utter aloofness from his fellows gave him an almost supernatural distinction, and cut him off from all such trifling intimacy with them as love implies. And it was his success in producing this very curious and very imposing effect that made for Barry Sullivan, in his best days (I am not now speaking of the period after 1870 or thereabout), a unique provincial and Australian reputation which carried him over parts he could not play at all, such as Othello, through which he walked as if the only line in the play that conveyed any idea to him was the description of Othello as 'perplexed in the extreme,' or Macbeth, who was simply Cibber's Richard (a favorite part of his) in mutton-chop whiskers. No doubt his temperament, with its exceptional combination of imaginative energy with coldness and proud timidity of the sympathetic passions, accentuated the superhuman pretension in the style of acting which he practised; but his predecessor, Macready (if I may judge from that extremely depressing document, his diary), must have been much more like him than like Sir Henry Irving. At all events, both Macready and Sullivan had abominable tempers, and relied for their stage climaxes on effects of violence and impetuosity, and for their ordinary impressiveness on grandiose assumption of style. Once, when my father mentioned to me that he had seen Macready play Coriolanus, and I asked him what it was like, he replied that it was like a mad bull. I do not offer this as evidence that my critical faculty is an inherited one—clearly there must have been some artistic method in the bull's madness to have gained such a reputation—but I feel quite sure that when Sir Henry Irving fulfils his promise to appear as Coriolanus, no father will describe him to his son as my father described Macready to me. Barry Sullivan, then, represented the grandiose and the violent on its last legs, and could do nothing for the young Irving but mislead him. Irving's mission was to re-establish on the stage the touching, appealing nobility of sentiment and affection—the dignity which only asserts itself when it is wounded; and his early attempts to express these by the traditional methods of the old domineering, self-assertive, ambitious, thundering, superb school led him for a time into a grotesque confusion of style. In playing villains, too, his vein of callous, humorous impishness, with its occasional glimpses of a latent bestial dangerousness, utterly defied the methods of expression proper to the heaven-defying, man-quelling tyrant, usurper, and murderer, who was the typical villain of the old school, and whose flavorless quintessence will be found by the curious distilled into that instructive Shakespearean forgery, Ireland's Vortigern. In short, Irving had to find the right expression for a perfectly new dignity and a perfectly new indignity; and it was not until he had done this that he really accomplished his destiny, broke the old tradition, and left Barry Sullivan and Macready half a century behind. I will not say that he also left Shakespear behind: there is too much of the 'not for an age but for all time' about our bard for that; but it is a pity that the new acting was not applied to a new author. For though Sir Henry Irving's acting is no longer a falsification of the old style, his acting versions are falsifications of the old plays. His Hamlet, his Shylock, his Lear, though interesting in their own way, are spurious as representations of Shakespear. His Othello I have never seen: his Macbeth I thought fine and genuine, indicating that his business is with Shakespear's later plays and not with his earlier ones. But he owes it to literature to connect his name with some greater modern dramatist than the late Wills, or Tennyson, who was not really a dramatist at all. There is a nice bishop's part in Ibsen's—— but I digress.

My point is that Sir Henry Irving's so-called training under the old stock-company system not only did not give him the individuality of his style—for to that it did not pretend—but that it failed to give him even those generalities of stage deportment which are common to all styles. The stock actor, when the first travelling companies came along, vanished before them, unwept, unhonored, and unsung, because the only sentiment he had inspired in the public was an intense desire for some means of doing without him. He was such an unpresentable impostor that the smart London person, well dressed and well spoken, figuring in plays ingeniously contrived so as to dispense with any greater powers of acting than every adroit man of the world picks up, came as an inexpressible relief. Dare I now confess that I am beginning to have moments of regret for him. The smart nullity of the London person is becoming intolerably tedious; and the exhaustion of the novelty of the plays constructed for him has stripped them of their illusion and left their jingling, rickety mechanism patent to a disgusted public. The latest generation of 'leading ladies' and their heroes simply terrify me: Mr Bourchier, who had the good fortune to learn his business as an amateur, towers above them as an actor. And the latest crop of plays has been for the most part deliberately selected for production because of the very abjectness and venality which withered them, harvestless, almost as soon as they were above ground.

And yet there is more talent now than ever—more skill now than ever—more artistic culture—better taste, better acting, better theatres, better dramatic literature. Mr Tree, Mr Alexander, Mr Hare, have made honorable experiments; Mr Forbes Robertson's enterprise at the Lyceum is not a sordid one; Mr Henry Arthur Jones and Mr Pinero are doing better work than ever before, and doing it without any craven concession to the follies of 'the British public.' But it is still necessary, if you want to feel quite reassured, to turn your back on the ordinary commercial west end theatre, with its ignoble gambling for 'a catch-on,' and its eagerly envious whisperings of how much Mr Penley has made by Charley's Aunt, to watch the forlorn hopes that are led from time to time by artists and amateurs driven into action by the starvation of their artistic instincts. The latest of these is the Elizabethan Stage Society; and I am delighted to be able to taunt those who missed the performance in Gray's Inn Hall with being most pitiably out of the movement. The Lyceum itself could not have drawn a more distinguished audience; and the pleasant effect of the play, as performed on the floor of the hall without proscenium or fittings of any kind, and played straight through in less than an hour and a half without any division into acts, cannot be as much as imagined by any frequenter of our ordinary theatres. The illusion, which generally lapses during performances in our style whenever the principal performers are off the stage, was maintained throughout: neither the torchbearers on the stage nor the very effective oddity of the Dromio costumes interfering with it in the least. Only, the modern dresses of the audience, the gasaliers, and the portrait of Manisty next that of Bacon, were anachronisms which one had to ignore. The stage management was good as regards the exits, entrances, and groupings—not so good in the business of the speeches, which might have been made more helpful to the actors, especially to Adriana, whose best speeches were underdone. On the whole the acting was fair—much better than it would have been at an average professional performance. Egeon, one of the Dromios, and the courtezan distinguished themselves most. The evening wound up with a Dolmetsch concert of lute and viol, virginal and voice, a delectable entertainment which defies all description by the pen.

Plays of the Week

THE PRISONER OF ZENDA. *A romantic play in a prologue and four acts. Adapted from* Anthony Hope's *story by* Edward Rose. *St James's Theatre,* 7 *January* 1896.

THE SIGN OF THE CROSS. *In four acts. By* Wilson Barrett. *Lyric Theatre,* 4 *January* 1896.

[11 *January* 1896]

MR ANTHONY HOPE's Prisoner of Zenda was an amusing attempt to get a Scott-Dumas romance out of modern life. To take the nineteenth-century hero, give him a sword and a horse, a forest to gallop through and a castle to besiege, enemies to pursue him, persons with wrists of steel to fence with, princesses to love and rescue, and all the other luxuries of a D'Artagnan, was a laudable enterprise, in pursuit of which Mr Hope went to the shores of the Baltic, and carved an imaginary State of Ruritania out of Mecklenburg. He was so far successful that the book made pleasant reading up to within a few chapters of the end. Then the reader's heavily taxed powers of make-believe gave out. At least, that was my experience. At about the point where Rassendyl began his swimming exploits in the moat, I found it impossible any longer to forget that the whole book was a great piece of nonsense. Mere incident in a romance is not interesting unless you believe in the reality of the people to whom the incidents occur. Scott and Dumas could create real men and women for you: their merest supernumeraries, from the innkeepers whom the Musketeers cheat to Higg the son of Snell, are more solid acquaintances than Mr Hope's heroes.

Rassendyl is really nothing but a pasteboard pattern of manly attitudes to be struck in the act of doing one's duty under difficult circumstances, a figure motived by conventionalities, without individual will, and therefore without reality or humanity. If it were not for Mr Hope's light touch and sense of fun, the whole book would be as dull and mechanical a rigmarole of adventure as its last chapters. As it is, all the attempts to indicate the serious worth and rarity of the qualities which Rassendyl carries so lightly, bore and jar us by threatening to awake our common sense, which, if aroused, must immediately put a summary stop to the somewhat silly Ruritanian gambols of our imagination.

This weakness of characterization is perpetuated in the play with some added disadvantages. The liveliest character in the book is Captain Hentzau, because, though he is not a very possible scoundrel, at least his conduct is wilful, and not obviously made to order for the British Wholesale Association for the Supply of Moral Fiction. On the stage he acquires possibility, but loses fascination. The flimsiness of Rassendyl is terribly exposed by the footlights. The notion that in England every futile, harum-scarum, goodnaturedly selfish Johnny is a hero who only needs opportunity to display the noblest qualities, and have his hand kissed by veterans and high-souled ladies, is as popular, because as widely flattering, as that other idea that our yachts constitute a reserve fleet, and our shopmen a reserve army which in case of invasion would rush from behind the counter to hurl the foe back in confusion from the soil of England. It is, of course, pleasant to think that valuable qualities are dirt cheap in our own country; but I, unluckily, am constitutionally sceptical as to the heroism of people who never do anything heroic. However disgusting this cynicism of mine may appear, I noticed that Rassendyl pleased the audience at the St James's in all the passages where he appears as a reckless young gentleman impersonating the King of Ruritania for a lark, and rubbed it the wrong way in all his attempts to pose as a king of men. The only qualities needed for his exploit are impudence and the not very uncommon sort of dare-devilry that induces young men to risk breaking their necks at bodily exercises for the mere excitement of the thing. The real author and hero of it is Colonel Sapt, who risks his life as much as Rassendyl, besides taking his chance of the English stranger breaking down or backing out. All the anxiety is his, as well as all the serious purpose and contrivance. When he addresses the sham king as 'You damned young fool!' for exposing himself idly to an unnecessary risk of discovery, the audience is sympathetic and satisfied. When he kneels down and kisses Rassendyl's hand in homage to the innate princeliness which that gentleman has in no wise displayed, it is impossible not to feel revolted. And there you have the false note of the play.

Perhaps the most serious consequence of this mistake is the Prologue. Mr Rose knows far too much about the theatre to suppose that the resemblance of Rassendyl to the King of Ruritania needed any explanation. An audience will always accept a resemblance with eagerness as a freak of nature. What Mr Rose wanted to do was to place Rassendyl under a moral obligation to risk his life for the red Elphberg because the red Elphberg's grandfather sacrificed his life for Rassendyl's grandmother. Now, I submit not only that the motive appeals to that bogus-kingly side of Rassendyl's character which had better have been left out, but that even so its compulsion is ridiculously unconvincing. If a gentleman were to ask me to lend him half a crown on the strength of a relationship based on the following circumstances: to wit, that his grandfather had seduced my grandmother; fought a duel with my grandmother's husband, in the course of which he had been run through during a moment of inattention caused by the entry of the lady; declared with his last breath that he had died for her; and finally walked out of the house in his blood-stained shirt in apparently robust health, I should refer that gentleman to the Charity Organization Society.

Besides, Mr Rose has written the Prologue in the spirit of the nineteenth-century fancier of the eighteenth century rather than in that of the eighteenth century itself. It is a pomandering sort of Prologue, thrown in, not by dramatic necessity, but for the sake of hoops and patches, snuff-boxes and silk coats—above all, a duel by candlelight, without which no eighteenth-century drama would be complete. Mr Rose has often written pleasantly about these and other more remote and lavendery antiquities; but in giving way to them on the stage he has been beset by the temptation to lay the scene out not only for obsolete dresses and incidents, but for obsolete acting, and even obsolete drama. I should not be surprised to learn that he had pleaded hard with Mr Alexander to have a door knocked through the proscenium in order that Miss Mabel Hackney might enter through it with two black pages carrying her train, as the stage custom was in those days. The Prologue, in short, exhibits Mr Rose as the man of sentimental fancies and antiquarian learning rather than as the playwright. It will be useful as a curtain-raiser; but it is not essential to the comprehension or enjoyment of the play.

The play itself, as far as the novel will let it, brings into action Mr Rose's best qualities as a dramatist: his humor, his intelligence in the more generous issues of human feeling, and his insight, which is engagingly disabled—especially in the case of his feminine characters—by a certain shy anxiety to apologize to the lady for the intrusion, and present her with a favorable construction for what he has discovered. It is a thousand pities that the novel contained no figures sufficiently rounded and solid to make the drama really live. Still, unsubstantial as they are, they are superficially natural; and the play hops genially and adventurously along to the final speeches of Flavia and Rassendyl, which make a very pretty ending. A strong ending could only have been achieved by throwing the novel over, and changing the drunken imbecile of a king into an able but unlovable man, as whose consort Flavia might reasonably feel that her high destiny (rather a sentimental fancy, by the way, that high destiny!) would be better fulfilled than with the lovable but feather-brained Rassendyl.

The performance is a curiously haphazard one, considering its costliness and elaboration. Though the prevalent style of play is in the usual quiet St James's key, some of the characters rush on the stage supercharged with dramatic excitement, and momentarily upset all congruity of style. Mr Cautley or Mr Alexander will certainly either kill or be killed some night, unless the sabre fight at the end is more carefully preconcerted than it was on the first night. What is called the coronation scene—meaning the scene in which Rassendyl goes off the stage to be crowned and comes back when the ceremony is over—seems a very quiet little drawing room party business to a musical critic nursed on Le Prophète and the Wagnerian music drama; but it is enjoyable in its unsensational way. The dresses are recklessly expensive and not unhandsome. If I had never been taught to use my eyes as a critic of pictures, I might, perhaps, have been satisfied with the sunset scene in the forest of Zenda: as it was, the hopeless absurdity of the foreground light where Mr Alexander lay at the foot of the tree, set me speculating as to when some serious attempt will be made to produce any of the subtler effects of open air on the stage. The acting was mostly very easy. Mr Vernon, as Colonel Sapt, had the best part—indeed, in a sense the only part—and he left all the rest far behind in it. Mr Alexander was capital in the comedy passages, and delivered his speeches in the last scene finely, but was bad in the drunken episode, which he played like a seasoned teetotaller. The rest of his part, or rather parts, was the wrong side of Rassendyl, which nothing could make really effective. Mr Waring did what was possible to give an air of substance to the nullity called Duke Michael; and Mr Lawrence Cautley had not the material in his lines for producing the dashingly diabolical effect of the Hentzau of the novel. The truth is that half the company are doing nothing but 'supering,' although they are of course neither lineless nor nameless. Miss Millard has apparently taken the most heroic measures to transform herself into a true red Elphberg. She played with a touch of passion in the later scenes; but she was a little flat in the second act through her deficiency in comedy, her sense of humor resolutely refusing to express itself artistically. Miss Olga Brandon had nothing to do but embody the description of the Mayor's wife as a pretty woman;

but though the part is nothing, Miss Brandon certainly got the last inch out of it, and something over, making more of her curtsey than a good many actresses make of a speech. Miss Lily Hanbury was fairly successful in grappling with Antoinette de Mauban; and Miss Mabel Hackney, not as yet a very finished executant, conceived her part in the Prologue excellently.

Mr Wilson Barrett has given me such unbounded delight by his feat of persuading the London critics that several of the most characteristic passages in his Sign of the Cross are quotations from the Bible that I have nothing but praise for him. Sterne's 'tempering the wind to the shorn lamb' need never again be quoted as the champion instance of scripturization. It is true that Mr Wilson Barrett, following the universal law of art development, has founded his Sermon on the Mount to some extent on the original one; but I can assure the public that the text of The Sign of the Cross is essentially original; and if Mr Wilson Barrett writes to the papers to assure us, in the usual terms, that so far from his having taken his play from the Bible, he has never even read that volume, I am quite prepared to believe him. His literary style is altogether different. The play is a monument of sacred and profane history. The influence of Ibsen is apparent throughout, the Norwegian keynote being struck by Mr Barrett himself in the words: 'How many crimes are committed under the cloak of duty!' With scathing, searching irony, and with resolute courage in the face of the prejudiced British public, he has drawn a terrible contrast between the Romans ('Pagans, I regret to say,' as Mr Pecksniff remarked of the sirens), with their straightforward sensuality, and the strange, perverted voluptuousness of the Christians, with their shuddering exaltations of longing for the whip, the rack, the stake, and the lions. The whole drama lies in the spectacle of the hardy Roman prefect, a robust soldier and able general, gradually falling under the spell of a pale Christian girl, white and worn with spiritual ecstasy, and beautiful as Mary Anderson. As she gradually throws upon him the fascination of suffering and martyrdom, he loses his taste for wine; the courtezans at his orgies disgust him; heavenly visions obsess him; undreamt-of raptures of sacrifice, agony, and escape from the world to indescribable holiness and bliss tempt him; and finally he is seen, calm and noble, but stark mad, following the girl to her frightfully voluptuous death. It is a tremendous moral lesson; and though I am pagan enough to dislike most intensely the flogging and racking and screaming on the stage (I really am such a bloodless creature that I take no delight in torture), yet no doubt it helps to drive the irony of the theme home.

On the intellectual side, Christianity hardly receives justice from Mr Wilson Barrett. 'Christianity is not in itself a crime,' says Marcus to Nero. 'Marcus argues strongly, Cæsar,' is Poppea's comment. I must say I think Poppea is rather too easily satisfied. But, after all, we do not want to hear the case argued at this time of day. What we enjoy is being so familiarly in Rome that it sounds quite natural when such directions to wayfarers as 'Fourth on the right from the statue of Hercules' are given by the lictors. We come into the presence of Nero, and hear him ordering a set of living torches for that evening, and boasting of what an artist he is. We see the Roman ladies at home sticking pins into their slaves, and the Roman diner-out exhausted by his second vomit. We hear the thunder of the chariot race, and see the gladiator enter the arena. And we have, as aforesaid, whips and racks, chains and dungeons, uplifted crosses and Christian martyrs, not to mention plenty of music well handled by Mr Edward Jones, with hymns for the Christians, waltzes for the Romans, and Sullivan's Thou'rt passing hence, my brother, and Gounod's Nazareth on the cornet and sackbut between the acts.

The mounting is handsome, and the stage management good and unselfish, all the parts being played with quite extraordinary spirit, and in no way sacrificed to the actor-manager's. I have never seen better work got out of a company. Mr Wilson Barrett has honestly sunk the actor in the author, and done his best for the play, instead of for himself personally. Indeed, the one conspicuous and laughable oversight is in Mr Barrett's own make-up. Instead of wearing the proper cropped Roman wig, he wears his own hair in his old familiar feminine fashion, with the result that when he first steps on the stage he presents such an amazing resemblance to Miss Victor that, instead of applauding him, I stared with a shocked conviction that I had that lady before me in the costume of a Roman warrior. The effect is amusing; but it spoils an otherwise manly picture.

Michael and His Lost Angel

MICHAEL AND HIS LOST ANGEL. *A new and original play of modern English life. In five acts. By* Henry Arthur Jones. *Lyceum Theatre,* 15 *January* 1896.

[18 *January* 1896]

ONE of the great comforts of criticizing the work of

Mr Henry Arthur Jones is that the critic can go straight to the subject matter without troubling about the dramatic construction. In the born writer the style is the man; and with the born dramatist the play is the subject. Mr Jones's plays grow: they are not cut out of bits of paper and stuck together. Mr Grundy or Sardou, at their respective worsts, perform such feats of carpentry in constructing show-cases for some trumpery little situation, that the critics exhaust all their space in raptures over the mechanical skill displayed. But Mr Jones's technical skill is taken as a matter of course. Nobody ever dreams of complimenting him about it: we proceed direct to abusing his ideas without delay. This is quite right and natural. If you invent a mechanical rabbit, wind it up, and set it running round the room for me, I shall be hugely entertained, no matter how monstrously unsuccessful it may be as a representation of nature; but if you produce a real rabbit which begins running about without being wound up at all, I simply say 'Why shouldnt it?' and take down my gun. Similarly, on Mr Jones producing a live play, which starts into perfectly natural action on the rising of the curtain without being wound up during an act or two of exposition, I say 'Why shouldnt it?' and, as aforesaid, take down my gun.

When I respond to the appeal of Mr Jones's art by throwing myself sympathetically into his characteristic attitude of mind, I am conscious of no shortcoming in Michael and his Lost Angel. It then seems to me to be a genuinely sincere and moving play, feelingly imagined, written with knowledge as to the man and insight as to the woman by an author equipped not only with the experience of an adept playwright, and a kindly and humorous observer's sense of contemporary manners, but with that knowledge of spiritual history in which Mr Jones's nearest competitors seem so stupendously deficient. Its art is in vital contact with the most passionate religious movement of its century, as fully quickened art always has been. On comparing it in this relation with the ordinary personal sentiment of Mr Grundy, and with those grotesque flounderings after some sort of respectably pious foothold which have led Mr Pinero to his rescue of the burning Bible from Mrs Ebbsmith's stove, and his redemption of Mrs Fraser by the social patronage of the Bishop's wife, I unhesitatingly class Mr Jones as first, and eminently first, among the surviving fittest of his own generation of playwrights.

But when, instead of throwing myself sympathetically into Mr Jones's attitude, I remain obstinately in my own, I find myself altogether unable to offer to Michael that final degree of complete sympathy and approval which is implied in the conviction that I would have written the play myself if I could. As to the first two acts, I ask nothing better; but at the beginning of the third comes the parting of our ways; and I can point out the exact place where the roads fork. In the first act Michael, a clergyman, compels a girl who has committed what he believes to be a deadly sin to confess it publicly in church. In the second act he commits that sin himself. At the beginning of the third he meets the lady who has been his accomplice; and the following words pass between them:

AUDRIE. Youre sorry?
MICHAEL. No. And you?
AUDRIE. No.

Now, after this, what does the clergyman do?

Without giving another thought to that all-significant fact that he is not sorry—that at the very point where, if his code and creed were valid, his conscience would be aching with remorse, he is not only impenitent, but positively glad, he proceeds to act as if he really were penitent, and not only puts on a hair shirt, but actually makes a confession to his congregation in the false character of a contrite sinner, and goes out from among them with bowed head to exile and disgrace, only waiting in the neighborhood until the church is empty to steal back and privily contradict his pious imposture by picking up and hiding a flower which the woman has thrown on the steps of the altar. This is perfectly true to nature: men do every day, with a frightful fatalism, abjectly accept for themselves as well as others all the consequences of theories as to what they ought to feel and ought to believe, although they not only do not so feel or believe, but often feel and believe the very reverse, and find themselves forced to act on their real feeling and belief in supreme moments which they are willing with a tragically ridiculous self-abnegation to expiate afterwards even with their lives.

Here you have the disqualification of Michael and his Lost Angel for full tragic honors. It is a play without a hero. Let me rewrite the last three acts, and you shall have your Reverend Michael embracing the answer of his own soul, thundering it from the steps of his altar, and marching out through his shocked and shamed parishioners, with colors flying and head erect and unashamed, to the freedom of faith in his own real conscience. Whether he is right or wrong is nothing to me as a dramatist: he must follow his star, right or wrong, if he is to be a hero. In Hamlet one cannot approve unreservedly of the views of Fortinbras;

but, generations of foolish actor-managers to the contrary notwithstanding, what true Shakespearean ever thinks of Hamlet without seeing Fortinbras, in his winged helmet, swoop down at the end, and take, by the divine right of a born 'captain of his soul,' the crown that slips through the dead fingers of the philosopher who went, at the bidding of his father's ghost, in search of a revenge which he did not feel and a throne which he did not want? Fortinbras can, of course, never be anything more than an Adelphi hero, because his bellicose instincts and imperial ambitions are comfortably vulgar; but both the Adelphi hero and the tragic hero have fundamentally the same qualification—fearless pursuit of their own ends and championship of their own faiths *contra mundum.*

Michael fails to satisfy this condition in an emergency where a heroic self-realization alone could save him from destruction; and if this failure were the subject of Mr Jones's last three acts, then the play without a hero might be as tragic as Rosmersholm. But Mr Jones does not set Michael's situation in that light: he shares his fatalism, accepting his remorse, confession, and disgrace as inevitable, with a monastery for the man and death for the woman as the only possible stage ending—surely not so much an ending as a slopping up of the remains of the two poor creatures. The last act is only saved from being a sorry business by the man's plucking a sort of courage out of abandonment, and by a humorous piteousness in the dying woman, who, whilst submitting, out of sheer feebleness of character, to Michael's attitude, is apologetically conscious of having no sincere conviction of sin. When the priest offers his services, she replies, 'No, thanks, Ive been dreadfully wicked—

doesnt much matter, eh? Cant help it now. Havnt strength to feel sorry. So sorry I cant feel sorry.' This gives a pleasant quaintness to the hackneyed pathos of a stage death; but it does not obliterate the fact that Audrie is dying of nothing but the need for making the audience cry, and that she is a deplorable disappointment considering her promise of force and originality in the first two acts. A play without a hero may still be heroic if it has a heroine; and had Mr Jones so laid out his play as to pose the question, 'What will this woman do when she discovers that the saint of Cleveheddon is nothing but a hysterical coward, whose religion is a morbid perversion of his sympathetic instincts instead of the noblest development of them?' the answer of a capable woman to such a question might have given the last three acts the attraction of strength and hope, instead of their present appeal *ad misericordiam* of sentimental despair and irrelevant bodily disease. But Audrie, though she has a certain salt of wit in her, is as incapable of taking her fate into her own hands as Michael; and the two, hypnotized by public opinion, let themselves be driven abjectly, she to the shambles and he to the dustbin, without a redeeming struggle.

It is clear, I think, that if the public were of my way of thinking, the play, good as it is of its kind, would fail; for the public is not sympathetic enough to throw itself into Mr Jones's attitude, and enjoy the play from his point of view, unless it can do so without going out of its own way. And I cannot help thinking that the public dislike a man of Michael's stamp. After all, stupid as we are, we are not Asiatics. The most pigheaded Englishman has a much stronger objection to be crushed or killed by institutions and conventions, however sacred or even respectable, than a Russian peasant or a Chinaman. If he commits a sin, he either tells a lie and sticks to it, or else demands 'a broadening of thought' which will bring his sin within the limits of the allowable. To expiation, if it can possibly be avoided, he has a wholesome and energetic objection. He is an individualist, not a fatalist: with all his apparent conventionality there is no getting over the fact that institutions—moral, political, artistic, and ecclesiastical—which in more Eastern lands have paralysed whole races, making each century a mere stereotype of the one before, are mere footballs for the centuries in England. It is an instinct with me personally to attack every idea which has been full grown for ten years, especially if it claims to be the foundation of all human society. I am prepared to back human society against any idea, positive or negative, that can be brought into the field against it. In this—except as to my definite intellectual consciousness of it—I am, I believe, a much more typical and popular person in England than the conventional man; and I believe that when we begin to produce a genuine national drama, this apparently anarchic force, the mother of higher law and humaner order, will underlie it, and that the public will lose all patience with the conventional collapses which serve for last acts to the serious dramas of today. Depend upon it, the miserable doctrine that life is a mess, and that there is no way out of it, will never nerve any man to write a truly heroic play west of the Caucasus. I do not for a moment suspect Mr Jones of really holding that doctrine himself. He has written Michael as a realist on the unheroic plane, simply taking his contemporaries as he finds them on that plane.

Perhaps it is unfair to Mr Jones to substitute to this

extent a discussion of the philosophy of his play for a criticism of its merits on its own ground. But the performance at the Lyceum has taken all the heart out of my hopes of gaining general assent to my high estimate of Michael and his Lost Angel. The public sees the play as it is acted, not as it ought to be acted. The sooner Mr Jones publishes it the better for its reputation. There never was a play more skilfully designed to fit the chief actors than this was for Mr Forbes Robertson and Mrs Patrick Campbell. But though Mr Jones was able to write for Mrs Campbell such a part as she is not likely to get the refusal of soon again, he had to depend on Mrs Campbell's own artistic judgment to enable her to perceive the value of the chance. The judgment was apparently not forthcoming: at all events, Mrs Patrick Campbell vanished from the bills as the day of battle drew nigh. In such an emergency your London manager has only one idea—send for Miss Marion Terry. Miss Marion Terry was accordingly sent for—sent for to play the bad angel; to be perverse, subtly malign, infernally beautiful; to sell her soul and her lover's to the Devil, and bite her arm through as a seal to the bargain; to do everything that is neither in her nature, nor within the scope of her utmost skill in dissimulation. The result was a touching little sham, very charming in the first act, where her entry rescued the play just as it was staggering under the weight of some very bad acting in the opening scene; and very affecting at the end, where she died considerately and prettily, as only an inveterately amiable woman could. But not for the most infinitesimal fraction of a second was she Audrie Lesden; and five acts of Michael and his Lost Angel without Audrie Lesden was not what the author intended. As to Mr Forbes

Robertson, Mr Jones had undertaken to make the actor's outside effective if he in return would look after the inside of the Reverend Michael. Mr Jones kept to his bargain: Mr Forbes Robertson was unable to fulfil his. He made the mistake—common in an irreligious age—of conceiving a religious man as a lugubrious one. All the sympathy in the first act depended on his making it clear that the force that swept Rose Gibbard to the altar to confess was the priest's rapturous faith in the gladness of an open and contrite heart, natural to a man made over-sanguine by spiritual joy. Mr Forbes Robertson threw away all this sympathy, and set the audience against him and against the play from the outset by adopting the solemn, joyless, professional manner and the preachy utterance of the Low-Church apostle of mortification and wrath. It is quite impossible to exaggerate the disastrous effect of this initial mistake on the performance. The more saintly Mr Robertson looked, the slower, gloomier, more depressingly monotonous he became, until at last, in spite of Miss Terry's spoonfuls of sweet syrup, I half expected to see the infuriated author rush on the stage and treat us to a realistic tableau of the stoning of St Stephen. What is the use of the dramatist harmonizing the old Scarlet-Letter theme in the new Puseyite mode if the actor is to transpose it back again into the old Calvinistic minor key?

As to the rest, their woodenness is not to be described, though woodenness is hardly the right word for Mr Mackintosh, in whose performance, however, I could discover neither grace nor verisimilitude. Miss Brooke need not be included in this wholesale condemnation; but her part was too small to make any difference to the general effect. The melancholy truth of the matter is that the English stage got a good play, and was completely and ignominiously beaten by it. Mr Jones has got beyond the penny novelette conventions which are actable in our theatre. I fear there is no future for him except as a dramatic critic.

The play is well mounted, though the church scene is an appalling example of the worst sort of German 'restoration.' And it has the inevitable defect of all stage churches: the voices will not echo nor the footsteps ring through its canvas naves and aisles. Mr Forbes Robertson has been specially generous in the matter of the band. Mr Armbruster was able to give between the acts a genuine orchestral performance of the slow movement from Raff's Im Walde Symphony, and as much of the andante of Mendelssohn's Italian Symphony as there was time for.

The Immortal William

The Shakespear Anniversary Celebration at the Métropole Theatre, Camberwell, 23 *April* 1896.

[2 *May* 1896]

WITHIN reason, I am always prepared to do honor to Shakespear. Annual celebrations are all very well in theory, and are almost as popular with the people who dont take any part in them, and dont intend to, as Annual Parliaments are with the people who never vote and never electioneer; but outside that large circle they are too much of a good thing. I have long ceased to celebrate my own birthday; and I do not see why I should celebrate Shakespear's. There can be no objection in the world to Mr Benson, or Mr Greet, or anyone else in the Shakespearean business taking the fullest advantage of an anniversary to give that business a fillip; but whoever expects me to put myself every 23 April in an attitude at all differing from my attitude on the 23 October is doomed to disappointment. I went to Camberwell on the afternoon of last Thursday week because, on the whole, I thought it my business to be there; but when the Irving Dramatic Club wanted me to resume work the moment I got back to the west end by going to Cymbeline at St George's Hall, I struck. Shakespear is for an afternoon, but not for all time. Under ordinary circumstances I should have done the other thing—that is, gone to see the amateurs in the evening instead of the professionals in the afternoon; but it happened on this occasion that the professional cast was the fresher, younger, and more interesting of the two; so I went to Camberwell. Let me not, however, exaggerate my own virtue by leaving it to be inferred that I got there in time. The hour appointed was half-past two; and though I spared neither energy nor expense in my journey, making no less than three separate embarkations in train, bus, and tram, at a total cost of fourpence, it was three o'clock before the Métropole was sighted. This had two grave consequences. First, Camberwell had rallied round the Bard so multitudinously that the offer of untold gold could procure me nothing better than a mere skylight of a box, from which my view of the legitimate drama was considerably foreshortened. Second, I was late for Miss Dorothy Dene's Juliet. This I greatly regretted; for I have not seen Miss Dorothy Dene since the now almost remote days when Mr Henry Arthur Jones was making his reputation by writing melodramas for Mr Wilson Barrett at the Princess's. Why? Here was a young lady who had, not the painted show of beauty which is so common on the stage, and so tedious, but that honest reality of it which is useful to painters. Her speech shewed unusual signs of artistic cultivation; she had plastic grace; she took herself and her profession seriously; and her appearances in leading parts were not unpopular. The mystery is, what became of her? Did she fall into the abyss of opulent matrimony? Did the studio violently reclaim its adored model? Did she demand impossible terms? Or were the managers obdurate in their belief that there is only one safe sort of actress—the woman who is all susceptibility and no brains? Far be it from me to deny that every deviation from this type involves a certain risk of unpopularity—of a demand on the part of the actress, or rather the woman, that in the intercourse between her and the public the wooing and the worth shall not all be on one side. Further still be it from me to forget the fact that in cases of positive genius for the stage no question as to the dignity of the actress's occupation can arise. For instance, Duse is clearly a most laborious artist hard at work, and not a pretty woman making an exhibition of herself. But the appearance of a Duse is as rare on the stage as that of a woman who absolutely cannot act at all. Most of the routine of our leading theatrical work in London is done by ladies who are not altogether artists and not altogether exhibitions, but who eke out a little art with more or less personal attractiveness. Probably the reason our managers prefer the brainless-susceptible woman is that she is a ready-made actress as far as she can act at all; and small blame to them, since we have no apprenticeship system to secure to a manager the services of an actress whom he trains, and no system of training to replace the apprenticeship system. But I get so tired of the brainless-susceptible heroine that even an American lecturer would sometimes be a relief to the eternal sympathetic leading lady, who is called sweetly womanly because, having nothing but her sex to insist on, she insists on that continually. And yet, since women of the other sort get no engagements, it ends in her being the only one who gets sufficient stage practice to be trusted with important parts, whence it comes that the important parts never are important. We want more women of the clever, positive type on the stage (also men). We also want more objectively beautiful women on the stage; for your brainless-susceptible one is often your beauty-less-susceptible: she may appeal to your sentimentality; but a sculptor or a painter would not look twice at her from his dry business point of view; and her graces of carriage and movement are of the cheapest. Her hold on the stage is largely a result of the stage's hold on her through her disadvantage of being fit for nothing else; so that economic necessity does for her what irresistible vocation does for an actress of genius —gives her, that is, the unconditional singleness of aim and pertinacity which move mountains in the long run. The clever, positive woman, on the other hand, has alternative activities: she has ability and character enough to make her living in other professions, or to discharge social and domestic duties as the wife of a Philistine citizen in a responsible, capable, respectable way. Granted that she may have only the makings of a second-rate actress in her, she would probably make second-rate acting much more important than a good deal of what passes as first-rate acting at present; and her influence on the drama would be highly beneficial owing to her demand for real parts in which to put forth her brains and skill against the rivals who rely on sex and sympathy in every kind of part. It takes all sorts to make a stage, just as it takes all sorts to make a world; and we do not get all sorts at present. We get the geniuses and the *hystériques*; but the intermediate talents, however promising, are driven back from a profession in which brains and self-respect have no chance against emotional facility and neurotic sexuality. The latter are invaluable, the former quite useless, in any empty part which is nothing but the merest cue to the imagination of the audience; but confront the facile, neurotic, empty-headed actress with a part which demands not only sympathy but intelligence and trained nervous energy; not only 'womanly' softnesses and graces but plastic, picturesque, vigorous action; nay, ask her to deliver a ten-line speech—not a hysterical explosion, but a speech with thought as well as feeling in it—and you will soon find how a dramatic author is hampered at present by the limited compass of the instruments at his disposal. There are always clever, educated, ambitious young women ready to try their fortune on the stage; but how are they to get the necessary experience to make skilled artists of them? It takes years of practice to develop the power of emotional expression; for most educated women have been trained to fight against emotional expression because it is a mode of self-betrayal. Now self-betrayal, magnified to suit the optics of the theatre, is the whole art of acting; and the strong, continent woman, unless she is descended from generations of actors, is certain to be beaten at first on the stage by the hysterical, incontinent one, or even by the stupid, prosaic hereditary actress who, within certain limits, acts as a duck swims. Under present conditions this handicap is sufficient to baffle the clever recruit drawn from the newly emancipated women of the middle class in her quest for engagements, thus depriving her of the practice necessary to train her, and so defeating her attempt to gain a footing on the stage. The theatre is unable to keep and drill able-bodied and able-minded recruits; and the result is that the class of work which would in any other profession be perfectly within the competence of the rank and file, has to be entrusted to the leaders. And even the leaders are often more remarkable for what is called social charm than for any rarer artistic qualification.

On the whole, perhaps it is as well that I did not see Miss Dorothy Dene; for it is not conceivable that disuse has matured her powers, or years increased her natural suitability to the part of Juliet. Just at present I am more anxious about Miss Dorothea Baird, whom I did see, as Rosalind. Rosalind is to the actress what Hamlet is to the actor—a part in which, reasonable presentability being granted, failure is hardly possible. It is easier than Trilby up to a certain point, though it will of course hold much more acting. Miss Baird plays it intelligently and nicely; and this, to such a very pretty Ganymede, is enough to secure success. How far the niceness and intelligence of the pretty young lady will develop into the passion and intuition of the artist, or whether the prettiness will develop into the 'handsome is as handsome does' fascination which holds the stage for many years against Time, remains to be seen. All that can be said at present is that Miss Baird's Rosalind is bright and pleasant, with sufficient natural charm to secure indulgence for all its shortcomings. Of these the most serious is Miss Baird's delivery of the lines. Everybody by this time knows how a modern high-schoolmistress talks—how she repudiates the precision, the stateliness, the awe-inspiring oracularity of the old-fashioned schoolmistress who knew nothing, and cloaks her mathematics with a pretty little voice, a pretty little manner, and all sorts of self-conscious calineries and unassumingnesses. 'Poor little me! what do *I* know about conic sections?' is the effect she aims at. Miss Baird's Rosalind has clearly been to the high school and modelled herself upon her pet mistress, if not actually taught there herself. But that dainty, pleading, narrow-lipped little torrent of gabble will not do for Shakespear. It is so unintelligible across the footlights that even I, who know As You Like It almost as well as I know Beethoven's Pastoral Symphony, could not always catch what she was saying. This being so, it may safely be taken that Camberwell did not catch more than a very small conic section of it. For even an expert cannot make sense of Elizabethan blank verse at a first hearing when it is delivered at the rate of 200 words a minute and upwards. Besides, its lyrical flow, if such a tiny ladylike patter can be credited with so broad a quality, is not that of Shakespear's verse. The effect is like a canary trying to sing Handel.

Mr H. B. Irving is in the full flood of that Shakespearean enthusiasm which exalts the Bard so far above common sense that any prosaic suiting of the action to the word and the word to the action seems to be a degradation of his genius to what Nicholas Rowe called 'a mere light of reason.' Mr Irving gave us the closet scene from Hamlet. He entered, surcharged with Fate, and instead of Hamlet's sharp, dry, 'Now, mother: whats the matter?' followed by his reply to her affected 'Thou has thy father much offended,' with the purposely blunt 'Mother: *you* have my father much offended,' gave us a most tragic edition of the conversation, with the yous altered to thous, and an agitated slip or two to enhance the effect. When he lifted the arras and found that he had killed Polonius instead of the King, he betrayed not the smallest surprise, but said, in a superior tone, 'Thou wretched, rash, intruding fool, farewell!' much as if he were dismissing a deservedly and quite intentionally flogged schoolboy. He was resolved to make an effect by seizing the Queen and throwing her down on the floor; and the moment he selected was in the middle of the following passage:

At your age
The heyday in the blood is tame: it's humble,
And waits upon the judgment; and what judgment
Would step from this to this?

The Queen was floored after the phrase 'and waits upon the judgment,' shewing that at Mr Irving's age the heyday in the blood does not wait upon the judgment, but has its fling (literally) regardless of reason. The only dramatic profit from this proceeding was the point given to the Ghost's 'But see! amazement on thy mother sits.' Nevertheless, the performance, nonsensical as it was, was not ridiculous. Mr Irving is not altogether unsuccessful in his attempts to be tragic and to make effects; and if he could only bring his tragedy and his effects into some intelligent relation to the drama in hand, he would find himself highly complimented in the Saturday Review. To be abstractly and irrelevantly tragic; to brandish a sword; to discourse in blank verse; to stagger and fall and hurl frail heroines away, is just as absurd in Hamlet, if done at the wrong moment, as it would be in Box and Cox. There are people so unfit for the stage that they could not do these things even at the right moment without making the audience laugh. That is not Mr Irving's case. When he learns what to do and when to do it, he will not be at a loss as to how to do it. More than that it is impossible to grant him at present. The scenes from As You Like It included nothing of Jaques except the few scraps of dialogue between the pessimist and Orlando; and no exception can be taken to the way in which these were handled by Mr Irving. He dressed and looked the part well.

The best bit of work was Mr Bernard Gould's Orlando; the worst, Mr Ben Greet's Touchstone. Mr Greet put himself out of the question before he had been two minutes on the stage by the profound stroke of picking one of Orlando's sonnets from a tree, and reading from it the impromptu burlesque:

> If a hart do lack a hind,
> Let him seek out Rosalind, etc.

This was a new reading with a vengeance. He was not much more successful as executant than as Shakespearean student. He completely missed the piled-up climax of the speech to William, and was, in short, as bad a Touchstone as a critic could desire to see. It is no disgrace to an actor to be unable to play Touchstone; but why, under these circumstances, and being a manager, he should cast himself for it, passes my understanding. Mr Rawson Buckley played Oliver very well, but persisted, as usual, in dressing himself smartly, and then describing himself as 'a wretched ragged man, o'ergrown with hair.' Mr Gould managed his part, especially the difficulties of the sham courtship with Ganymede, better than I can remember having seen it managed before; and some of his lines were finely spoken; but he was not Orlando. Orlando's intelligence is the intelligence of the heart: he always comes out best as an amiable, strong, manly, handsome, shrewd-enough-to-take-care-of-himself, but safely stupid and totally unobservant young man. Now, Mr Gould plays with his head; his intelligence is always on the alert; and he is so observant that in spite of his many valuable stage qualities he almost disqualifies himself as an actor by his draughtsman's habit of watching himself and everyone else so keenly and interestedly that he is more apt to forget his part than to forget himself in it. The born actor looks in: Mr Gould looks on. He acts like a good critic, and probably represses his tendencies—if he has any—to the maudlin self-sympathy, the insane egotism, the bottomless folly, the hysterical imaginative mendacity which—with the help of alcohol—make acting easy to some men who are for all other purposes the most hopeless wastrels. However, I do not object: I recognize the fact that the ascendency of the sentimental amorphous actor means the ascendency of the sentimental amorphous drama, and that the critical actor, like Mr Gould, is indispensable to a drama with any brains in it. Still, the critical actor need not be also a draughtsman actor. I once elaborately explained to Mr Gould a part of which I was myself the author. He paid me the closest attention; retired to ponder my utterances; and presently returned with a perfectly accurate and highly characteristic drawing of me, which I shall probably never live down. And if I had been Shakespear explaining Orlando, it would have been just the same.

Henry IV

HENRY IV. PART I. *Haymarket Theatre,* 8 *May* 1896.

[16 *May* 1896]

THIS is a miserably incompetent world. The average doctor is a walking compound of natural ignorance and acquired witchcraft, who kills your favorite child, wrecks your wife's health, and orders you into habits of nervous dram-drinking before you have the courage to send him about his business, and take your chance like a gentleman. The average lawyer is a nincompoop, who contradicts your perfectly sound impressions on notorious points of law, involves you in litigation when your case is hopeless, compromises when your success is certain, and cannot even make your will without securing the utter defeat of your intentions if anyone takes the trouble to dispute them. And so on, down to the bootmaker whose boots you have to make your tortured feet fit, and the tailor who clothes you as if you were a cast-iron hot-water apparatus. You imagine that these people have professions; and you find that what they have is only, in the correct old word, their 'mystery'—a humbug, like all mysteries. And yet, how we help to keep up the humbug! I know men of quite exceptional intelligence—men so sceptical that they have freed their minds from all philosophic and religious dogma, who nevertheless read the Lancet and the British Medical Journal from end to end every week as devoutly as any superstitious washerwoman ever read Zadkiel or Old Moore, and not only believe it all, but long tremblingly for the next symptom that will give them an excuse for calling in the medicine man to mistake typhoid fever for influenza or paint their tonsils with caustic when their kidneys are out of order. Every week they have some joyful tidings for me. Another disease has been traced to its germ; an infallible destroyer of that germ has been discovered; the disease has been annihilated. What wonderful triumphs has not science enjoyed in my time! Small-pox has been made totally impossible; hydrophobia has vanished; epilepsy has yielded to the simplest of operations; the pangs of angina pectoris have been relieved as if by magic; consumption is a dream of the past; and now there is to be no more diphtheria. Instead of vainly seeking, as of old, for a universal remedy, we are the proud discoverers of a dozen, and can change with the fashion from one to another. Mercury, salicylic acid, iodide and bromide of potassium, hashed thyroid, antipyrine, with lymphs innumerable: there they are, making us all safe and happy until we are unfortunate enough to fall down in a fit, or get bitten by a mad dog, or fall sick with an ugly rash and a bad pain in our backs, when we promptly place ourselves in the hands of the very gentleman who wrote to The Times to pledge his honor and reputation, founded on a pyramid of vivisected rabbits, that such things could never happen again. Depend upon it, if Macbeth had killed Macduff, he would have gone back to the Witches next day to ask their advice as to the best way of dealing with Malcolm.

It is the same with all the professions. I have other friends who are law-mad—who believe that lawyers are wise, judges high-minded and impartial, juries infallible, and codes on the brink of perfection. The military-mad and the clergy-mad stalk at large throughout the kingdom. Men believe in the professions as they believe in ghosts, because they want to believe in them. Fact-blindness—the most common sort of blindness—and the resolute lying of respectable men, keep up the illusion. No mortal, however hard-headed, can feel very safe in his attempts to sift the gold of fact and efficiency out of the huge rubbish heap of professionalism.

My own weakness is neither medicine, nor law, nor tailoring, nor any of the respectable departments of bogusdom. It is the theatre. The mystery-man who takes me in is not the doctor nor the lawyer, but the actor. In this column I have prated again and again of the mission of the theatre, the art of the actor, of his labor, his skill, his knowledge, his importance as a civilizing agent, his function as a spiritual doctor. Surely I have been in this the most ridiculous of all dupes. But before you lay me down in derision, never to read my articles again, hear my excuse. There is one sort of human accomplishment that cannot be dismissed as a figment of the spectator's imagination. The skill with which a man does that which he has done every day for twenty years is no illusion. When the operative at his mule in the cotton mill pieces the broken yarn, when Paderewski at his Erard grand plays a sonata, he is not hypnotizing you, or inviting you to make-believe. He is actually doing things that would be miracles if done by an untrained man. Or take him who, with no eye to cotton cloth or the interpretation of Beethoven, does difficult things for the sake of their difficulty, simply as marvels: for instance, the acrobat. You cannot deny the reality of his feats. His complete physical self-possession, his ambidextrous grace, his power of making several deliberate movements in the space of a pang of terror—as when, for example, he will coolly alter the disposition of his body at a given moment, whilst he is falling headlong through the air: all these accomplishments of his really exist, and are by no means the product of the imagination of an innocent clergyman, sitting in the auditorium with his nose buried in a volume of Shakespear, and ready to take the word of the newspapers next day for what is happening on the stage. Now, am I to be greatly blamed for having supposed that the actor was a genuinely skilled artist like the acrobat, only adding to the skilled mastery of his powers of movement a mastery of his powers of speech, with an ear for verse, a sense of character, a cultivated faculty of observation and mimicry, and such higher qualities as Nature might throw into the bargain? There were great examples to mislead me: Kean was a harlequin as well as a Hamlet; Duse's Camille is positively enthralling as an exhibition of the gymnastics of perfect suppleness and grace; and I have seen Salvini come out before the curtain to accept a trophy from an admirer in a stage box with more art and more fascination—the whole thing being carried out in strict accordance with certain rules of his art—than an ordinary skirt dancer could get into the clumsy imposture she calls dancing after two years' hard practice. Further, it has been a matter of common observation in my generation that the burlesque of the Byron-Farnie-Reece-Burnand period did not, as it turned out, prove a bad training for the people who played in it. Nobody will contend, I imagine, that the training was intellectual: the secret lay in the music, the dancing, the marching, the fantastic walks round, the boundless scope for physical agility, the premium which the very barrenness and vulgarity of the entertainment placed on personal feats and on mimicry. Even that terrible stage calamity the stock actor of the old régime learnt something more from the Christmas pantomime than he would have known without it .

I plead, then, that acting is potentially an artistic profession, and that by training and practice a person can qualify himself or herself to come to a manager or author and say, 'Within the limits imposed by my age and sex, I can do all the ordinary work of the stage with perfect certainty. I know my vowels and consonants as a phonetic expert, and can speak so as to arrest the attention of the audience whenever I open my mouth, forcibly, delicately, roughly, smoothly, prettily, harshly, authoritatively, submissively, but always artistically, just as you want it. I can sit, stand, fall, get up, walk, dance, and otherwise use my body with the complete command of it that marks the physical artist.' An actor might know all this, and yet, for want of the power to interpret an author's text and invent the appropriate physical expression for it, never, without coaching, get beyond Rosencrantz or Seyton. It is, therefore, only the minimum qualification of a skilled stage hand; and if an actor is not that, then he is merely a stage-struck unskilled laborer or handy man, and his 'conceptions' of Ibsen or Shakespear are mere impertinences. I naturally concluded that the minimum was in force, and acting a real profession. Alas! that only proves that my desire and hope got the better of my observation—my imagination of my experience.

However, I am cured now. It is all a delusion: there is no profession, no art, no skill about the business at all. We have no actors: we have only authors, and not many of them. When Mendelssohn composed Son and Stranger for an amateur performance, he found that the bass could only sing one note. So he wrote the bass part all on that one note; and when it came to the fateful night, the bass failed even at that. Our authors do as Mendelssohn did. They find that the actors have only one note, or perhaps, if they are very clever, half a dozen. So their parts are confined to these notes, often with the same result as in Mendelssohn's case. If you doubt me, go and see Henry IV at the Haymarket. It is as good work as our stage can do; but the man who says that it is skilled work has neither eyes nor ears; the man who mistakes it for intelligent work has no brains; the man who finds it even good fun may be capable of Christy Minstrelsy but not of Shakespear. Everything that charm of style, rich humor, and vivid natural characterization can do for a play are badly wanted by Henry IV, which has neither the romantic beauty of Shakespear's earlier plays nor the tragic greatness of the later ones. One can hardly forgive Shakespear quite for the worldly phase in which he tried to thrust such a Jingo hero as his Harry V down our throats. The combination of conventional propriety and brute masterfulness in his public capacity with a low-lived blackguardism in his private tastes is not a pleasant one. No doubt he is true to nature as a picture of what is by no means uncommon in English society, an able young Philistine inheriting high position and authority, which he holds on to and goes through with by keeping a tight grip on his conventional and legal advantages, but who would have been quite in his place if he had been born a gamekeeper or a farmer. We do not in the first part of Henry IV see Harry sending Mrs Quickly and Doll Tearsheet to the whipping-post, or handing over Falstaff to the Lord Chief Justice with a sanctimonious lecture; but he repeatedly makes it clear that he will turn on them later on, and that his self-indulgent good-fellowship with them is consciously and deliberately treacherous. His popularity, therefore, is like that of a prizefighter: nobody feels for him as for Romeo or Hamlet. Hotspur, too, though he is stimulating as ginger cordial is stimulating, is hardly better than his horse; and King Bolingbroke, preoccupied with his crown exactly as a miser is preoccupied with his money, is equally useless as a refuge for our affections, which are thus thrown back undivided on Falstaff, the most human person in the play, but none the less a besotted and disgusting old wretch. And there is neither any subtlety nor (for Shakespear) much poetry in the presentation of all these characters. They are labelled and described and insisted upon with the roughest directness; and their reality and their humor can alone save them from the unpopularity of their unlovableness and the tedium of their obviousness. Fortunately, they offer capital opportunities for interesting acting. Bolingbroke's long discourse to his son on the means by which he struck the imagination and enlisted the snobbery of the English people gives the actor a chance comparable to the crafty early scenes in Richelieu. Prince Hal's humor is seasoned with sportsmanlike cruelty and the insolence of conscious mastery and contempt to the point of occasionally making one shudder. Hotspur is full of energy; and Falstaff is, of course, an unrivalled part for the right sort of comedian. Well acted, then, the play is a good one in spite of there not being a single tear in it. Ill acted—O heavens!

Of the four leading parts, the easiest—Hotspur—becomes pre-eminent at the Haymarket, not so much by Mr Lewis Waller's superiority to the rest as by their inferiority to him. Some of the things he did were astonishing in an actor of his rank. At the end of each of his first vehement speeches, he strode right down the stage and across to the prompt side of the proscenium on the frankest barnstorming principles, repeating this absurd 'cross'—a well-known convention of the booth for catching applause—three times, step for step, without a pretence of any dramatic motive. In the camp scene before the battle of Shrewsbury, he did just what I blamed Miss Violet Vanbrugh for trying to do in Monsieur de Paris: that is, to carry through a long crescendo of excitement by main force after beginning fortissimo. Would it be too far-fetched to recommend Mr Waller to study how Mozart, in rushing an operatic movement to a spirited conclusion, knew how to make it, when apparently already at its utmost, seem to bound forward by a sudden pianissimo and lightsome change of step, the speed and force of the execution being actually reduced instead of intensified by the change? Such skilled, resourceful husbandry is the secret of all effects of this kind; and it is in the entire absence of such husbandry that Mr Waller shewed how our miserable theatre has left him still a novice for the purposes of a part which he is fully equipped by nature to play with most brilliant success, and which he did play very strikingly considering he was not in the least sure how to set about it, and hardly dared to stop blazing away at full pitch for an instant lest the part should drop flat on the boards. Mr Mollison presented us with an assortment of effects, and tones, and poses which had no reference, as far as I could discover, to the part of Bolingbroke at any single point. I did not catch a glimpse of the character from one end of his performance to the other, and so must conclude that Shakespear has failed to convey his intention to him. Mr Gillmore's way of playing Hal was as bad as the traditional way of playing Sheridan. He rattled and swaggered and roystered, and followed every sentence with a forced explosion of mirthless laughter, evidently believing that, as Prince Hal was reputed to be a humorous character, it was his business to laugh at him. Like most of his colleagues, he became more tolerable in the plain sailing of the battle scene, where the parts lose their individuality in the general warlike excitement, and an energetic display of the commonest sort of emotion suffices. Mr Tree only wants one thing to make him an excellent Falstaff, and that is to get born over again as unlike himself as possible. No doubt, in the course of a month or two, when he begins to pick up a few of the lines of the part, he will improve on his first effort; but he will never be even a moderately good Falstaff. The basket-work figure, as expressionless as that of a Jack in the Green; the face, with the pathetic wandering eye of Captain Swift belying such suggestion of character as the lifeless mask of paint and hair can give; the voice, coarsened, vulgarized, and falsified without being enriched or colored; the hopeless efforts of the romantic imaginative actor, touching only in unhappy parts, to play the comedian by dint of mechanical horseplay: all that is hopeless, irremediable. Mr Tree might as well try to play Juliet; and if he were wise he would hand over his part and his breadbasket to Mr Lionel Brough, whose Bardolph has the true comic force which Mr Tree never attains for a moment.

Two ideas have been borrowed from the last London revival of Henry V by Mr Coleman at the Queen's Theatre in Long Acre. One is the motionless battle tableau, which is only Mr Coleman's Agincourt over again, and which might just as well be cut out of cardboard. The other is the casting of Miss Kate Phillips for Mrs Quickly. As Mrs Quickly is plainly a slovenly, greasy, Gampish old creature, and Miss Phillips is unalterably trim, smart, and bright, a worse choice could not have been made. One would like to have seen Miss Mansfield in the part. Mrs Tree, as Lady Percy, did what I have never seen her do before: that is, played her part stupidly. The laws of nature seem to be suspended when Shakespear is in question. A Lady Percy who is sentimentally affectionate, who recites her remonstrance with Percy in the vein of Clarence's dream in Richard III, and who comes on the stage to share the applause elicited by the combats in the battle of Shrewsbury, only makes me rub my eyes and wonder whether I am dreaming.

Besides Mr Lionel Brough and Mr Lewis Waller, there were three performers who came off with credit. Mr Holman Clark played Glendower like a reasonable man who could read a Shakespearean play and understand it—a most exceptional achievement in his profession, as it appears. Mr D. J. Williams, who played William in As You Like It the other day at the Métropole, and played him well, was a Smike-like and effective Francis; and Miss Marion Evans was a most musical Lady Mortimer, both in her Welsh song and Welsh speech.

The chief merit of the production is that the play has been accepted from Shakespear mainly as he wrote it. There are cuts, of course, the worst of them being the sacrifice of the nocturnal innyard scene, a mutilation which takes the reality and country midnight freshness from the Gadshill robbery, and reduces it to a vapid interlude of horseplay. But the object of these cuts is to save time: there is no alteration or hotch-potch, and consequently no suspicion of any attempt to demonstrate the superiority of the manager's taste and judgment to Shakespear's, in the Daly fashion. This ought to pass as a matter of course; but as things are at present it must be acknowledged as highly honorable to Mr Tree. However, it is not my cue just now to pay Mr Tree compliments. His *tours de force* in the art of make-up do not impose on me: any man can get into a wicker barrel and pretend to be Falstaff, or put on a false nose and call himself Svengali. Such tricks may very well be left to the music-halls: they are altogether unworthy of an artist of Mr Tree's pretensions. When he returns to the serious pursuit of his art by playing a part into which he can sincerely enter without disguise or mechanical denaturalization, may I be there to see! Until then let him guard the Haymarket doors against me; for I like him best when he is most himself.

The Second Dating of Sheridan

THE SCHOOL FOR SCANDAL. *By* Sheridan. *Lyceum Theatre,* 20 *June* 1896.

ON THE MARCH. *A musical comedy in two acts. Prince of Wales Theatre,* 22 *June* 1896.

[27 *June* 1896]

IT is impossible to see The School for Scandal without beginning to moralize. I am going to moralize: let the reader skip if he will.

As the world goes on, manners, customs, and morals change their aspect with revolutionary completeness, whilst man remains almost the same.

Honor and decency, coats and shirts, cleanliness and politeness, eating and drinking, may persist as names; but the actual habits which the names denote alter so much that no century would tolerate those of its forerunner or successor. Compare the gentleman of Sheridan's time with the gentleman of today. What a change in all that is distinctively gentlemanly!—the dress, the hair, the watch-chain, the manners, the point of honor, the meals, the ablutions, and so on! Yet strip the twain, and they are as like as two eggs: maroon them on Juan Fernandez, and what difference will there be between their habits and those of Robinson Crusoe? Nevertheless, men do change, not only in what they think and what they do, but in what they are. Sometimes they change, just like their fashions, by the abolition of one sort and color of man and the substitution of another—white for black or yellow for red, white being the height of fashion with us. But they also change by slow development of the same kind of man; so that whilst the difference between the institutions of the eighteenth and twentieth centuries may be as complete as the difference between a horse and a bicycle, the difference between the men of those periods is only a trifling increment of efficiency, not nearly so great as that which differentiated Shakespear from the average Elizabethan. That is why Shakespear's plays, though obsolete as representations of fashion and manners, are still far ahead of the public as dramatic studies of humanity.

But I must cut my argument more finely than this. To say that fashions change more rapidly than men is a very crude statement of extremes. Everything has its own rate of change. Fashions change more quickly than manners, manners more quickly than morals, morals more quickly than passions, and, in general, the conscious, reasonable, intellectual life more quickly than the instinctive, wilful, affectionate one. The dramatist who deals with the irony and humor of the relatively durable sides of life, or with their pity and terror, is the one whose comedies and tragedies will last longest—sometimes so long as to lead a book-struck generation to dub him 'Immortal,' and proclaim him as 'not for an age, but for all time.' Fashionable dramatists begin to 'date,' as the critics call it, in a few years: the accusation is rife at present against the earlier plays of Pinero and Grundy, though it is due to these gentlemen to observe that Shakespear's plays must have 'dated' far more when they were from twenty to a hundred years old than they have done since the world gave up expecting them to mirror the passing hour. When Caste and Diplomacy were fresh, London Assurance had begun to date most horribly: nowadays Caste and Diplomacy date like the day-before-yesterday's tinned salmon; whereas if London Assurance were revived (and I beg that nothing of the kind be attempted), there would be no more question of dating about it than about the plays of Garrick or Tobin or Mrs Centlivre.

But now observe the consequences, as to this dating business, of the fact that morals change more slowly than costumes and manners, and instincts and passions than morals. It follows, does it not, that every 'immortal' play will run the following course? First, like London Assurance, its manners and fashions will begin to date. If its matter is deep enough to tide it over this danger, it will come into repute again, like the comedies of Sheridan or Goldsmith, as a modern classic. But after some time—some centuries, perhaps —it will begin to date again in point of its ethical conception. Yet if it deals so powerfully with the instincts and passions of humanity as to survive this also, it will again regain its place, this time as an antique classic, especially if it tells a capital story. It is impossible now to read, without a curdling of the blood and a bristling of the hair, the frightful but dramatically most powerful speech which David, on his death-bed, delivers to his son about the old enemy whom he had himself sworn to spare. 'Thou art a wise man and knowest what thou oughtest to do unto him; but his hoar head bring thou down to the grave with blood.' Odysseus, proud of outwitting all men at cheating and lying, and intensely relishing the blood of Penelope's suitors, is equally outside our morality. So is Punch. But David and Ulysses, like Punch and Judy, will survive for many a long day yet. Not until the change has reached our instincts and passions will their stories begin to 'date' again for the last time before their final obsolescence.

I have been led into this investigation of 'dating' by the fact that The School for Scandal, which has got over its first attack of that complaint so triumphantly that its obsolete costumes and manners positively heighten its attraction, dated very perceptibly last Saturday night at the Lyceum in point of morals. Its thesis of the superiority of the good-natured libertine to the ill-natured formalist and hypocrite may pass, though it is only a dramatization of Tom Jones, and hardly demurs to the old morality further than to demonstrate that a bad man is not so bad as a worse. But there is an ancient and fishlike smell about the 'villainy' of Joseph and the ladylikeness of Lady Teazle. If you want to bring The School for Scandal up to date, you must make Charles a woman, and Joseph a perfectly sincere moralist. Then you will be in the atmosphere of Ibsen and of The Greatest of These—at once. And it is because there is no sort of hint of this now familiar atmosphere—because Joseph's virtue is a pretence instead of a reality, and because the women in the play are set apart and regarded as absolutely outside the region of free judgment in which the men act, that the play, as aforesaid, 'dates.'

Formerly, nothing shocked us in the screen scene except Charles's caddishness in making fun of Sir Peter and his wife under very painful circumstances. But, after all, Charles was not so bad as Hamlet rallying Ophelia at the play or Mercutio chaffing the Nurse. What now jars on us is the caddishness of Lady Teazle, whose conduct for the first time begins to strike us as it would if it were the conduct of a man in the like circumstances. Society forbids a man to compromise a woman; but it also requires him, if he nevertheless does compromise her, to accept as one of the consequences of his action the obligation not to betray her, even if he has to go into the witness box and swear to her innocence. Suppose Lady Teazle, on being surprised by Sir Peter in Joseph's rooms, had invented a plausible excuse, and had asked Joseph to confirm her. Suppose Joseph had thereupon said, 'No, it is false, every word. My slumbering conscience awakens; and I return to the sacred path of truth and duty. Your wife, Sir Peter, is an abandoned woman who came here to tempt me from the path of honor. But for your arrival I might have fallen; but now I see the blackness of her conduct in all its infamy; and I ask you to pardon me, and to accept the sincerity of my contrition as a pledge for my future good conduct.' Would any extremity of blackballing, cutting, even kicking, be considered too severe for the man who should try to extricate himself at the expense of his accomplice in that straightforward manner? And yet that is exactly what Lady Teazle does without the least misgiving on the part of the dramatist as to the entire approval and sympathy of the audience. In this, as far as I am concerned, the dramatist is mistaken, and the play consequently dates. I cannot for the life of me see why it is less dishonorable for a woman to kiss and tell than a man. It is sometimes said that the social consequences of exposure are worse for a woman than for a man; but that is certainly not the case in these days of Parnell overthrows and ruinous damages, whatever it may have been in the time of Sheridan—and the commonplace assumptions with regard to that period are probably as erroneous as those current about our own. At all events, when a married woman comes to a man's rooms with the deliberate intention of enjoying a little gallantry, and, on being caught, pleads for sympathy and forgiveness as an innocent young creature misled and seduced by a villain, she strikes a blow at the very foundations of immorality.

The fact that this is not altogether a wise thing to do—that artificial systems of morality, like other dangerous engines, explode when they are worked at high pressure without safety-valves—was cynically admitted in Sheridan's time with regard to men, and sentimentally repudiated with regard to women. But now see what has happened. A terrible, gifted person, a woman speaking for women, Madame Sarah Grand to wit, has arisen to insist that if the morality of her sex can do without safety-valves, so can the morality of 'the stronger sex,' and to demand that the man shall come to the woman exactly as moral as he insists that she shall come to him. And, of course, not a soul dares deny that claim. On the other hand, the fact that there is an obvious alternative way out of the difficulty does not escape those to whom Madame Sarah Grand's position is a *reductio ad absurdum* of our whole moral system; and accordingly we have Mrs Kendal asking every night at the Garrick why Man—meaning Woman—should be so much more moral than God. As for me, it is not my business as a dramatic critic to pursue the controversy: it concerns me only as the explanation of how Lady Teazle's position is changed by the arrival of audiences who read edition after edition of The Heavenly Twins, and who nightly applaud the point made by the author of The Greatest of These—. Whether they are for greater rigor with the novelist, or for greater charity with the dramatist, they are equally learning to drop the old fast-and-loose system of a masculine morality for the man and a feminine morality for the woman, and to apply instead a human standard impartially to both sexes. And so The School for Scandal dates on the Woman Question almost as badly as The Taming of the Shrew.

That the play is well acted goes without saying. Sheridan wrote for the actor as Handel wrote for the singer, setting him a combination of strokes which, however difficult some of them may be to execute finely, are familiar to all practised actors as the strokes which experience has shewn to be proper to the nature and capacity of the stage-player as a dramatic instrument. With Sheridan you are never in the plight of the gentleman who stamped on a sheet of Beethoven's music in a rage, declaring that what cannot be played should not be written. That difficulty exists today with Ibsen, who abounds in passages that our actors do not know how to play; but

The School for Scandal is like Acis and Galatea: you may have the voice and the skill for it or you may not (probably not); but at all events you are never in doubt as to how it ought to be done. To see Mr William Farren play Sir Peter after a long round of modern 'character acting' is like hearing Santley sing Nasce al bosco after a seasonful of goat-bleating Spanish tenors and tremulous French baritones shattering themselves on passionately sentimental dithyrambs by Massenet and Saint-Saëns. Mr Forbes Robertson is an excellent Joseph Surface. He gets at the centre of the part by catching its heartlessness and insincerity, from which his good looks acquire a subtle ghastliness, his grace a taint of artifice, and all the pictorial qualities which make him so admirable as a saint or medieval hero an ironical play which has the most delicate hypocritical effect. Mr Fred Terry not only acts as Charles Surface, but acts well. I do not expect this statement to be believed in view of such prior achievements of his as A Leader of Men, The Home Secretary, and so forth; but I am bound to report what I saw. Mr Terry has grown softer—fatter, if he will excuse the remark; and he has caught some of the ways of Miss Julia Neilson, the total result being to make his playing more effeminate than it used to be; but it cannot be denied that he plays Charles Surface with a vivacity and a pleasant adipose grace that has nothing of the stickishness of his modern Bond Street style about it. Mrs Patrick Campbell struck me as being exactly right, for modern purposes, in her performance. In the fourth act she was Lady Teazle, and not an actress using the screen scene as a platform for a powerful but misplaced display of intense emotional acting. No doubt an actress—if she is able to do it—is greatly tempted to say to Joseph Surface 'I think we had better leave honor out of the question' with all the dignity and depth of Imogen rebuking Iachimo, and to reveal herself, when the screen falls, as a woman of the richest nature tragically awakened for the first time to its full significance. In ten years' time we shall have Mrs Campbell doing this as unscrupulously as Miss Rehan or any other past-mistress of her art does it now. But it is not the play: it upsets the balance of the comedy and belittles Sir Peter. Nothing deeper is wanted than commonplace thoughtlessness, good-nature, and a girl's revulsion of feeling at the end; and this Mrs Patrick Campbell gives prettily and without exaggeration, with the result that the comedy is seen in its true proportions for the first time within the memory of this generation. It may be held, of course, that the play has only been kept alive by overacting that particular scene; but this view is not borne out by a general comparison of the effect of the Daly and the Lyceum revivals. On Miss Rose Leclercq, Mr Cyril Maude, and Mr Edward Righton as Mrs Candour, Sir Benjamin Backbite, and Sir Oliver, I need not waste compliments: their success was a foregone conclusion. Maria was hardly in Miss Brooke's line; but then Maria is not in anybody's line. Mr Forbes Robertson's reception was extraordinarily enthusiastic. It is evident that the failure of Magda and the escapade of Michael have not shaken his popularity, whatever else it may have cost him. Towards Mrs Campbell, however, there was a disposition to be comparatively sane and critical as well as very friendly. I attribute this, not to any improvement in the public brain, but to a make-up which, though cleverly in character with Lady Teazle, hid all the magnetic fascination of Paula Tanqueray and Fedora.

On the March, at the Prince of Wales Theatre (now in the hands of Miss Cissy Grahame), is prodigiously superior to Biarritz, which seems to have perished miserably, as it certainly deserved to. It is a variety entertainment of no particular pretensions to smartness; and it must be admitted that the primitive funniments and outlandish dialect of Mr Thomas Murray, the Irish-American comedian who succeeds Mr Arthur Roberts, smacks of the village rather than of the West End. But he is imperturbably good-humored, sings in tune, and surprises the audience into laughing at his childlike jokes several times, on which scores much is forgiven to him. For the rest, the people who come forward to dance can dance, and the singers can sing—one of them, Miss Maud Boyd, so exceptionally well that she recalled the night on which the public first discovered Miss Marie Tempest. Miss Alice Atherton, who is in some danger of bodily outgrowing her reputation, is supported by Mr Horace Mills, a highly successful disciple of Mr Dan Leno. Mr Brookfield throws himself away pitiably for half the evening in order to recover himself very funnily during the other half as an amateur Valentine in Faust. On the whole, though I do not defend the entertainment as 'a musical comedy,' or the charging of theatre prices for what is really a music-hall entertainment; still, there is no incompetence, no parading of the unskilled, flashy girls who get engaged in theatres solely because their ineptitudes would not be tolerated for a moment in a music-hall; and the music is not rowdy and tiresome, but pretty, with fairly elegantly scored accompaniments. Let On the March, therefore, pass as good of its simple kind.

'The Spacious Times'

DOCTOR FAUSTUS. *By* Christopher Marlowe. *Acted by members of the Shakespear Reading Society at St George's Hall, on a stage after the model of the Fortune Playhouse, 2 July* 1896.

THE MUMMY. *A new and original farce in three acts. By* George D. Day *and* Allan Reed. *Comedy Theatre, 2 July* 1896.

SCENES FROM ROMEO AND JULIET, FEDORA, and THE COUNTRY GIRL. *By* Miss Elizabeth Tyree. *Comedy Theatre, 3 July* 1896.

BEHIND THE SCENES. *A farcical comedy adapted from The First Night. By* Felix Morris *and* George P. Hawtrey. *Comedy Theatre, 4 July* 1896.

[11 *July* 1896]

MR WILLIAM POEL, in drawing up an announcement of the last exploit of the Elizabethan Stage Society, had no difficulty in citing a number of eminent authorities as to the superlative merits of Christopher Marlowe. The dotage of Charles Lamb on the subject of the Elizabethan dramatists has found many imitators, notably Mr Swinburne, who expresses in verse what he finds in books as passionately as a poet expresses what he finds in life. Among them, it appears, is a Mr G. B. Shaw, in quoting whom Mr Poel was supposed by many persons to be quoting me. But though I share the gentleman's initials, I do not share his views. He can admire a fool: I cannot, even when his folly not only expresses itself in blank verse, but actually invents that art form for the purpose. I admit that Marlowe's blank verse has charm of color and movement; and I know only too well how its romantic march caught the literary imagination and founded that barren and horrible worship of blank verse for its own sake which has since desolated and laid waste the dramatic poetry of England. But the fellow was a fool for all that. He often reminds me, in his abysmally inferior way, of Rossini. Rossini had just the same trick of beginning with a magnificently impressive exordium, apparently pregnant with the most tragic developments, and presently lapsing into arrant triviality. But Rossini lapses amusingly; writes 'Excusez du peu' at the double bar which separates the sublime from the ridiculous; and is gay, tuneful and clever in his frivolity. Marlowe, the moment the exhaustion of the imaginative fit deprives him of the power of raving, becomes childish in thought, vulgar and wooden in humor, and stupid in his attempts at invention. He is the true Elizabethan blank-verse beast, itching to frighten other people with the superstitious terrors and cruelties in which he does not himself believe, and wallowing in blood, violence, muscularity of expression and strenuous animal passion as only literary men do when they become thoroughly depraved by solitary work, sedentary cowardice, and starvation of the sympathetic centres. It is not surprising to learn that Marlowe was stabbed in a tavern brawl: what would be utterly unbelievable would be his having succeeded in stabbing anyone else. On paper the whole obscene crew of these blank-verse rhetoricians could outdare Lucifer himself: Nature can produce no murderer cruel enough for Webster, nor any hero bully enough for Chapman, devout disciples, both of them, of Kit Marlowe. But you do not believe in their martial ardor as you believe in the valor of Sidney or Cervantes. One calls the Elizabethan dramatists imaginative, as one might say the same of a man in delirium tremens; but even that flatters them; for whereas the drinker can imagine rats and snakes and beetles which have some sort of resemblance to real ones, your typical Elizabethan heroes of the mighty line, having neither the eyes to see anything real nor the brains to observe it, could no more conceive a natural or convincing stage figure than a blind man can conceive a rainbow or a deaf one the sound of an orchestra. Such success as they have had is the success which any fluent braggart and liar may secure in a pothouse. Their swagger and fustian, and their scraps of Cicero and Aristotle, passed for poetry and learning in their own day because their public was Philistine and ignorant. Today, without having by any means lost this advantage, they enjoy in addition the quaintness of their obsolescence, and, above all, the splendor of the light reflected on them from the reputation of Shakespear. Without that light they would now be as invisible as they are insufferable. In condemning them indiscriminately, I am only doing what Time would have done if Shakespear had not rescued them. I am quite aware that they did not get their reputations for nothing; that there were degrees of badness among them; that Greene was really amusing, Marston spirited and silly-clever, Cyril Tourneur able to string together lines of which any couple picked out and quoted separately might pass as a fragment of a real organic poem, and so on. Even the brutish pedant Jonson was not heartless, and could turn out prettily affectionate verses and foolishly affectionate criticisms; whilst the plausible firm of Beaumont and Fletcher, humbugs as they were, could produce plays which were, all things considered, not worse than The Lady of Lyons. But these distinctions are not worth making now. There is much variety in a dust-heap, even when the rag-picker is done with it; but we throw it indiscriminately into the 'destructor' for all that. There is only one use left for the Elizabethan dramatists, and that is the purification of Shakespear's reputation from its spurious elements. Just as you can cure people of talking patronizingly about 'Mozartian melody' by shewing that the tunes they imagine to be his distinctive characteristic were the commonplaces of his time, so it is possible, perhaps, to cure people of admiring, as distinctively characteristic of Shakespear, the false, forced rhetoric, the callous sensation-mongering in murder and lust, the ghosts and combats, and the venal expenditure of all the treasures of his genius on the bedizenment of plays which are, as wholes, stupid toys. When Sir Henry Irving presently revives Cymbeline at the Lyceum, the numerous descendants of the learned Shakespearean enthusiast who went down on his knees and kissed the Ireland forgeries will see no difference between the great dramatist who changed Imogen from a mere name in a story to a living woman, and the manager-showman who exhibited her with the gory trunk of a newly beheaded man in her arms. But why should we, the heirs of so many greater ages, with the dramatic poems of Goethe and Ibsen in our hands, and the music of a great dynasty of musicians, from Bach to Wagner, in our ears—why should we waste our time on the rank and file of the Elizabethans, or encourage foolish modern persons to imitate them, or talk about Shakespear as if his moral platitudes, his jingo claptraps, his tavern pleasantries, his bombast and drivel, and his incapacity for following up the scraps of philosophy he stole so aptly, were as admirable as the mastery of poetic speech, the feeling for nature, and the knack of character-drawing, fun, and heart wisdom which he was ready, like a true son of the theatre, to prostitute to any subject, any occasion, and any theatrical employment? The fact is, we are growing out of Shakespear. Byron declined to put up with his reputation at the beginning of the nineteenth century; and now, at the beginning of the twentieth, he is nothing but a household pet. His characters still live; his word pictures of woodland and wayside still give us a Bank-holiday breath of country air; his verse still charms us; his sublimities still stir us; the commonplaces and trumperies of the wisdom which age and experience bring to all of us are still expressed by him better than by anybody else; but we have nothing to hope from him and nothing to learn from him—not even how to write plays, though he does that so much better than most modern dramatists. And if this is true of Shakespear, what is to be said of Kit Marlowe?

Kit Marlowe, however, did not bore me at St George's Hall as he has always bored me when I have tried to read him without skipping. The more I see of these performances by the Elizabethan Stage Society, the more I am convinced that their method of presenting an Elizabethan play is not only the right method for that particular sort of play but that any play performed on a platform amidst the audience gets closer home to its hearers than when it is presented as a picture framed by a proscenium. Also, that we are less conscious of the artificiality of the stage when a few well-understood conventions, adroitly handled, are substituted for attempts at an impossible scenic verisimilitude. All the old-fashioned tale-of-adventure plays, with their frequent changes of scene, and all the new problem plays, with their intense intimacies, should be done in this way.

The E. S. S. made very free with Doctor Faustus. Their devils, Baliol and Belcher to wit, were not theatrical devils with huge pasteboard heads, but pictorial Temptation-of-St-Anthony devils such as Martin Schongauer drew. The angels were Florentine fifteenth-century angels, with their draperies sewn into Botticellian folds and tucks. The Emperor's bodyguard had Maximilianesque uniforms copied from Holbein. Mephistophilis made his first appearance as Mr Joseph Pennell's favorite devil from the roof of Notre Dame, and, when commanded to appear as a Franciscan friar, still proclaimed his modernity by wearing an electric bulb in his cowl. The Seven Deadly Sins were *tout ce qu'il y a de plus fin de siècle*, the five worst of them being so attractive that they got rounds of applause on the strength of their appearance alone. In short, Mr William Poel gave us an artistic rather than a literal presentation of Elizabethan conditions, the result being, as always happens in such cases, that the picture of the past was really a picture of the future. For which result he is, in my judgment, to be highly praised. The performance was a wonder of artistic discipline in this lawless age. It is true, since the performers were only three or four instead of fifty times as skilful as ordinary professional actors, that Mr Poel has had to give up all impetuosity and spontaneity of execution, and to have the work done very slowly and carefully. But it is to be noted that even Marlowe, treated in this thorough way, is not tedious; whereas Shakespear, rattled and rushed and spouted and clattered through in the ordinary professional manner, all but kills the audience with tedium. For instance, Mephistophilis was as joyless and leaden as a devil need be—it was clear that no stage-manager had ever exhorted him, like a lagging horse, to get the long speeches over as fast as possible, old chap—and yet he never for a moment bored us as Prince Hal and Poins bore us at the Haymarket. The actor who hurries reminds the spectators of the flight of time, which it is his business to make them forget. Twenty years ago the symphonies of Beethoven used to be rushed through in London with the sole object of shortening the agony of the audience. They were then highly unpopular. When Richter arrived he took the opposite point of view, playing them so as to prolong the delight of the audience; and Mottl dwells more lovingly on Wagner than Richter does on Beethoven. The result is that Beethoven and Wagner are now popular. Mr Poel has proved that the same result will be attained as soon as blank-verse plays are produced under the control of managers who like them, instead of openly and shamelessly treating them as inflictions to be curtailed to the utmost. The representation at St George's Hall went without a hitch from beginning to end, a miracle of diligent preparedness. Mr Mannering, as Faustus, had the longest and the hardest task; and he performed it conscientiously, punctually, and well. The others did no less with what they had to do. The relief of seeing actors come on the stage with the simplicity and abnegation of children, instead of bounding on to an enthusiastic reception with the 'Here I am again' expression of the popular favorites of the ordinary stage, is hardly to be described. Our professional actors are now looked at by the public from behind the scenes; and they accept that situation and glory in it for the sake of the 'personal popularity' it involves. What a gigantic reform Mr Poel will make if his Elizabethan Stage should lead to such a novelty as a theatre to which people go to see the play instead of to see the cast!

There has been a plague of matinées lately; but the matinée is the opportunity of the incompetent casual acting-manager; and the incompetent casual acting-manager's opportunity often proves the holiday of the eminent dramatic critic, whose invitation, being the main thing that the casual one is engaged to look after, is generally forgotten. Nevertheless, I was captured no less than thrice last week. The Mummy is ingenious enough to have a narrow miss of being a successful play; but unfortunately in these matters a miss is as good as a mile. What is wrong with it is the perfunctory flimsiness of the figures who surround the mummy. It is not enough to provide a squad of rag dolls for your mummy to confuse himself in: they must be real people in whom we can feel some interest, and who can make us believe that an ancient Egyptian is actually walking about in a modern household. The play only lives whilst Mr Brough, whose trained physical self-command and professional skill were never more useful, is on the stage. Our younger generation of stage bunglers, who take such prodigious trouble to prevent perfectly simple effects from making themselves, doubtless often ask themselves why the public can be so unjust and foolish as to laugh at an actor who can apparently do nothing but stare helplessly at his own success. The reason is, of course, that Mr Lionel Brough never stands between the public and Mr Lionel Brough's part. This seems simple but just try to do it, and you will appreciate the training that it costs to make a capable actor.

Miss Elizabeth Tyree, late of Mr Daniel Frohman's company at the Lyceum Theatre, New York, invited London to see what she could do as Juliet, Fedora, and the Country Girl. Like most American executive artists, musical and dramatic, Miss Tyree shewed signs of having attempted to qualify herself by some systematic physical training for her profession. But she does not appreciate the degree of beauty of execution and distinction of style that are required by such parts as Juliet and Fedora. She played Juliet, amusingly enough, to Mr Will Dennis's Romeo, exactly as Miss Maude Millet plays the comic relief young lady in a modern comedy to Mr Sidney Brough's comic relief young gentleman. The performance proved, not that Miss Tyree can play Juliet, but that the balcony scene makes a capital one-act comedietta. Her Fedora was out of the question: it was as remote from the effect planned by Sardou as Brixton is from St Petersburg. The Country Girl was adequate; but then we have a dozen young ladies on our own stage who could do it as well if any one wanted them to. Frankly, since Miss Tyree must be understood as asking whether she has the power that crosses frontiers, I must reply, Not yet. The work she can do so far can be done in any country without sending to America for assistance. And the sort of character for which she seems best fitted by her temperament is precisely that in which English actresses excel. If Miss Elizabeth Robins or Miss Olga Brandon were to return to their native shores, it would not be easy to name their successors in their best parts, not only because of their professional skill, but because their temperaments are of a kind that England does not produce very freely. We can and do produce Miss Tyree's temperament by the dozen.

I congratulate Mr Felix Morris on the success with which, returning to this country after a long absence, he has persuaded us to revive two hopelessly obsolete plays for his sake. On 'Change was pardonable; but a new version of The First Night is really too much; Achille Dufard is as dead as Alfred Wigan. There are, however, three scenes in the new version which should be rescued from Dufard's grave. The outfaced dunning grocer, with his 'Arf a mo: give a man a chance,' is very funny; and the rehearsal, with the leading lady on the rampage, as well as the scene at the end of the first act, should certainly be seen again, if only to let London enjoy a most amusing and spontaneous piece of acting by Miss Alma Stanley. Shade of Lady Dedlock, who would have supposed that she could have done this excellent thing! Mr Ernest Cosham was capital as the grocer. The piece was, indeed, exceptionally well played on all hands; but Mr Felix Morris and Miss Sarah Brooke, though they did all that was possible, could not justify the survival of their part of the business. Mr Morris's French accent, by the way, was a triumph of accurate aural observation.

Blaming the Bard

CYMBELINE. *By* Shakespear. *Lyceum Theatre,* 22 *September* 1896.

[26 *September* 1896]

I CONFESS to a difficulty in feeling civilized just at present. Flying from the country, where the gentlemen of England are in an ecstasy of chicken-butchering, I return to town to find the higher wits assembled at a play three hundred years old, in which the sensation scene exhibits a woman waking up to find her husband reposing gorily in her arms with his head cut off.

Pray understand, therefore, that I do not defend Cymbeline. It is for the most part stagey trash of the lowest melodramatic order, in parts abominably written, throughout intellectually vulgar, and, judged in point of thought by modern intellectual standards, vulgar, foolish, offensive, indecent, and exasperating beyond all tolerance. There are moments when one asks despairingly why our stage should ever have been cursed with this 'immortal' pilferer of other men's stories and ideas, with his monstrous rhetorical fustian, his unbearable platitudes, his pretentious reduction of the subtlest problems of life to commonplaces against which a Polytechnic debating club would revolt, his incredible unsuggestiveness, his sententious combination of ready reflection with complete intellectual sterility, and his consequent incapacity for getting out of the depth of even the most ignorant audience, except when he solemnly says something so transcendently platitudinous that his more humble-minded hearers cannot bring themselves to believe that so great a man really meant to talk like their grandmothers. With the single exception of Homer, there is no eminent writer, not even Sir Walter Scott, whom I can despise so entirely as I despise Shakespear when I measure my mind against his. The intensity of my impatience with him occasionally reaches such a pitch, that it would positively be a relief to me to dig him up and throw stones at him, knowing as I do how incapable he and his worshippers are of understanding any less obvious form of indignity. To read Cymbeline and to think of Goethe, of Wagner, of Ibsen, is, for me, to imperil the habit of studied moderation of statement which years of public responsibility as a journalist have made almost second nature in me.

But I am bound to add that I pity the man who cannot enjoy Shakespear. He has outlasted thousands of abler thinkers, and will outlast a thousand more. His gift of telling a story (provided some one else told it to him first); his enormous power over language, as conspicuous in his senseless and silly abuse of it as in his miracles of expression; his humor; his sense of idiosyncratic character; and his prodigious fund of that vital energy which is, it seems, the true differentiating property behind the faculties, good, bad, or indifferent, of the man of genius, enable him to entertain us so effectively that the imaginary scenes and people he has created become more real to us than our actual life—at least, until our knowledge and grip of actual life begins to deepen and glow beyond the common. When I was twenty I knew everybody in Shakespear, from Hamlet to Abhorson, much more intimately than I knew my living contemporaries; and to this day, if the name of Pistol or Polonius catches my eye in a newspaper, I turn to the passage with more curiosity than if the name were that of—but perhaps I had better not mention any one in particular.

How many new acquaintances, then, do you make in reading Cymbeline, provided you have the patience to break your way into it through all the fustian, and are old enough to be free from the modern idea that Cymbeline must be the name of a cosmetic and Imogen of the latest scientific discovery in the nature of a hitherto unknown gas? Cymbeline is nothing; his queen nothing, though some attempt is made to justify her description as 'a woman that bears all down with her brain;' Posthumus, nothing—most fortunately, as otherwise he would be an unendurably contemptible hound; Belarius, nothing—at least, not after Kent in King Lear (just as the Queen is nothing after Lady Macbeth); Iachimo, not much—only a *diabolus ex machina* made plausible; and Pisanio, less than Iachimo. On the other hand, we have Cloten, the prince of numbskulls, whose part, indecencies and all, is a literary masterpiece from the first line to the last; the two princes—fine presentments of that impressive and generous myth, the noble savage; Caius Lucius, the Roman general, urbane among the barbarians; and, above all, Imogen. But do, please, remember that there are two Imogens. One is a solemn and elaborate example of what, in Shakespear's opinion, a real lady ought to be. With this unspeakable person virtuous indignation is chronic. Her object in life is to vindicate her own propriety and to suspect everybody else's, especially her husband's. Like Lothaw in the jeweller's shop in Bret Harte's burlesque novel, she cannot be left alone with unconsidered trifles of portable silver without officiously assuring the proprietors that she has stolen naught, nor would not, though she had found gold strewed i' the floor. Her fertility and spontaneity in nasty ideas is not to be described: there is hardly a speech in her part that you can read without wincing. But this Imogen has another one tied to her with ropes of blank verse (which can fortunately be cut)—the Imogen of Shakespear's genius, an enchanting person of the most delicate sensitiveness, full of sudden transitions from ecstasies of tenderness to transports of childish rage, and reckless of consequences in both, instantly hurt and instantly appeased, and of the highest breeding and courage. But for this Imogen, Cymbeline would stand about as much chance of being revived now as Titus Andronicus.

The instinctive Imogen, like the real live part of the rest of the play, has to be disentangled from a mass of stuff which, though it might be recited with effect and appropriateness by young amateurs at a performance by the Elizabethan Stage Society, is absolutely unactable and unutterable in the modern theatre, where a direct illusion of reality is aimed at, and where the repugnance of the best actors to play false passages is practically insuperable. For the purposes of the Lyceum, therefore, Cymbeline had to be cut, and cut liberally. Not that there was any reason to apprehend that the manager would flinch from the operation: quite the contrary. In a true republic of art Sir Henry Irving would ere this have expiated his acting versions on the scaffold. He does not merely cut plays: he disembowels them. In Cymbeline he has quite surpassed himself by extirpating the antiphonal third verse of the famous dirge. A man who would do that would do anything—cut the coda out of the first movement of Beethoven's Ninth Symphony, or shorten one of Velasquez's Philips into a kitcat to make it fit over his drawing room mantlepiece. The grotesque character tracery of Cloten's lines, which is surely not beyond the appreciation of an age educated by Stevenson, is defaced with Cromwellian ruthlessness; and the patriotic scene, with the Queen's great speech about the natural bravery of our isle, magnificent in its Walkürenritt swing, is shorn away, though it might easily have been introduced in the Garden scene. And yet, long screeds of rubbish about 'slander, whose edge is sharper than the sword,' and so on, are preserved with superstitious veneration.

This curious want of connoisseurship in literature would disable Sir Henry Irving seriously if he were an interpretative actor. But it is, happily, the fault of a great quality—the creative quality. A prodigious deal of nonsense has been written about Sir Henry Irving's conception of this, that, and the other Shakespearean character. The truth is that he has never in his life conceived or interpreted the characters of any author except himself. He is really as incapable of acting another man's play as Wagner was of setting another man's libretto; and he should, like Wagner, have written his plays for himself. But as he did not find himself out until it was too late for him to learn that supplementary trade, he was compelled to use other men's plays as the framework for his own creations. His first great success in this sort of adaptation was with the Merchant of Venice. There was no question then of a bad Shylock or a good Shylock: he was simply not Shylock at all; and when his own creation came into conflict with Shakespear's, as it did quite openly in the Trial scene, he simply played in flat contradiction of the lines, and positively acted Shakespear off the stage. This was an original policy, and an intensely interesting one from the critical point of view; but it was obvious that its difficulty must increase with the vividness and force of the dramatist's creation. Shakespear at his highest pitch cannot be set aside by any mortal actor, however gifted; and when Sir Henry Irving tried to interpolate a most singular and fantastic notion of an old man between the lines of a fearfully mutilated acting version of King Lear, he was smashed. On the other hand, in plays by persons of no importance, where the dramatist's part of the business is the merest trash, his creative activity is unhampered and uncontradicted; and the author's futility is the opportunity for the actor's masterpiece. Now I have already described Shakespear's Iachimo as little better than any of the lay figures in Cymbeline—a mere *diabolus ex machina.* But Irving's Iachimo is a very different affair. It is a new and independent creation. I knew Shakespear's play inside and out before last Tuesday; but this Iachimo was quite fresh and novel to me. I witnessed it with unqualified delight: it was no vulgar bagful of 'points,' but a true impersonation, unbroken in its life-current from end to end, varied on the surface with the finest comedy, and without a single lapse in the sustained beauty of its execution. It is only after such work that an artist can with perfect naturalness and dignity address himself to his audience as 'their faithful and loving servant;' and I wish I could add that the audience had an equal right to offer him their applause as a worthy acknowledgment of his merit. But when a house distributes its officious first-night plaudits impartially between the fine artist and the blunderer who roars a few lines violently and rushes off the stage after compressing the entire art of How Not to Act into five intolerable minutes, it had better be told to reserve its impertinent and obstreperous demonstrations until it has learnt to bestow them with some sort of discrimination. Our first-night people mean well, and will, no doubt, accept my assurance that they are donkeys with all possible good humor; but they should remember that to applaud for the sake of applauding, as schoolboys will cheer for the sake of cheering, is to destroy our own power of complimenting those who, as the greatest among us, are the servants of all the rest.

Over the performances of the other gentlemen in the cast let me skate as lightly as possible. Mr Norman Forbes's Cloten, though a fatuous idiot rather than the brawny 'beef-witted' fool whom Shakespear took from his own Ajax in Troilus and Cressida, is effective and amusing, so that one feels acutely the mangling of his part, especially the cutting of that immortal musical criticism of his upon the serenade. Mr Gordon Craig and Mr Webster are desperate failures as the two noble savages. They are as spirited and picturesque as possible; but every pose, every flirt of their elfin locks, proclaims the wild freedom of Bedford Park. They recite the poor maimed dirge admirably, Mr Craig being the more musical of the twain; and Mr Webster's sword-and-cudgel fight with Cloten is very lively; but their utter deficiency in the grave, rather sombre, uncivilized primeval strength and Mohican dignity so finely suggested by Shakespear, takes all the ballast out of the fourth act, and combines with the inappropriate prettiness and sunniness of the landscape scenery to handicap Miss Ellen Terry most cruelly in the trying scene of her awakening by the side of the flower-decked corpse: a scene which, without every accessory to heighten its mystery, terror, and pathos, is utterly and heartbreakingly impossible for any actress, even if she were Duse, Ristori, Mrs Siddons, and Miss Terry rolled into one. When I saw this gross and palpable oversight, and heard people talking about the Lyceum stage management as superb, I with difficulty restrained myself from tearing out my hair in handfuls and scattering it with imprecations to the four winds. That cave of the three mountaineers wants nothing but a trellised porch, a bamboo bicycle, and a nice little bed of standard roses, to complete its absurdity.

With Mr Frederic Robinson as Belarius, and Mr Tyars as Pisanio, there is no reasonable fault to find, except that they might, perhaps, be a little brighter with advantage; and of the rest of their male colleagues I think I shall ask to be allowed to say nothing at all, even at the cost of omitting a tribute to Mr Fuller Mellish's discreet impersonation of the harmless necessary Philario. There remains Miss Geneviève Ward, whose part, with the Neptune's park speech lopped off, was not worth her playing, and Miss Ellen Terry, who invariably fascinates me so much that I have not the smallest confidence in my own judgment respecting her. There was no Bedford Park about the effect she made as she stepped into the King's garden; still less any of the atmosphere of ancient Britain. At the first glance, we were in the Italian fifteenth century; and the house, unversed in the cinquecento, but dazzled all the same, proceeded to roar until it stopped from exhaustion. There is one scene in Cymbeline, the one in which Imogen receives the summons to 'that same blessed Milford,' which might have been written for Miss Terry, so perfectly does its innocent rapture and frank gladness fit into her hand. Her repulse of Iachimo brought down the house as a matter of course, though I am convinced that the older Shakespeareans present had a vague impression that it could not be properly done except by a stout, turnip-headed matron, with her black hair folded smoothly over her ears and secured in a classic bun. Miss Terry had evidently cut her own part; at all events the odious Mrs Grundyish Imogen had been dissected out of it so skilfully that it went without a single jar. The circumstances under which she was asked to play the fourth act were, as I have explained, impossible. To wake up in the gloom amid the wolf and robber-haunted mountain gorges which formed the Welsh mountains of Shakespear's imagination in the days before the Great Western existed is one thing: to wake up at about three on a nice Bank-holiday afternoon in a charming spot near the valley of the Wye is quite another. With all her force, Miss Terry gave us faithfully the whole process which Shakespear has presented with such dramatic cunning—Imogen's bewilderment, between dreaming and waking, as to where she is; the vague discerning of some strange bedfellow there; the wondering examination of the flowers with which he is so oddly covered; the frightful discovery of blood on the flowers, with the hideous climax that the man is headless and that his clothes are her husband's; and it was all ruined by that blazing, idiotic, prosaic sunlight in which everything leapt to the eye at once, rendering the mystery and the slowly growing clearness of perception incredible and unintelligible, and spoiling a scene which, properly stage-managed, would have been a triumph of histrionic intelligence. Cannot somebody be hanged for this?—men perish every week for lesser crimes. What consolation is it to me that Miss Terry, playing with infinite charm and delicacy of appeal, made up her lost ground in other directions, and had more than as much success as the roaring gallery could feel the want of?

A musical accompaniment to the drama has been specially composed; and its numbers are set forth in the bill of the play, with the words 'LOST PROPERTY' in conspicuous red capitals in the margin. Perhaps I can be of some use in restoring at least some of the articles to their rightful owner. The prelude to the fourth act belongs to Beethoven—first movement of the Seventh Symphony. The theme played by 'the ingenious instrument' in the cave is Handel's, and is familiar to lovers of Judas Maccabeus as O never bow we down to the rude stock or sculptured stone. J. F. R. will, I feel sure, be happy to carry the work of identification further if necessary.

Sir Henry Irving's next appearance will be on Bosworth Field. He was obviously astonished by the startling shout of approbation with which the announcement was received. We all have an old weakness for Richard. After that, Madame Sans-Gêne, with Sardou's Napoleon.

Little Eyolf

LITTLE EYOLF. *A play in three acts. By* Henrik Ibsen. *Avenue Theatre,* 23 *November* 1896.

[28 *November* 1896]

THE happiest and truest epithet that has yet been applied to the Ibsen drama in this country came from Mr Clement Scott when he said that Ibsen was 'suburban.' That is the whole secret of it. If Mr Scott had only embraced his discovery instead of quarrelling with it, what a splendid Ibsen critic he would have made! Suburbanity at present means modern civilization. The active, germinating life in the households of today cannot be typified by an aristocratic hero, an ingenuous heroine, a gentleman-forger abetted by an Artful Dodger, and a parlormaid who takes half-sovereigns and kisses from the male visitors. Such interiors exist on the stage, and nowhere else: therefore the only people who are accustomed to them and at home in them are the dramatic critics. But if you ask me where you can find the Helmer household, the Allmers household, the Solness household, the Rosmer household, and all the other Ibsen households, I reply, 'Jump out of a train anywhere between Wimbledon and Haslemere; walk into the first villa you come to; and there you are.' Indeed you need not go so far: Hampstead, Maida Vale, or West Kensington will serve your turn; but it is as well to remind people that the true suburbs are now the forty-mile radius, and that Camberwell and Brixton are no longer the suburbs, but the overflow of Gower Street—the genteel slums, in short. And this suburban life, except in so far as it is totally vegetable and undramatic, is the life depicted by Ibsen. Doubtless some of our critics are quite sincere in thinking it a vulgar life, in considering the conversations which men hold with their wives in it improper, in finding its psychology puzzling and unfamiliar, and in forgetting that its bookshelves and its music cabinets are laden with works which did not exist for them, and which are the daily bread of young women educated very differently from the sisters and wives of their day. No wonder they are not at ease in an atmosphere of ideas and assumptions and attitudes which seem to them bewildering, morbid, affected, extravagant, and altogether incredible as the common currency of suburban life. But Ibsen knows better. His suburban drama is the inevitable outcome of a suburban civilization (meaning a civilization that appreciates fresh air); and the true explanation of Hedda Gabler's vogue is that given by Mr Grant Allen—'I take her in to dinner twice a week.'

Another change that the critics have failed to reckon with is the change in fiction. Byron remarked that

> Romances paint at full length people's wooings,
> But only give a bust of marriages.

That was true enough in the days of Sir Walter Scott, when a betrothed heroine with the slightest knowledge of what marriage meant would have shocked the public as much as the same ignorance today would strike it as tragic if real, and indecent if simulated. The result was that the romancer, when he came to a love scene, had frankly to ask his 'gentle reader' to allow him to omit the conversation as being necessarily too idiotic to interest anyone. We have fortunately long passed out of that stage in novels. By the time we had reached Vanity Fair and Middlemarch —both pretty old and prim stories now—marriage had become the starting point of our romances. Love is as much the romancer's theme as ever; but married love and the courtships of young people who are appalled by the problems of life and motherhood have left the governesses and curates, the Amandas and Tom Joneses of other days, far out of sight. Ten years ago the stage was as far behind Sir Walter Scott as he is behind Madame Sarah Grand. But when Ibsen took it by the scruff of the neck just as Wagner took the Opera, then, willy nilly, it had to come along. And now what are the critics going to do? The Ibsen drama is pre-eminently the drama of marriage. If dramatic criticism receives it in the spirit of the nurse's husband in Romeo and Juliet, if it grins and makes remarks about 'the secrets of the alcove,' if it pours forth columns which are half pornographic pleasantry and the other half sham propriety, then the end will be, not in the least that Ibsen will be banned, but that dramatic criticism will cease to be read. And what a frightful blow that would be to English culture!

LITTLE EYOLF

Little Eyolf is an extraordinarily powerful play, although none of the characters are as fascinatingly individualized as Solness or Rosmer, Hedda or Nora. The theme is a marriage—an ideal marriage from the suburban point of view. A young gentleman, a student and an idealist, is compelled to drudge at teaching to support himself. He meets a beautiful young woman. They fall in love with one another; and by the greatest piece of luck in the world (suburbanly considered) she has plenty of money. Thus he is set free by his marriage to live his own life in his own way. That is just where an ordinary play leaves off, and just where an Ibsen play begins. The husband begins to make those discoveries which everybody makes, except, apparently, the dramatic critics. First, that love, instead of being a perfectly homogeneous, unchanging, unending passion, is of all things the most mutable. It will pass through several well-marked stages in a single evening, and, whilst seeming to slip back to the old starting point the next evening, will yet not slip quite back, so that in the course of years it will appear that the moods of an evening were the anticipation of the evolution of a lifetime. But the evolution does not occur in different people at the same time or in the same order. Consequently the hero of Little Eyolf, being an imaginative, nervous, thoughtful person, finds that he has had enough of caresses, and wants to dream alone among the mountain peaks and solitudes, whilst his wife, a warm-blooded creature, has only found her love intensified to a fiercely jealous covetousness of him. His main refuge from this devouring passion is in his peacefully affectionate relations with his sister, and in certain suburban dreams very common among literary amateurs living on their wives' incomes: to wit, forming the mind and character of his child, and writing a great book (on Human Responsibility if you please). Of course the wife, in her jealousy, hates the sister, hates the child, hates the book, hates her husband for making her jealous of them, and hates herself for her hatreds with the frightful logic of greedy, insatiable love. Enter then our old friend, Ibsen's divine messenger. The Ratwife, alias the Strange Passenger, alias the Button Moulder, alias Ulrik Brendel, comes in to ask whether there are any little gnawing things there of which she can rid the house. They do not understand—the divine messenger in Ibsen is never understood, especially by the critics. So the little gnawing thing in the house—the child—follows the Ratwife and is drowned, leaving the pair awakened by the blow to a frightful consciousness of themselves, the woman as a mere animal, the man as a moonstruck nincompoop, keeping up appearances as a suburban lady and gentleman with nothing to do but enjoy themselves. Even the sister has discovered now that she is not really a sister—also a not unprecedented suburban possibility—and sees that the passionate stage is ahead of her too; so, though she loves the husband, she has to get out of his way by the pre-eminently suburban expedient of marrying a man whom she does not love, and who, like Rita, is warm-blooded and bent on the undivided unshared possession of the object of his passion. At last the love of the woman passes out of the passionate stage; and immediately, with the practical sense of her sex, she proposes, not to go up into the mountains or to write amateur treatises, but to occupy herself with her duties as landed proprietress, instead of merely spending the revenues of her property in keeping a monogamic harem. The gentleman asks to be allowed to lend a hand; and immediately the storm subsides, easily enough, leaving the couple on solid ground. This is the play, as actual and near to us as the Brighton and South Coast Railway—this is the mercilessly heart-searching sermon, touching all of us somewhere, and some of us everywhere, which we, the critics, have summed up as 'secrets of the alcove.' Our cheeks, whose whiteness Mr Arthur Roberts has assailed in vain, have mantled at 'the coarseness and vulgarity which are noted characteristics of the author' (I am quoting, with awe, my fastidiously high-toned colleague of the Standard). And yet the divine messenger only meant to make us ashamed of ourselves. That is the way divine messengers always do muddle their business.

The performance was of course a very remarkable one. When, in a cast of five, you have the three best yet discovered actresses of their generation, you naturally look for something extraordinary. Miss Achurch was the only one who ran any risk of failure. The Ratwife and Asta are excellent parts; but they are not arduous ones. Rita, on the other hand, is one of the heaviest ever written: any single act of it would exhaust an actress of no more than ordinary resources. But Miss Achurch was more than equal to the occasion. Her power seemed to grow with its own expenditure. The terrible outburst at the end of the first act did not leave a scrape on her voice (which appears to have the compass of a military band) and threw her into victorious action in that tearing second act instead of wrecking her. She played with all her old originality and success, and with more than her old authority over her audience. She had to speak some dangerous lines—lines of a kind that usually find out the vulgar spots in an audience and give an excuse for a laugh—but nobody laughed or wanted to laugh at Miss Achurch. 'There stood your champagne; but you tasted it not,' neither shirked nor slurred, but driven home to the last syllable, did not elicit an audible breath from a completely dominated audience. Later on I confess I lost sight of Rita a little in studying the surprising capacity Miss Achurch shewed as a dramatic instrument. For the first time one clearly saw the superfluity of power and the vehemence of intelligence which make her often so reckless as to the beauty of her methods of expression. As Rita she produced almost every sound that a big human voice can, from a creak like the opening of a rusty canal lock to a melodious tenor note that the most robust Siegfried might have envied. She looked at one moment like a young, well-dressed, very pretty woman: at another she was like a desperate creature just fished dripping out of the river by the Thames Police. Yet another moment, and she was the incarnation of impetuous, ungovernable strength. Her face was sometimes winsome, sometimes listlessly wretched, sometimes like the head of a statue of Victory, sometimes suffused, horrible, threatening, like Bellona or Medusa. She would cross from left to right like a queen, and from right to left with, so to speak, her toes turned in, her hair coming down, and her slippers coming off. A more utter recklessness, not only of fashion, but of beauty, could hardly be imagined: beauty to Miss Achurch is only one effect among others to be produced, not a condition of all effects. But then she can do what our beautiful actresses cannot do: attain the force and terror of Sarah Bernhardt's most vehement explosions without Sarah's violence and abandonment, and with every appearance of having reserves of power still held in restraint. With all her cleverness as a realistic actress she must be classed technically as a heroic actress; and I very much doubt whether we shall see her often until she comes into the field with a repertory as highly specialized as that of Sir Henry Irving or Duse. For it is so clear that she would act an average London success to pieces and play an average actor-manager off the stage, that we need not expect to see much of her as that useful and pretty auxiliary, a leading lady.

Being myself a devotee of the beautiful school, I like being enchanted by Mrs Patrick Campbell better than being frightened, harrowed, astonished, conscience-stricken, devastated, and dreadfully delighted in general by Miss Achurch's untamed genius. I have seen Mrs Campbell play the Ratwife twice, once quite enchantingly, and once most disappointingly. On the first occasion Mrs Campbell divined that she was no village harridan, but the messenger of heaven. She played supernaturally, beautifully: the first notes of her voice came as from the spheres into all that suburban prose: she played to the child with a witchery that might have drawn him not only into the sea, but into her very bosom. Nothing jarred except her obedience to Ibsen's stage direction in saying 'Down where all the rats are' harshly, instead of getting the effect, in harmony with her own inspired reading, by the most magical tenderness. The next time, to my unspeakable fury, she amused herself by playing like any melodramatic old woman, a profanation for which, whilst my critical life lasts, never will I forgive her. Of Miss Robins's Asta it is difficult to say much, since the part, played as she plays it, does not exhibit anything like the full extent of her powers. Asta is a study of a temperament—the quiet, affectionate, enduring, reassuring, faithful, domestic temperament. That is not in the least Miss Robins's temperament: she is nervous, restless, intensely self-conscious, eagerly energetic. In parts which do not enable her to let herself loose in this, her natural way, she falls back on pathos, on mute misery, on a certain delicate plaintive note in her voice and grace in her bearing which appeal to our sympathy and pity without realizing any individuality for us. She gave us, with instinctive tact and refinement, the 'niceness,' the considerateness, the ladylikeness, which differentiate Asta from the wilful, passionate, somewhat brutal Rita. Perhaps only an American playing against an Englishwoman could have done it so discriminately; but beyond this and the pathos there was nothing: Asta was only a picture, and, like a picture, did not develop. The picture, being sympathetic and pretty, has been much admired; but those who have not seen Miss Robins play Hilda Wangel have no idea of what she is like when she really acts her part instead of merely giving an urbanely pictorial recommendation of it. As to Allmers, how could he recommend himself to spectators who saw in him everything that they are ashamed of in themselves? Mr Courtenay Thorpe played very intelligently, which, for such a part, and in such a play, is saying a good deal; but he was hampered a little by the change from the small and intimate auditorium in which he has been accustomed to play Ibsen, to the Avenue, which ingeniously combines the acoustic difficulties of a large theatre with the pecuniary capacity of a small one. Master Stewart Dawson, as Eyolf, was one of the best actors in the company. Mr Lowne, as Borgheim, was as much out of tone as a Leader sunset in a Rembrandt picture—no fault of his, of course (the audience evidently liked him), but still a blemish on the play.

And this brings me to a final criticism. The moment I put myself into my old attitude as musical critic, I at once perceive that the performance, as a whole, was an unsatisfactory one. You may remonstrate, and ask me how I can say so after admitting that the performers shewed such extraordinary talent —even genius. It is very simple, nevertheless. Suppose you take Isaye, Sarasate, Joachim, and Hollmann, and tumble them all together to give a scratch performance of one of Beethoven's posthumous quartets at some benefit concert. Suppose you also take the two De Reszkes, Calvé, and Miss Eames, and set them to sing a glee under the same circumstances. They will all shew prodigious individual talent; but the resultant performances of the quartet and glee will be inferior, as wholes, to that of an ordinary glee club or group of musicians who have practised for years together. The Avenue performance was a parallel case. There was nothing like the atmosphere which Lugné Poë got in Rosmersholm. Miss Achurch managed to play the second act as if she had played it every week for twenty years; but otherwise the performance, interesting as it was, was none the less a scratch one. If only the company could keep together for a while! But perhaps that is too much to hope for at present, though it is encouraging to see that the performances are to be continued next week, the five matinées—all crowded, by the way—having by no means exhausted the demand for places.

Several performances during the past fortnight remain to be chronicled; but Ibsen will have his due; and he has not left me room enough to do justice to any one else this week.

Ibsen Without Tears

[12 *December* 1896]

LITTLE EYOLF, which began at the Avenue Theatre only the other day as an artistic forlorn hope led by Miss Elizabeth Robins, has been promoted into a full-blown fashionable theatrical speculation, with a Morocco Bound syndicate in the background, unlimited starring and bill-posting, and everything complete. The syndicate promptly set to work to shew us how Ibsen should really be done. They found the whole thing wrong from the root up. The silly Ibsen people had put Miss Achurch, an Ibsenite actress, into the leading part, and Mrs Patrick Campbell, a fashionable actress, into a minor one. This was soon set right. Miss Achurch was got rid of altogether, and her part transferred to Mrs Campbell. Miss Robins, though tainted with Ibsenism, was retained, but only, I presume, because, having command of the stage-right in the play, she could not be replaced—say by Miss Maude Millet—without her own consent. The rest of the arrangements are economical rather than fashionable, the syndicate, to all appearance, being, like most syndicates, an association for the purpose of getting money rather than supplying it.

Mrs Patrick Campbell has entered thoroughly into the spirit of the alterations. She has seen how unladylike, how disturbing, how full of horror even, the part of Rita Allmers is, acted as Miss Achurch acted it. And she has remedied this with a completeness that leaves nothing to be desired—or perhaps only one thing. Was there not a Mr Arcedeckne who, when

Thackeray took to lecturing, said, 'Have a piano, Thack'? Well, Rita Allmers wants a piano. Mrs Tanqueray had one, and played it so beautifully that I have been her infatuated slave ever since. There need be no difficulty about the matter: the breezy Borgheim has only to say, 'Now that Alfred is back, Mrs Allmers, wont you give us that study for the left hand we are all so fond of?' and there you are. However, even without the piano, Mrs Campbell succeeded wonderfully in eliminating all unpleasantness from the play. She looked charming; and her dresses were beyond reproach: she carried a mortgage on the 'gold and green forests' on her back. Her performance was infinitely reassuring and pretty: its note was, 'You silly people: what are you making all this fuss about? The secret of life is charm and self-possession, and not tantrums about drowned children.' The famous line 'There stood your champagne; but you tasted it not,' was no longer a 'secret of the alcove,' but a good-humored, mock petulant remonstrance with a man whom there was no pleasing in the matter of wine. There was not a taste of a nasty jealousy: this Rita tolerated her dear old stupid's preoccupation with Asta and Eyolf and his books as any sensible (or insensible) woman would. Goodness gracious, I thought, what things that evil-minded Miss Achurch did read into this harmless play! And how nicely Mrs Campbell took the drowning of the child! Just a pretty waving of the fingers, a moderate scream as if she had very nearly walked on a tin tack, and it was all over, without tears, without pain, without more fuss than if she had broken the glass of her watch.

At this rate, it was not long before Rita thoroughly gained the sympathy of the audience. We felt that if she could only get rid of that ridiculous, sentimental

Asta (Miss Robins, blind to the object lesson before her, persisted in acting Ibsenitically), and induce her fussing, self-conscious, probably underbred husband not to cry for spilt milk, she would be as happy as any lady in the land. Unfortunately, the behaviour of Mr Allmers became more and more intolerable as the second act progressed, though he could not exhaust Rita's patient, slily humorous tolerance. As usual, he wanted to know whether she would like to go and drown herself; and the sweet, cool way in which she answered, 'Oh, I don't know, Alfred. No: I think I should have to stay here with *you*—a *litt*-le while' was a lesson to all wives. What a contrast to Miss Achurch, who so unnecessarily filled the stage with the terror of death in this passage! This is what comes of exaggeration, of over-acting, of forgetting that people go to the theatre to be amused, and not to be upset! When Allmers shook his fist at his beautiful wife—O unworthy the name of Briton!—and shouted '*You* are the guilty one in this,' her silent dignity overwhelmed him. Nothing could have been in better taste than her description of the pretty way in which her child had lain in the water when he was drowned—his mother's son all over. All the pain was taken out of it by the way it was approached. 'I got Borgheim to go down to the pier with me [so nice of Borgheim, dear fellow!].' 'And what,' interrupts the stupid Allmers, 'did you want there?' Rita gave a little laugh at his obtuseness, a laugh which meant 'Why, you dear silly,' before she replied, 'To question the boys as to how it happened.' After all, it is these Ibsenite people that create the objections to Ibsen. If Mrs Campbell had played Rita from the first, not a word would have been said against the play; and the whole business would have been quietly over and the theatre closed by this time. But nothing would serve them but their Miss Achurch; and so, instead of a pretty arrangement of the 'Eyolf' theme for boudoir pianette, we had it flung to the 'Götterdämmerung' orchestra, and blared right into our shrinking souls.

In the third act, the smoothness of the proceedings was somewhat marred by the fact that Mrs Campbell, not knowing her words, had to stop acting and frankly bring the book on the stage and read from it. Now Mrs Campbell reads very clearly and nicely; and the result of course was that the Ibsenite atmosphere began to assert itself, just as it would if the play were read aloud in a private room. However, that has been remedied, no doubt, by this time; and the public may rely on an uninterruptedly quiet evening.

The main drawback is that it is impossible not to feel that Mrs Campbell's Rita, with all her charm, is terribly hampered by the unsuitability of the words Ibsen and Mr Archer have put into her mouth. They were all very well for Miss Achurch, who perhaps, if the truth were known, arranged her acting to suit them; but they are forced, strained, out of tune in all sorts of ways in the mouth of Mrs Campbell's latest creation. Why cannot the dialogue be adapted to her requirements and harmonized with her playing, say by Mr William Black? Ibsen is of no use when anything really ladylike is wanted: you might as well put Beethoven to compose Chaminades. It is true that no man can look at the new Rita without wishing that Heaven had sent him just such a wife, whereas the boldest man would hardly have envied Allmers the other Rita if Miss Achurch had allowed him a moment's leisure for such impertinent speculations; but all the same, the evenings at the Avenue Theatre are likely to be a little languid. I had rather look at a beautiful picture than be flogged, as a general thing; but if I were offered my choice between looking at the most beautiful picture in the world continuously for a fortnight and submitting to, say, a dozen, I think I should choose the flogging. For just the same reason, if I had to choose between seeing Miss Achurch's Rita again, with all its turns of beauty and flashes of grandeur obliterated, and nothing left but its insane jealousy, its agonizing horror, its lacerating remorse, and its maddening unrest, the alternative being another two hours' contemplation of uneventful feminine fascination as personified by Mrs Patrick Campbell, I should go like a lamb to the slaughter. I prefer Mrs Campbell's Rita to her photograph, because it moves and talks; but otherwise there is not so much difference as I expected. Mrs Campbell, as Magda, could do nothing with a public spoiled by Duse. I greatly fear she will do even less, as Rita, with a public spoiled by Miss Achurch.

The representation generally is considerably affected in its scale and effect by the change of Ritas. Mr Courtenay Thorpe, who, though playing *con tutta la forza*, could hardly avoid seeming to underact with Miss Achurch, has now considerable difficulty in avoiding overacting, since he cannot be even in earnest and anxious without producing an effect of being good-humoredly laughed at by Mrs Campbell. Miss Robins, as Asta, has improved greatly on the genteel misery of the first night. She has got complete hold of the part; and although her old fault of resorting to the lachrymose for all sorts of pathetic expression produces something of its old monotony, and the voice clings to one delicate register until the effect verges on affectation, yet Asta comes out as a distinct person about whose history the audience has learnt something, and not as an actress delivering a string of lines and making a number of points more or less effectively. The difficulty is that in this cheap edition of Little Eyolf Asta, instead of being the tranquillizing element, becomes the centre of disturbance; so that the conduct of Allmers in turning for the sake of peace and quietness from his pretty, coaxing, soothing wife to his agitated high-strung sister becomes nonsensical. I pointed out after the first performance that Miss Robins had not really succeeded in making Asta a peacemaker; but beside Miss Achurch she easily seemed gentle, whereas beside Mrs Campbell she seems a volcano. It is only necessary to recall her playing of the frightful ending to the first act of Alan's Wife, and compare it with Mrs Campbell's finish to the first act of Little Eyolf, to realize the preposterousness of their relative positions in the cast. Mrs Campbell's old part of the Ratwife is now played by Miss Florence Farr. Miss Farr deserves more public sympathy than any of the other Ibsenite actresses; for they have only damaged themselves professionally by appearing in Ibsen's plays, whereas Miss Farr has complicated her difficulties by appearing in mine as well. Further, instead of either devoting herself to the most personally exacting of all the arts or else letting it alone, Miss Farr has written clever novels and erudite works on Babylonish lore; has managed a theatre capably for a season; and has only occasionally acted. For an occasional actress she has been rather successful once or twice in producing singular effects in singular parts—her Rebecca in Rosmersholm was remarkable and promising—but she has not pursued her art with sufficient constancy to attain any authoritative power of carrying out her conceptions, which are, besides, only skin deep. Her

Ratwife is a favorable example of her power of producing a certain strangeness of effect; but it is somewhat discounted by want of sustained grip in the execution. Miss Farr will perhaps remedy this if she can find time enough to spare from her other interests to attend to it. The rest of the cast is as before. One has no longer any real belief in the drowning of Master Stewart Dawson, thanks to the gentle method of Mrs Campbell. Mr Lowne's sensible, healthy superiority to all this morbid Ibsen stuff is greatly reinforced now that Rita takes things nicely and easily.

I cannot help thinking it a great pity that the Avenue enterprise, just as it seemed to be capturing that afternoon classical concert public to which I have always looked for the regeneration of the classical drama, should have paid the penalty of its success by the usual evolution into what is evidently half a timid speculation in a 'catch-on,' and half an attempt to slacken the rate at which the Avenue Theatre is eating its head off in rent. That evolution of course at once found out the utter incoherence of the enterprise. The original production, undertaken largely at Miss Robins's individual risk, was for the benefit of a vaguely announced Fund, as to the constitution and purpose of which no information was forthcoming, except that it proposed to produce Echegaray's Mariana, with Miss Robins in the title-part. But neither Miss Robins's nor anyone else's interests in this fund seem to have been secured in any way. The considerable profit of the first week of little Eyolf may, for all that is guaranteed to the contrary, be devoted to the production of an opera, a shadow play from Paris, or a drama in which neither Miss Robins nor any of those who have worked with her may be offered any part or share whatever. There is already just such a fund in existence in the treasury of the Independent Theatre, which strove hard to obtain Little Eyolf for production, and which actually guaranteed part of the booking at the Avenue. But here the same difficulty arose. Miss Achurch would no doubt have trusted the Independent, for the excellent reason that her husband is one of the directors; but no other artist playing for it would have had the smallest security that, had its fortunes been established through their efforts, they would ever have been cast for a part in its future productions. On the other hand, Miss Achurch had no hold on the new fund, which had specially declared its intention of supporting Miss Robins. This has not prevented the production of Little Eyolf, though it has greatly delayed it; for everybody finally threw security to the winds, and played by friendly arrangement on such terms as were possible. As it happened, there was a substantial profit, and it all went to the Fund. Naturally, however, when the enterprise entered upon a purely commercial phase, the artists at once refused to work for the profit of a syndicate on the enthusiastic terms (or no terms) on which they had worked for Ibsen and for one another. The syndicate, on the other hand, had no idea of wasting so expensive a star as Mrs Patrick Campbell on a small part that could be filled for a few pounds, when they could transfer her to the leading part and save Miss Achurch's salary. If they could have substituted an inferior artist for Miss Robins, they could have effected a still further saving, relying on Mrs Pat to draw full houses; but that was made impossible by Miss Robins's power over the stage-right. Consequently, the only sufferer was Miss Achurch; but it is impossible for Miss Robins and Mrs Campbell not to feel that the same thing might have happened to them if there had been no stage-right, and if the syndicate had realized that, when it comes to Ibsen, Miss Achurch is a surer card to play than Mrs Campbell.

Under these circumstances, what likelihood is there of the experiment being resumed or repeated on its old basis? Miss Robins will probably think twice before she creates Mariana without some security that, if she succeeds, the part will not immediately be handed over to Miss Winifred Emery or Miss Julia Neilson. Miss Achurch, triumphantly as she has come out of the comparison with her successor, is not likely to forget her lesson. Mrs Campbell's willingness to enlist in forlorn hopes in the humblest capacity may not improbably be received in future as Laocoon received the offer of the wooden horse. I do not presume to meddle in the affairs of all these actors and authors, patrons and enthusiasts, subscribers and guarantors, though this is quite as much my business as theirs; but after some years' intimate experience of the results of unorganized Ibsenism, I venture to suggest that it would be well to have some equitable form of theatrical organization ready to deal with Ibsen's new play, on the translation of which Mr Archer is already at work.

Richard Himself Again

RICHARD III. *Lyceum Theatre*, 19 *December* 1896.

[26 *December* 1896]

THE world being yet little better than a mischievous schoolboy, I am afraid it cannot be denied that Punch and Judy holds the field still as the most popular of dramatic entertainments. And of all its versions, except those which are quite above the head of the man in the street, Shakespear's Richard III is the best. It has abundant devilry, humor, and character, presented with luxuriant energy of diction in the simplest form of blank verse. Shakespear revels in it with just the sort of artistic unconscionableness that fits the theme. Richard is the prince of Punches: he delights Man by provoking God, and dies unrepentant and game to the last. His incongruous conventional appendages, such as the Punch hump, the conscience, the fear of ghosts, all impart a spice of outrageousness which leaves nothing lacking to the fun of the entertainment, except the solemnity of those spectators who feel bound to take the affair as a profound and subtle historic study.

Punch, whether as Jingle, Macaire, Mephistopheles, or Richard, has always been a favorite part with Sir Henry Irving. The craftily mischievous, the sardonically impudent, tickle him immensely, besides providing him with a welcome relief from the gravity of his serious impersonations. As Richard he drops Punch after the coronation scene, which, in deference to stage tradition, he makes a turning-point at which the virtuoso in mischief, having achieved his ambition, becomes a savage at bay. I do not see why this should be. In the tent scene, Richard says:

> There is no creature loves me;
> And if I die no soul will pity me.

Macbeth repeats this patch of pathos, and immediately proceeds to pity himself unstintedly over it; but Richard no sooner catches the sentimental cadence of his own voice than the mocker in him is awakened at once, and he adds, quite in Punch's vein,

> Nay, wherefore should they? since that I myself
> Find in myself no pity for myself.

Sir Henry Irving omits these lines, because he plays, as he always does, for a pathetically sublime ending. But we have seen the sublime ending before pretty often; and this time it robs us of such strokes as Richard's aristocratically cynical private encouragement to his entourage of peers:

> Our strong arms be our conscience, swords our law.
> March on; join bravely; let us to't pell-mell,
> If not to Heaven, then hand in hand to hell;

followed by his amusingly blackguardly public address to the rank and file, quite in the vein of the famous and more successful appeal to the British troops in the Peninsula. 'Will you that are Englishmen fed on beef let yourselves be licked by a lot of —— Spaniards fed on oranges?' Despair, one feels, could bring to Punch-Richard nothing but the exultation of one who loved destruction better than even victory; and the exclamation

> A thousand hearts are great within my bosom

is not the expression of a hero's courage, but the evil ecstasy of the destroyer as he finds himself, after a weak, piping time of peace, back at last in his native element.

Sir Henry Irving's acting edition of the play is so enormously superior to Cibber's, that a playgoer brought up, as I was, on the old version must needs find an overwhelming satisfaction in it. Not that I object to the particular lines which are now always flung in poor Cibber's face. 'Off with his head: so much for Buckingham!' is just as worthy of Shakespear as 'I'll hear no more. Die, prophet, in thy speech,' and distinctly better than 'Off with his son George's head.'

> Hark! the shrill trumpet sounds. To horse! Away!
> My soul's in arms, and eager for the fray,

is ridiculed because Cibber wrote it; but I cannot for the life of me see that it is inferior to

> Go muster men. My counsel is my shield.
> We must be brief when traitors brave the field.

'Richard's himself again' is capital of its kind. If you object to the kind, the objection is stronger against Shakespear, who set Cibber the example, and was proclaimed immortal for it, than against an unfortunate actor who would never have dreamt of inventing the art of rhetorical balderdash for himself. The plain reason why the public for so many generations could see no difference in merit between the famous Cibber points and

> A horse! A horse! My kingdom for a horse!

was that there was no difference to see. When it came to fustian, Jack was as good as his master.

The real objection to Cibber's version is that it is what we call a 'one man show.' Shakespear, having no room in a play so full of action for more than one real part, surrounded it with figures whose historical titles and splendid dresses, helped by a line or two at the right moment, impose on our imagination sufficiently to make us see the whole Court of Edward IV. If Hastings, Stanley, the 'jockey of Norfolk,' the 'deep revolving witty Buckingham,' and the rest, only bear themselves with sufficient address not to contradict absolutely the dramatist's suggestion of them, the audience will receive enough impression of their reality, and even of their importance, to give Richard an air of moving in a Court as the King's brother. But Cibber could not bear that anyone on the stage should have an air of importance except himself: if the subordinate members of the company could not act so well as he, it seemed to him, not that it was his business as the presenter of a play to conceal their deficiencies, but that the first principles of justice and fair dealing demanded before all things that his superiority should be made evident to the public. (And there are not half a dozen leading actors on the stage today who would not take precisely that view of the situation.) Consequently he handled Richard III so as to make every other actor in it obviously ridiculous and insignificant, except only that Henry VI, in the first act, was allowed to win the pity of the audience in order that the effect might be the greater when Richard stabbed him. No actor could have produced more completely, exactly, and forcibly the effect aimed at by Cibber than Barry Sullivan, the one actor who kept Cibber's Richard on the stage during the present half-century. But it was an exhibition, not a play. Barry Sullivan was full of force, and very clever: if his power had been less exclusively of the infernal order, or if he had devoted himself to the drama instead of devoting the drama to himself as a mere means of self-assertion, one might have said more for him. He managed to make the audience believe in Richard; but as he could not make it believe in the others, and probably did not want to, they destroyed the illusion almost as fast as he created it. This is why Cibber's Richard, though it is so simple that the character plays itself as unmistakeably as the blank verse speaks itself, can only be made endurable by an actor of exceptional personal force. The second and third acts at the Lyceum, with their atmosphere of Court faction and their presentation before the audience of Edward and Clarence, make all the difference between the two versions.

But the Lyceum has by no means emancipated itself from superstition—even gross superstition. Italian opera itself could go no further in folly than the exhibition of a pretty and popular young actress in tights as Prince Edward. No doubt we were glad to see Miss Lena Ashwell—for the matter of that we should have been glad to see Mrs John Wood as the other prince—but from the moment she came on the stage all serious historical illusion necessarily vanished, and was replaced by the most extreme form of theatrical convention. Probably Sir Henry Irving cast Miss Ashwell for the part because he has not followed her career since she played Elaine in King Arthur. She was then weak, timid, subordinate, with an insignificant presence and voice which, contrasted as it was with Miss Terry's, could only be described—if one had the heart to do it—as a squawl. Since then she has developed precipitously. If any sort of success had been possible for the plays in which she has appeared this year at the Duke of York's and Shaftesbury Theatres, she would have received a large share of the credit of it. Even in Carmen, when, perhaps for the sake of auld lang syne, she squawled and stood on the tips of her heels for the last time (let us hope), her scene with the dragoon in the first act was the one memorable moment in the whole of that disastrous business. She now returns to the Lyceum stage as an actress of mark, strong in womanly charm, and not in the least the sort of person whose sex is so little emphasized that it can be hidden by a doublet and hose. You might as well put forward Miss Ada Rehan as a boy. Nothing can be more absurd than the spectacle of Sir Henry Irving elaborately playing the uncle to his little nephew when he is obviously addressing a fine young woman in rational dress who is very thoroughly her own mistress, and treads the boards with no little authority and assurance as one of the younger generation knocking vigorously at the door. Miss Ashwell makes short work of the sleepiness of the Lyceum; and though I take urgent exception to her latest technical theory, which is, that the bridge of the nose is the seat of facial expression, I admit that she does all that can be done to reconcile us to the burlesque of her appearance in a part that should have been played by a boy.

Another mistake in the casting of the play was Mr Gordon Craig's Edward IV. As Henry VI, Mr Craig, who wasted his delicacy on the wrong part, would have been perfect. Henry not being available, he might have played Richmond with a considerable air of being a young Henry VII. But as Edward he was incredible: one felt that Richard would have had him out of the way years ago if Margaret had not saved him the trouble by vanquishing him at Tewkesbury. Shakespear took plenty of pains with the strong ruffian of the York family: his part in Henry VI makes it quite clear why he held his own both in and out of doors. The remedy for the misfit lay ready to the manager's hand. Mr Cooper, his too burly Richmond, shewed what a capital Edward he would have made when he turned at the entrance to his tent, and said, with the set air of a man not accustomed to be trifled with,

> O Thou, whose captain I account myself,
> Look on my forces with a gracious eye,
> Or you will have me to reckon with afterwards.

The last line was not actually spoken by Mr Cooper; but he looked it, exactly as Edward IV might have done.

As to Sir Henry Irving's own performance, I am not prepared to judge it, in point of execution, by what he did on the first night. He was best in the Court scenes. In the heavy single-handed scenes which Cibber loved, he was not, as it seemed to me, answering his helm satisfactorily; and he was occasionally a little out of temper with his own nervous condition. He made some odd slips in the text, notably by repeatedly substituting 'you' for 'I'—for instance, 'Shine out, fair sun, till you have bought a glass.' Once he inadvertently electrified the house by very unexpectedly asking Miss Milton to get further up the stage in the blank verse and penetrating tones of Richard. Finally, the worry of playing against the vein tired him. In the tent and battle scenes his exhaustion was too genuine to be quite acceptable as part of the play. The fight was, perhaps, a relief to his feelings; but to me the spectacle of Mr Cooper pretending to pass his sword three times through Richard's body, as if a man could be run through as easily as a cuttle-fish, was neither credible nor impressive. The attempt to make a stage combat look as imposing as Hazlitt's description of the death of Edmund Kean's Richard reads, is hopeless. If Kean were to return to life and do the combat for us, we should very likely find it as absurd as his habit of lying down on a sofa when he was too tired or too drunk to keep his feet during the final scenes.

Further, it seems to me that Sir Henry Irving should either cast the play to suit his acting or else modify his acting to suit the cast. His playing in the scene with Lady Anne—which, though a Punch scene, is Punch on the Don Giovanni plane—was a flat contradiction, not only of the letter of the lines, but of their spirit and feeling as conveyed unmistakeably by their cadence. This, however, we are used to: Sir Henry Irving never did and never will make use of a play otherwise than as a vehicle for some fantastic creation of his own. But if we are not to have the tears, the passion, the tenderness, the transport of dissimulation which alone can make the upshot credible—if the woman is to be openly teased and insulted, mocked, and disgusted, all through the scene as well as in the first 'keen encounter of their wits,' why not have Lady Anne presented as a weak, childish-witted, mesmerized creature, instead of as that most awful embodiment of virtue and decorum, the intellectual American lady? Poor Miss Julia Arthur honestly did her best to act the part as she found it in Shakespear; and if Richard had done the same she would have come off with credit. But how could she play to a Richard who would not utter a single tone to which any woman's heart could respond? She could not very well box the actor-manager's ears, and walk off; but really she deserves some credit for refraining from that extreme remedy. She partly had her revenge when she left the stage; for Richard, after playing the scene with her as if he were a Houndsditch salesman cheating a factory girl over a pair of second-hand stockings, naturally could not reach the raptures of the tremendous outburst of elation beginning

> Was ever woman in this humor wooed?
> Was ever woman in this humor won?

One felt inclined to answer, 'Never, I assure you,' and make an end of the scene there and then. I am prepared to admit that the creations of Sir Henry Irving's imagination are sometimes—in the case of his Iachimo, for example—better than those of the dramatists whom he is supposed to interpret. But what he did in this scene, as well as in the opening soliloquy, was child's play compared to what Shakespear meant him to do.

The rest of the performance was—well, it was Lyceum Shakespear. Miss Geneviève Ward was, of course, a very capable Margaret; but she missed the one touchstone passage in a very easy part—the tenderness of the appeal to Buckingham. Mr Macklin, equally of course, had no trouble with Buckingham; but he did not give us that moment which makes Richard say:

None are for me
That look into me with considerate eyes.

Messrs Norman Forbes and W. Farren (junior) played the murderers in the true Shakespearean manner: that is, as if they had come straight out of the pantomime of The Babes in the Wood; and Clarence recited his dream as if he were an elocutionary coroner summing up. The rest were respectably dull, except Mr Gordon Craig, Miss Lena Ashwell, and, in a page's part, Miss Edith Craig, the only member of the company before whom the manager visibly quails.

Better than Shakespear

THE PILGRIM'S PROGRESS. *A mystery play, with music, in four acts. By* G. G. Collingham; *founded on* John Bunyan's *immortal allegory. Olympic Theatre,* 24 *December* 1896.

BLACK-EY'D SUSAN; OR, ALL IN THE DOWNS. Douglas Jerrold's *famous nautical drama, in two acts. Preceded by* J. Maddison Morton's *domestic comedy, in two acts,* ALL THAT GLITTERS IS NOT GOLD. *Adelphi Theatre,* 23 *December* 1896.

THE EIDER DOWN QUILT. *Farcical comedy, in three acts. By* Tom S. Wotton. *Terry's Theatre,* 21 *December* 1896.

BETSY. *The celebrated comedy, in three acts. By* F. C. Burnand. *Revival. Criterion Theatre,* 29 *December* 1896.

HOLLY TREE INN. *Adapted by* Mrs Oscar Beringer *from* Charles Dickens's *story. In one act. Terry's Theatre,* 28 *December* 1896.

[2 *January* 1897]

WHEN I saw a stage version of The Pilgrim's Progress announced for production, I shook my head, knowing that Bunyan is far too great a dramatist for our theatre, which has never been resolute enough even in its lewdness and venality to win the respect and interest which positive, powerful wickedness always engages, much less the services of men of heroic conviction. Its greatest catch, Shakespear, wrote for the theatre because, with extraordinary artistic powers, he understood nothing and believed nothing. Thirty-six big plays in five blank verse acts, and (as Mr

Ruskin, I think, once pointed out) not a single hero! Only one man in them all who believes in life, enjoys life, thinks life worth living, and has a sincere, unrhetorical tear dropped over his death-bed; and that man—Falstaff! What a crew they are—these Saturday to Monday athletic stockbroker Orlandos, these villains, fools, clowns, drunkards, cowards, intriguers, fighters, lovers, patriots, hypochondriacs who mistake themselves (and are mistaken by the author) for philosophers, princes without any sense of public duty, futile pessimists who imagine they are confronting a barren and unmeaning world when they are only contemplating their own worthlessness, self-seekers of all kinds, keenly observed and masterfully drawn from the romantic-commercial point of view. Once or twice we scent among them an anticipation of the crudest side of Ibsen's polemics on the Woman Question, as in All's Well that Ends Well, where the man cuts as meanly selfish a figure beside his enlightened lady doctor wife as Helmer beside Nora; or in Cymbeline, where Posthumus, having, as he believes, killed his wife for inconstancy, speculates for a moment on what his life would have been worth if the same standard of continence had been applied to himself. And certainly no modern study of the voluptuous temperament, and the spurious heroism and heroinism which its ecstasies produce, can add much to Antony and Cleopatra, unless it were some sense of the spuriousness on the author's part. But search for statesmanship, or even citizenship, or any sense of the commonwealth, material or spiritual, and you will not find the making of a decent vestryman or curate in the whole horde. As to faith, hope, courage, conviction, or any of the true heroic qualities, you find nothing but death made sensational, despair made stage-sublime, sex made romantic, and barrenness covered up by sentimentality and the mechanical lilt of blank verse.

All that you miss in Shakespear you find in Bunyan, to whom the true heroic came quite obviously and naturally. The world was to him a more terrible place than it was to Shakespear; but he saw through it a path at the end of which a man might look not only forward to the Celestial City, but back on his life and say:—'Tho' with great difficulty I am got hither, yet now I do not repent me of all the trouble I have been at to arrive where I am. My sword I give to him that shall succeed me in my pilgrimage, and my courage and skill to him that can get them.' The heart vibrates like a bell to such an utterance as this: to turn from it to 'Out, out, brief candle,' and 'The rest is silence,' and 'We are such stuff as dreams are made on, and our little life is rounded with a sleep' is to turn from life, strength, resolution, morning air and eternal youth, to the terrors of a drunken nightmare.

Let us descend now to the lower ground where Shakespear is not disabled by his inferiority in energy and elevation of spirit. Take one of his big fighting scenes, and compare its blank verse, in point of mere rhetorical strenuousness, with Bunyan's prose. Macbeth's famous cue for the fight with Macduff runs thus:—

> Yet I will try the last: before my body
> I throw my warlike shield. Lay on, Macduff,
> And damned be him that first cries Hold, enough!

Turn from this jingle, dramatically right in feeling, but silly and resourceless in thought and expression, to Apollyon's cue for the fight in the Valley of Humiliation: 'I am void of fear in this matter. Prepare thyself to die; for I swear by my infernal den that thou shalt go no farther: here will I spill thy soul.' This is the same thing done masterly. Apart from its superior grandeur, force, and appropriateness, it is better claptrap and infinitely better word-music.

Shakespear, fond as he is of describing fights, has hardly ever sufficient energy or reality of imagination to finish without betraying the paper origin of his fancies by dragging in something classical in the style of the Cyclops' hammer falling 'on Mars's armor, forged for proof eterne.' Hear how Bunyan does it: 'I fought till my sword did cleave to my hand; and when they were joined together as if the sword grew out of my arm; and when the blood run thorow my fingers, then I fought with most courage.' Nowhere in all Shakespear is there a touch like that of the blood running down through the man's fingers, and his courage rising to passion at it. Even in mere technical adaptation to the art of the actor, Bunyan's dramatic speeches are as good as Shakespear's tirades. Only a trained dramatic speaker can appreciate the terse manageableness and effectiveness of such a speech as this, with its grandiose exordium, followed up by its pointed question and its stern threat: 'By this I perceive thou art one of my subjects; for all that country is mine, and I am the Prince and the God of it. How is it then that thou hast ran away from thy King? Were it not that I hope thou mayst do me more service, I would strike thee now at one blow to the ground.' Here there is no raving and swearing and rhyming and classical allusion. The sentences go straight to their mark; and their concluding phrases soar like the sunrise, or swing and drop like a hammer, just as the actor wants them.

I might multiply these instances by the dozen; but I had rather leave dramatic students to compare the two authors at first-hand. In an article on Bunyan lately published in the Contemporary Review—the only article worth reading on the subject I ever saw (yes, thank you: I am quite familiar with Macaulay's patronizing prattle about The Pilgrim's Progress)—Mr Richard Heath, the historian of the Anabaptists, shews how Bunyan learnt his lesson, not only from his own rough pilgrimage through life, but from the tradition of many an actual journey from real Cities of Destruction (under Alva), with Interpreters' houses and convoy of Greathearts all complete. Against such a man what chance had our poor immortal William, with his 'little Latin' (would it had been less, like his Greek!), his heathen mythology, his Plutarch, his Boccaccio, his Holinshed, his circle of London literary wits, soddening their minds with books and their nerves with alcohol (quite like us), and all the rest of his Strand and Fleet Street surroundings, activities, and interests, social and professional, mentionable and unmentionable? Let us applaud him, in due measure, in that he came out of it no blackguardly Bohemian, but a thoroughly respectable snob; raised the desperation and cynicism of its outlook to something like sublimity in his tragedies; dramatized its morbid, self-centred passions and its feeble and shallow speculations with all the force that was in them; disinfected it by copious doses of romantic poetry, fun, and common sense; and gave to its perpetual sex-obsession the relief of individual character and feminine winsomeness. Also—if you are a sufficiently good Whig—that after incarnating the spirit of the whole epoch which began with the sixteenth century and is ending (I hope) with the nineteenth, he is still the idol of all well-read children. But as he never thought a noble life worth living or a great work worth doing, because the commercial profit-and-loss sheet shewed that the one did not bring happiness nor the other money, he never struck the great vein—the vein in which Bunyan told of that 'man of a very stout countenance' who went up to the keeper of the book of life and said, not 'Out, out, brief candle,' but 'Set down my name, sir,' and immediately fell on the armed men and cut his way into heaven after receiving and giving many wounds.

Let me not, however, be misunderstood by the Anglo-American Theatrical Syndicate, Limited, which has introduced the entertainment at the Olympic described as The Pilgrim's Progress, a mystery play, by G. G. Collingham, founded on John Bunyan's Immortal Allegory. That syndicate has listened to the voice of Demas; and I wish it joy of the silver mines to which he has led it. As to Mr Collingham, he does not take my view of the excellence of Bunyan's language or ideas. It is true that his hero is called Christian, and the villain Apollion, on the analogy of Rapscallion, Scullion, and the like, instead of Appol Lyon, which is what Bunyan called him. Also, three of the scenes are called Vanity Fair, The Valley of the Shadow of Death, and Doubting Castle, from which Christian escapes with the key called Promise. I fancied, too, I detected a paraphrase of a Bunyan passage in the following couplet:

> Heed not this king: he never gives reward,
> But always leaves his followers in the lurch.

But, these points apart, it would not have occurred to me that Mr Collingham or anyone else connected with the Olympic production had ever read or heard of Bunyan. It has been stated publicly that 'Mr Collingham' is a lady who has been encouraged to venture a good deal of her private means on the production of a work which is perilously deficient in the stage qualities needed to justify such encouragement. If this is true, I need not say what I think of the enterprise. If not, I desire to treat it with respect because it has attracted capital; for the other day, when subscriptions were invited to produce Little Eyolf, several of those colleagues of mine who still devotedly keep knocking their heads against the Norwegian stone wall laid great stress on this failure on Ibsen's part to attract capital from the ordinary theatrical sources. I sardonically invite them to go and revel in The Pilgrim's Progress as a play which has attracted capital enough to produce Little Eyolf six times over.

The new bill at the Adelphi should not be missed by anyone who wishes to qualify as an experienced playgoer. All that Glitters is not Gold is a most fearful specimen of obsolete pinchbeck, in spite of the pleasant qualities of the author of Box and Cox. But, of course, what one goes for is Black-Ey'd Susan, not Wills's genteel edition, with which Mrs Kendal made us cry so at the St James's, but the real original, with San Domingo Billy, hornpipe, song about My sweet Willy-yum, and nautical lingo all complete. Mr Terriss makes brilliant play with his diamond shoebuckles in the hornpipe, justifies his ear in his song, and delivers the jargon of the first two scenes like a conjuror producing miles of ribbon from his mouth. Miss Millward, when rudely accosted by Mr Fulton as Captain Crosstree, says, 'He is intoxicated. I must hence,' as if that were the most natural observation possible for the wife of an able seaman. But Black-Ey'd Susan, when it once gets to business, is an excellent play. It is the second act that tries the actor; and here Mr Terriss plays with perfect judgment, producing just the right effect of humble but manly sincerity and naturalness in great distress by the most straightforward methods. Is it not odd that the Adelphi is the only theatre in London devoted to sentimental modern drama where the acting is not vulgar? In other houses the actors' subordination of drama to 'good taste,' their consciousness of the stalls, their restrained drawing room voices, made resonant enough for the theatre by clarionet effects from the nose, their perpetual thinking of their manners and appearance when they ought to be thinking of their work, all produce a detestable atmosphere of candidature for social promotion which makes me wish sometimes that the stage were closed to all classes except only those accustomed to take their position for granted and their own ways as the standard ways, or those who frankly make no social pretension at all. At the Adelphi the actors provide for their appearance in their dressing rooms, and when they come on the stage go straight for the play with all their force, as if their point of honor lay in their skill, and not in persuading smart parties in the boxes that it would be quite safe to send them cards for an 'At Home' in spite of their profession. The result is that they look better, dress better, and behave better than their competitors at the intentionally fashionable theatres. Instead of having caught the 'form' of South Kensington (and what an appalling complaint that is for anyone to catch!), they have universal good manners, the proof being that Mr Terriss, without the slightest self-disguise or 'character-acting' trickery of any sort, is equally engaging and equally natural as the officer in One of the Best and as the common sailor in Black-Ey'd Susan. Miss Millward, though she is, I am told, always so scrupulously in fashion that women's hearts sink if they see her sleeves vary by an inch from their latest frocks, is always in her part, and always fits it if there is any sort of possible humanity and charm in it. Mr Fulton, too, is a courageous and self-respecting actor who is at home everywhere on the stage. Even Mr Harry Nicholls, badly spoiled funny man as he is, has serious qualities as an actor, and can make real bricks when the author provides any straw. In short, the secret of the Adelphi is not, as is generally assumed, bad drama, but simply good acting and plenty of it. And, unlike most critics, I am fond of acting.

The Eider Down Quilt, at Terry's, a somewhat artlessly amusing piece, owes a good deal to the genius of Miss Fanny Brough as a lady who has, as she believes, sat on a man and smothered him, and to Mr de Lange, who tries the very dangerous experiment of taking a purely farcical figure (an Italian waiter disguised as a prince), and making a realistic character study of him. However, the result justifies the attempt; and Alberto da Bologna is another of Mr de Lange's successes.

Betsy has been revived at the Criterion to give Mr Wyndham a holiday. I hope he will enjoy it at least as much as I enjoyed Betsy, which, though funny, is somewhat too pre-Ibsenite for my taste.

The afternoon performances of Love in Idleness at Terry's now begin with Mrs Oscar Beringer's adaptation of Boots at the Holly Tree Inn, in which Master Stewart Dawson, late of Little Eyolf, and Miss Valli Valli play the tiny elopers. It is very prettily done, and just the sort of piece that old people like.

Satan Saved at Last

THE SORROWS OF SATAN. *A play in four acts. Adapted by* Herbert Woodgate *and* Paul M. Berton *from the famous novel of that name, by* Marie Corelli. *Shaftesbury Theatre,* 9 *January* 1897.

[16 *January* 1897]

I WISH this invertebrate generation would make up its mind either to believe in the devil or disbelieve in him. The Norwegians, we learn from Ibsen's Brand, prefer an easygoing God, whom they can get round, and who does not mean half what he says when he is angry. I have always thought that there is a good deal to be said for this amiable theology; but when it comes to the devil, I claim, like Brand, 'all or nothing.' A snivelling, remorseful devil, with his heart in the right place, sneaking about the area railings of heaven in the hope that he will presently be let in and forgiven, is an abomination to me. The Lean Person in Peer Gynt, whose occupation was gone because men sinned so half-heartedly that nobody was worth damning, gained my sympathy at once. But a devil who is himself half-hearted—whose feud with heaven is the silliest sort of lovers' quarrel—who believes that he is in the wrong and God in the right—pah! He reminds me of those Sunday School teachers who cannot keep from drinking and gambling, though they believe in teetotalism and long to be the most respectable men in the parish. I cannot conceive how such a creature can charm the imagination of Miss Marie Corelli. It will be admitted that she is not easy to please when fashionable women and journalists are in question. Then why let the devil off so cheaply?

Let me not, however, dismiss The Sorrows of Satan too cavalierly; for I take Miss Marie Corelli to be one of the most sincere and independent writers at present before the public. Early in 1886, when she made her mark for the first time with A Romance of Two Worlds, she took her stand boldly as the apostle of romantic religion. 'Believe,' she said, 'in anything or everything miraculous and glorious—the utmost reach of your faith can with difficulty grasp the majestic reality and perfection of everything you can see, desire, or imagine.' Here we have that sure mark of romantic religion—the glorification of the miraculous. Again, 'walking on the sea can be accomplished now by anyone who has cultivated sufficient inner force.' Two years later, A Romance of Two Worlds was prefaced by a list of testimonials from persons who had found salvation in the Electric Christianity of the novel. Lest anyone should suppose that Electric Christianity was a fictitious religion, Miss Corelli took the opportunity to say of it, 'Its tenets are completely borne out by the New Testament, which sacred *little book* [italics mine], however, has much of its mystical and true meaning obscured nowadays through the indifference of those who read and the apathy of those who hear. . . . My creed has its foundation in Christ alone . . . only Christ, only the old old story of Divine love and sacrifice. . . . The proof of the theories set forth in the Romance is, as I have stated, easily to be found in the New Testament. . . . I merely endeavored to slightly shadow forth the miraculous powers which

I *know* are bestowed on those who truly love and understand the teachings of Christ.' The miraculous powers, I may mention, included making trips round the solar system, living for ever, seeming to improvise on the pianoforte by playing at the dictation of angels, knocking people down with electric shocks at will and without apparatus, painting pictures in luminous paint, and cognate marvels. When I say that Miss Corelli is sincere, I of course do not mean that she has ever acted on the assumption that her 'religion' is real. But when she takes up her pen, she imagines it to be real, because she has a prodigiously copious and fluent imagination, without, as far as I have been able to ascertain, the knowledge, the training, the observation, the critical faculty, the humor, or any other of the acquirements and qualities which compel ordinary people to distinguish in some measure (and in some measure only; for the best of us is not wholly un-Corellian) between what they may sanely believe and what they would like to believe. Great works in fiction are the arduous victories of great minds over great imaginations: Miss Corelli's works are the cheap victories of a profuse imagination over an apparently commonplace and carelessly cultivated mind. The story of the Passion in the New Testament not being imaginative enough for her, and quite superfluously thoughtful and realistic, she rewrote it to her taste; and the huge circulation of her version shows that, to the minds of her readers, she considerably improved it. Having made this success with the hero of Barabbas, she next turned her attention to Satan, taking all the meaning out of him, but lavishing imagination on him until he shone all over with stage fire. I do not complain of the process: I neither grudge Miss Corelli to her disciples nor her disciples to Miss Corelli; but

I must warn my readers that nothing that I have to say about the play must be taken as implying that it is possible, real, or philosophically coherent.

Let me now come down from my high horse, and take the play on its own ground. The romantic imagination is the most unoriginative, uncreative faculty in the world, an original romance being simply an old situation shewn from a new point of view. As John Gabriel Borkman says, 'the eye, born anew, transforms the old action.' Miss Corelli's eye, not having been born anew, transforms nothing. Only, it was born recently enough to have fallen on the music dramas of Wagner; and just as she gave us, in Thelma, a version of the scene in Die Walküre where Brynhild warns Siegmund of his approaching death, so in The Sorrows of Satan she reproduces Vanderdecken, the man whose sentence of damnation will be cancelled if he can find one soul faithful to the death. Wagner's Vanderdecken is redeemed by a woman; but Miss Corelli, belonging to that sex herself, knows better, and makes the redeemer a man. I am bound to say that after the most attentive study of the performance, I am unable to report the logical connection between the drowning of Geoffrey Tempest in the shipwreck of Satan-Vanderdecken Rimanez' yacht in the Antarctic circle, and the immediate ascension to heaven of Satan in a suit of armor; but I have no doubt it is explained in the novel: at all events, the situation at the end of the Flying Dutchman, with the ship sinking, and the redeemed man rising from the sea in glory, is quite recognizable. It seems hard that Geoffrey Tempest should be left in the cold water; but the spectacle of Satan ascending in fifteenth-century splendor, with his arm round a gentleman in shirt and trousers, evidently would not do; so poetic justice has to be sacrificed to stage effect.

The most forcible scene in the play is that in the fourth act, where the villain of the piece, Lady Sybil, plays false to her trusting husband by trying to seduce the virtuous demon. In an ordinary man-made play the villain would be a man and the sympathetic personages women; but as The Sorrows of Satan are woman-made, the sexes are reversed. This novelty is heightened by the operatic culture of the author, which enables her to blend the extremity of modern fashionableness with the extremity of medieval superstition, in the assured foreknowledge that the public will not only stand it but like it. All the essentials of the church scene from Gounod's Faust are in that fourth act, with even some of the accessories—the organ, for instance. The scene succeeds, as certain other scraps of the play succeed, because Miss Corelli has the courage and intensity of her imagination. This does not, of course, save her from absurdity—indeed it rather tends to involve her in it—but absurdity is the one thing that does not matter on the stage, provided it is not psychological absurdity. Still, a dramatist had better not abuse his immunity from common sense. It is true that if a man goes into the National Gallery, and raises the objection that all these pretended figures and landscapes and interiors are nothing but canvas and colored clay, there is nothing for it but to conduct him to the entrance and shoot him gently over the balustrade into the prosaic street. All the same, the more completely a painter can make us overlook that objection the better. Miss Corelli is apt to forget this. The introduction of a devil in footman's livery passed off excellently; but when he subsequently turned his hand to steering the yacht, and adopted a cardinal's costume as the most convenient for that duty, I confess I began to realize what a chance the management lost in not securing Mr Harry Nicholls for the part. The young nobleman who played baccarat so prodigally did not shatter my illusions until he suddenly staked his soul, at which point I missed Meyerbeer's Robert le Diable music rather badly. On the other hand, I have no objection whatever to Satan, after elaborately disguising himself as a modern *chevalier d'industrie*, giving himself away by occasional flashes of lightning. Without them the audience would not know that he was the devil: besides, it reminds one of Edmund Kean.

These, however, are trifles: any play can be ridiculed by simply refusing to accept its descriptive conventions. But, as I have said, a play need not be morally absurd. Real life, in spite of the efforts of States, Churches, and individuals to reduce its haphazards to order, *is* morally absurd for the most part: Prometheus gains but little on Jupiter; and his defeats are the staple of tragedy. It is the privilege of the drama to make life intelligible, at least hypothetically, by introducing moral design into it, even if that design be only to shew that moral design is an illusion, a demonstration which cannot be made without some counter-demonstration of the laws of life with which it clashes. If the dramatist repudiates moral interest, and elects to depend on humor, sensuousness, and romance, all the more must he accept the moral conventions which have become normal on the stage. Now Miss Corelli has flatly no humor—positively none at all. She is, in a very bookish way, abundantly sensuous and romantic; but she vehemently repudiates the conventional moral basis, professing, for instance, a loathing for the normal course of fashionable society, with its marriage market, its spiritual callousness, and its hunt for pleasure and money. But if Miss Corelli did not herself live in the idlest of all worlds, the world of dreams and books (so idle that people do not even learn to ride and shoot and sin in it), she would know that it is vain to protest against a necessary institution, however corrupt, until you have an efficient and convincing substitute ready. 'Electric Christianity' (symbolized in the play by Satan's flashes of lightning) will not convince anybody with a reasonably hard head on his or her shoulders that it is an efficient substitute even for the morals of Mayfair. The play is morally absurd from beginning to end. Satan is represented, not as the enemy of God, but as his victim and moral superior: nevertheless he worships God and is rewarded by reconciliation with him. He is neither Lucifer nor Prometheus, but a sham revolutionist bidding for a seat in the Cabinet. Lady Sybil is stigmatized as a 'wanton' because she marries for money; but the man who buys her in the marriage market quite openly by offering to take 'The Hall, Willowsmere,' if she will marry him, as a set-off to the disagreeableness of living with a man she does not care for, not only passes without reproach, and is permitted to strike virtuous attitudes at her expense, but actually has his death accepted as a sufficient atonement to redeem the devil. Please observe that he is thereby placed above Christ, whose atonement and resistance to the temptation in the desert were ineffectual as far as Satan was concerned. At the same time we are permitted to take to our bosoms an American girl, because, to gratify her Poppa's love of a title without forfeiting her own self-respect, she has heroically refused a silly young Duke and married a venal old

Earl. Further, the parade of contempt for wealth and fashion is accompanied by the rigid exclusion of all second-class, poor or lowly persons from the play except in the capacity of servants. The male characters are a Prince, a millionaire, an Earl, a Viscount, a Duke, and a Baronet, with their servants, two caricatured solicitors and a publisher being introduced for a moment to be laughed at for their vulgarity. The feminine side is supplied by Lady Sybil, Lady Mary, Miss Charlotte Fitzroy (who, lest her name should fail to inspire awe, is carefully introduced as 'Lord Elton's sister-in-law'), a millionairess, a Duchess, one vulgar but only momentary landlady, and Mavis Clare. Mavis Clare might be Miss Corelli herself, so haughtily does she scorn the minions of fashion and worms of the hour (as Silas Wegg put it) who provide her with the only society she seems to care for.

The adaptation from Miss Corelli's novel has been made by Messrs Herbert Woodgate and Paul Berton. I nevertheless hold Miss Corelli responsible for it. She is quite as capable of dramatizing her novels as anyone who is likely to save her the trouble; and a little work in this direction would do her no harm. A good deal of the dialogue is redundant, slovenly, and full of reach-me-down phrases which vulgarize every scene in which the author has not been stirred up by strong feeling. Most of the critics of whose hostility Miss Corelli complains so bitterly could teach her to double the distinction of her style in ten lessons. No doubt she could return the compliment by elevating their imaginations; so the lessons could be arranged on reciprocal terms.

The play has not called forth any great display of acting at the Shaftesbury. Mr Lewis Waller, by a touch or two on his eyebrows, makes himself passably like the famous devil on the roof of Notre Dame, and keeps up appearances so well that he appears to be talking impressively and cleverly even when he is observing at a garden party that 'the man who pretends to understand women betrays the first symptoms of insanity.' Mr Yorke Stephens, with unquenchable politeness and unassailable style, fulfils his obligations to Miss Corelli and the audience most scrupulously, but with the air of a man who has resolved to shoot himself the moment the curtain is down. He lacks that priceless gift of stupidity which prevents most leading men from knowing a bad part from a good one; and so, though he plays Geoffrey Tempest expertly, he cannot wallow in him as a worse actor might. His address never fails him; but as he is essentially a sceptical actor, his function of the Redeemer of Satan does not seem to impress him; and there is a remarkably reassuring ring in his 'O Lucio, Lucio, my heart is broken!' Miss Granville would do very well as Lady Sybil if only she were trained hard enough to get the requisite force of execution and to maintain her grip firmly all through. As it is, she hardly gets beyond a string of creditable attempts to act. The other parts are of no great importance.

There is a play without words at the Prince of Wales Theatre, entitled A Pierrot's Dream, about which I have more to say[1] than there is room for this week. Meanwhile I may admit that I found it a very delectable entertainment, Mlle Litini's Pierrot having a quite peculiar charm in addition to the accomplishments which one expects as a matter of course from Pierrots. Rossi's Pochinet, in a rougher way, is also excellent.

[1] See below, p. 202 ff.

The New Ibsen Play

JOHN GABRIEL BORKMAN. *A play in four acts. By* Henrik Ibsen. *Translated by* William Archer. *London: Heinemann.* 1897.

[30 *January* 1897]

THE appearance some weeks ago in these columns of a review of the original Norwegian edition of Ibsen's new play, John Gabriel Borkman, relieves me from repeating here what I have said elsewhere concerning Mr William Archer's English version. In fact, the time for reviewing it has gone by: all who care about Ibsen have by this time pounced on the new volume, and ascertained for themselves what it is like. The only point worth discussing now is the play's chances of performance.

Everybody knows what happened to Little Eyolf. None of our managers would touch it; and it was not until the situation was made very pressing indeed by the advent of the proof-sheets of its successor that it was produced. As it happened, a certain section of the public—much the same section, I take it, as that which supplies the audiences for our orchestral concerts—jumped at the opportunity; and the experiment, in its original modesty, proved handsomely remunerative. Then commercial enterprise, always dreaming of 'catches-on,' long runs, and 'silver mines,' attempted to exploit the occasion in the usual way, and of course made an inglorious mess of it. A fashionable run of one of Ibsen's dramatic studies of modern society is about as feasible as a fashionable run of Beethoven's posthumous quartets. A late Ibsen play will not bring in twenty thousand pounds: it will only bring in fifteen hundred or two thousand. On the other hand, the play which *may* bring in twenty thousand pounds also may, and in nine cases out of ten does, bring in less than half its very heavy expenses; whereas the expenses of an Ibsen play, including a rate of profit for the entrepreneur which would be considered handsome in any ordinary non-speculative business, can be kept well within its practically certain returns, not to mention a high degree of artistic credit and satisfaction to all concerned. Under these circumstances, it can hardly be contended that Ibsen's plays are not worth producing. In legitimate theatrical business Ibsen is as safe and profitable as Beethoven and Wagner in legitimate musical business.

Then, it will be asked, why do not the syndicates and managers take up Ibsen? As to the syndicates, the answer is simple. Enterprises with prospects limited to a profit of a few hundred pounds on a capital of a thousand do not require syndicates to finance them. An energetic individual enthusiast and a subscription can get over the business difficulties. The formation of a wealthy syndicate to produce a Little Eyolf would be like the promotion of a joint-stock company to sweep a crossing. As to the managers, there are various reasons. First, there is the inevitable snobbery of the fashionable actor-manager's position, which makes him ashamed to produce a play without spending more on the stage mounting alone than an Ibsen play will bring in. Second, our managers, having for the most part only a dealer's knowledge of art, cannot appreciate a new line of goods.

It is clear that the first objection will have to be got over somehow. If every manager considers it due to himself to produce nothing cheaper than The

Prisoner of Zenda, not to mention the splendors of the Lyceum, then goodbye to high dramatic art. The managers will, perhaps, retort that if high dramatic art means Ibsen, then they ask for nothing better than to get rid of it. I am too polite to reply, bluntly, that high dramatic art *does* mean Ibsen; that Ibsen's plays are at this moment the head of the dramatic body; and that though an actor-manager can, and often does, do without a head, dramatic art cannot. Already Ibsen is a European power: this new play has been awaited for two years, and is now being discussed and assimilated into the consciousness of the age with an interest which no political or pontifical utterance can command. Wagner himself did not attain such a position during his lifetime, because he was regarded merely as a musician—much the same thing as regarding Shakespear merely as a grammarian. Ibsen is translated promptly enough nowadays; yet no matter how rapidly the translation comes on the heel of the original, newspapers cannot wait for it: detailed accounts based on the Norwegian text, and even on stolen glimpses of the proof-sheets, fly through the world from column to column as if the play were an Anglo-American arbitration treaty. Sometimes a foolish actor informs the public that Ibsen is a noisome nuisance. The public instantly loses whatever respect it may previously have had, not only for that foolish actor's critical opinion, but for his good sense. But if Ibsen were to visit London, and express his opinion of our English theatre—as Wagner expressed his opinion of the Philharmonic Society, for example—our actors and managers would go down to posterity as exactly such persons as Ibsen described them. He is master of the situation, this man of genius; and when we complain that he does not share our trumpery little notions of life and society; that the themes that make us whine and wince have no terrors for him, but infinite interest; and that he is far above the barmaid's and shop superintendent's obligation to be agreeable to Tom, Dick, and Harry (which naturally convinces Tom, Dick, and Harry that he is no gentleman), we are not making out a case against him, but simply stating the grounds of his eminence. When any person objects to an Ibsen play because it does not hold the mirror up to his own mind, I can only remind him that a horse might make exactly the same objection. For my own part, I do not endorse all Ibsen's views: I even prefer my own plays to his in some respects; but I hope I know a great man from a little one as far as my comprehension of such things goes. Criticism may be pardoned for every mistake except that of not knowing a man of rank in literature when it meets one.

It is quite evident, then, that Ibsen can do without the managers. There remains the question: Can they do without Ibsen? And it is certainly astounding how long English stupidity can stave off foreign genius. It took Mozart's Don Giovanni, the greatest opera in the world, guaranteed by contemporary critics to be void of melody and overwhelmed with noisy orchestration, thirty years to reach London; and Wagner's Tristan und Isolde made its way last year into the repertory of our Royal Italian Opera thirty-eight years after its composition. But even at this moderate rate of progress Ibsen may be regarded as fairly due by this time. The play which stands out among his works as an ideal Lyceum piece, The Pretenders, was his tenth play; and yet it was written thirty-four years ago. Peer Gynt is over thirty. Why, even A Doll's House is eighteen years old. These figures are significant, because there is an enormous difference between the effects of Ibsen's ideas on his own contemporaries and on those who might be his sons and grandsons. Take my own case. I am a middle-aged, old-fashioned person. But I was only two years old when The Vikings at Helgeland was written. Now, considering that Little Eyolf, written only a couple of years ago, already attracts an audience sufficiently numerous to pay for its production with a handsome little profit, is it to be believed that playgoers from ten to twenty years younger than I am are not yet ready for at least the great spectacular dramas, charged with romantic grandeur and religious sentiment, which Ibsen wrote between 1855 (the date of Lady Inger) and 1866 (the date of Peer Gynt)?

But alas! our managers are older in their ideas than Ibsen's grandmother. It is Sir Henry Irving's business, as the official head of his profession—*tu t'as voulu, Georges Dandin*—to keep before us the noble side of that movement in dramatic art of which The Sign of the Cross and The Sorrows of Satan are the cheap and popular manifestations. But how can he bring his transfigurations and fantasies to bear on the realities of the modern school? They have no more to do with Ibsen than with Shakespear or any other author save only Henry Irving himself. His theatre is not really a theatre at all: an accident has just demonstrated that nobody will go there to see a play, especially a play by Shakespear! They go only to see Sir Henry Irving or Miss Ellen Terry. When he sprains his knee and Miss Terry flies south leaving only Shakespear and the Lyceum company—O that company!—in possession, the theatre becomes a desert: Shakespear will not pay for gas enough to see him by. Back comes Miss Terry; up goes Shakespear, Wills, Sardou, anybody; the public rallies; and by the time the sprain is cured, all will be well. No: the Lyceum is incorrigible: its debt to modern dramatic art is now too far in arrear ever to be paid. After all, why, after inventing a distinct *genre* of art, and an undeniably fascinating one at that, should Sir Henry Irving now place himself at the disposition of Ibsen, and become the Exponent of Another on the stage which he has hitherto trodden as the Self-Expounded? Why should Miss Terry, whom we have adored under all sorts of delicious, nonsensical disguises, loving especially those which made her most herself, turn mere actress, and be transformed by Norwegian enchantments into an embodiment of those inmost reproaches of conscience which we now go to the Lyceum to forget? It is all very well for Mr Walkley to point out that Sir Henry Irving, Miss Ellen Terry and Miss Geneviève Ward would exactly suit the parts of Borkman, Ella and Gunhild in the new play; but what Sir Henry Irving wants to know is not whether he would suit the part, since he has good reason to consider himself actor enough to be able to suit many parts not worth his playing, but whether the part would suit him, which is quite another affair. That is the true centripetal force that keeps Ibsen off the stage.

Unfortunately when we give up the Lyceum, we give up the only theatre of classic pretensions, officially recognized as such, in London. Mr Oscar Barrett, when the details of his next pantomime are disposed of, might conceivably try one of the big spectacular Ibsen plays at Drury Lane; but the experiment would be more of a new departure for him and for the theatre than for Sir Henry Irving and the

Lyceum. Mr Wyndham acts better than anybody else; he makes his company act better than any other company—so well that they occasionally act him off his own stage for months together; and he has not only the cleverness of the successful actor-manager, which is seldom more than the craft of an ordinary brain stimulated to the utmost by an overwhelming professional instinct, but the genuine ability of a good head, available for all purposes. But the pre-Ibsenite drama, played as he plays it, will last Mr Wyndham's time; and the public mind still copes with the Ibsenite view of life too slowly and clumsily for the Criterion. The most humorous passages of Ibsen's work—three-fourths of The Wild Duck, for instance—still seem to the public as puzzling, humiliating, and disconcerting as a joke always does to people who cannot see it. Comedy must be instantly and vividly intelligible or it is lost: it must therefore proceed on a thoroughly established intellectual understanding between the author and the audience —an understanding which does not yet exist between Ibsen and our playgoing public. But tragedy, like Handel's 'darkness that might be felt,' is none the worse theatrically for being intellectually obscure and oppressive. The pathos of Hedwig Ekdal's suicide or Little Eyolf's death is quite independent of any 'explanation' of the play; but most of the fun of Hjalmar Ekdal, Gregers Werle, Relling, Molvik and Gina, to an audience still dominated by conventional ideals, must be as imperceptible, except when it hurts, as it is to Hjalmar himself. This puts the comedy houses out of the question, and leaves us with only Mr Alexander and Mr Tree to look to. Both of them have been more enterprising than the public had any right to expect them to be. Mr Tree actually produced

An Enemy of The People; but I doubt if he has ever realized that his Stockman, though humorous and entertaining in its way, was, as a character creation, the polar opposite of Ibsen's Stockman. None the less, Mr Tree's notion of feeding the popular drama with ideas, and gradually educating the public, by classical *matinées,* financed by the spoils of the popular plays in the evening bill, seems to have been the right one. Mr Alexander's attempts to run Guy Domville and The Divided Way fairly proved that such plays should not be substituted for The Prisoner of Zenda and Shakespear; for I submit that we do not want to suppress either Rose-Hope or Shakespear, and that we can spare Sudermann, Ibsen, and Mr Henry James from the footlights better than we could spare the entertainments which please everybody. But why not have both? If Mr Alexander, instead of handing over Magda to fail in the evening bill at another theatre, had produced it and Sodom's Ende and so forth at a series of *matinées* of the Saturday Pop class, financing them from the exchequer of the kingdom of Ruritania, and aiming solely at the nourishment of the drama and the prevention of stagnation in public taste, he might have laid the foundations of a genuine classic theatre, in which the cultivated people who never dream of going to the theatre now would take their boxes and stalls by the season, and the hundred thousand people who go to the St James's twice a year would be represented financially by four thousand going once a week.

At all events, the time for forlorn hopes has gone by. I observe by the publisher's columns that Mr Charles Charrington, the only stage-manager of genius the new movement has produced, and quite its farthest-seeing pioneer, has taken to literature.

Miss Janet Achurch has relapsed into Shakespear, and is going to play Cleopatra at the forthcoming Calvertian revival in Manchester, after which I invite her to look Ibsen in the face again if she can. Miss Robins is devoting the spoils of Little Eyolf to Echegaray's Mariana, which must, for business reasons, be produced very soon. There are no signs of a fresh campaign on Miss Farr's part. The only other Ibsenite enthusiast is Mrs Patrick Campbell, who is busy studying Emma Hamilton, the heroine of 'the celestial bed,' which will, I trust, figure duly in the forthcoming Nelson drama at the Avenue.

Altogether, the prospects of a speedy performance of John Gabriel Borkman are not too promising.

Olivia

OLIVIA. *A play in four acts. By the late* W. G. Wills. *Founded on an episode in The Vicar of Wakefield. Revival. Lyceum Theatre,* 30 *January* 1897.

THE FREE PARDON. *An original domestic drama in four acts. By* F. C. Philips *and* Leonard Meyrick. *Olympic Theatre,* 28 *January* 1897.

THE PRODIGAL FATHER. *An extravagant farce in three acts. By* Glen Macdonough. *Strand Theatre,* 1 *February* 1897.

[6 *February* 1897]

THE world changes so rapidly nowadays that I hardly dare speak to my juniors of the things that won my affections when I was a sceptical, imperturbable, hard-headed young man of twenty-three or thereabouts. Now that I am an impressionable, excitable, sentimental—if I were a woman everybody would say hysterical—party on the wrong side of forty, I am conscious of being in danger of making myself ridiculous unless I confine my public expressions of enthusiasm to great works which are still before their time. That is why, when Olivia was revived at the Lyceum last Saturday, I blessed the modern custom of darkening the auditorium during the performance, since it enabled me to cry secretly. I wonder what our playgoing freshmen think of Olivia. I do not, of course, mean what they think of its opening by the descent of two persons to the footlights to carry on an expository conversation beginning, 'It is now twenty-five years since, etc.,' nor the antediluvian asides of the 'I do but dissemble' order in Thornhill's part, at which the gallery burst out laughing. These things are the mere fashions of the play, not the life of it. And it is concerning the life of it that I ask how the young people who see it today for the first time as I saw it nearly twenty years ago at the old Court Theatre feel about it.

I must reply that I have not the least idea. For what has this generation in common with me, or with Olivia, or with Goldsmith? The first book I ever possessed was a Bible bound in black leather with gilt metal rims and a clasp, slightly larger than my sisters' Bibles because I was a boy, and was therefore fitted with a bigger Bible, precisely as I was fitted with bigger boots. In spite of the trouble taken to impress me with the duty of reading it (with the natural result of filling me with a conviction that such an occupation must be almost as disagreeable as going to church), I acquired a considerable familiarity with it, and indeed once read the Old Testament and the four Gospels straight through, from a vainglorious desire to do what nobody else had done. A sense of the sanctity of clergymen, and the holiness of Sunday, Easter, and Christmas—sanctity and holiness meaning to me a sort of reasonlessly inhibitory condition in which it was wrong to do what I liked and especially meritorious to make myself miserable—was imbibed by me, not from what is called a strict bringing-up (which, as may be guessed by my readers, I happily escaped), but straight from the social atmosphere. And as that atmosphere was much like the atmosphere of Olivia, I breathe it as one to the manner born.

The question is, then, has that atmosphere changed so much that the play is only half comprehensible to the younger spectators? That there is a considerable change I cannot doubt; for I find that if I mention Adam and Eve, or Cain and Abel, to people of adequate modern equipment under thirty, they do not know what I am talking about. The Scriptural literary style which fascinated Wills as it fascinated Scott is to them quaint and artificial. Think of the difference between the present Bishop of London's History of the Popes and anything that the Vicar of Wakefield could have conceived or written! Think of the eldest daughters of our two-horse-carriage vicars going out, as female dons with Newnham degrees, to teach the granddaughters of ladies shamefacedly conscious of having been educated much as Mrs Primrose was; and ponder well whether such domestic incidents can give any clue to poor Olivia going off by coach to be 'companion' to 'some old tabby' in Yorkshire, and—most monstrous of all—previously presenting her brothers with her Prayer-book and her Pilgrim's Progress, and making them promise to pray for her every night at their mother's knee. Read The Woman Who Did, bearing in mind its large circulation and the total failure of the attempt to work up the slightest public feeling against it; and then consider how obsolescent must be that part of the interest of Olivia which depends on her sense of a frightful gulf between her moral position as a legally married woman and that in which she feels herself when she is told that the legal part of the ceremony was not valid. Take, too, that old notion of the home as a sort of prison in which the parents kept their children locked up under their authority, and from which, therefore, a daughter who wished to marry without their leave had to escape through the window as from the Bastille! Must not this conception, which alone can give any reality to the elopement of Olivia, be very historical and abstract to the class of people to whom a leading London theatre might be expected to appeal? It is easy for me, taught my letters as I was by a governess who might have been Mrs Primrose herself, to understand the Wakefield vicarage; but what I want to know is, can it carry any conviction to people who are a generation ahead of me in years, and a century in nursery civilization?

If I, drowning the Lyceum carpet with tears, may be taken as one extreme of the playgoing body, and a modern lady who, when I mentioned the play the other day, dismissed it with entire conviction as 'beneath contempt,' as the other, I am curious to see whether the majority of those between us are sufficiently near my end to produce a renewal of the old success. If not, the fault must lie with the rate of social progress; for Olivia is by a very great deal the best nineteenth-century play in the Lyceum repertory; and it has never been better acted. The Ellen Terry of 1897 is beyond all comparison a better Olivia than the Ellen Terry of 1885. The enchanting delicacy and charm with which she first stooped to folly at the old Court Theatre was obscured at the Lyceum, partly, perhaps, by a certain wrathful energy of developed physical power, pride, strength, and success in the actress, but certainly, as I shall presently shew, by the Lyceum conditions. Today the conditions are altered; the vanities have passed away with the water under the bridges; and the delicacy and charm have returned. We have the original Olivia again, in appearance not discoverably a week older, and much idealized and softened by the disuse of the mere brute force of tears and grief, which Miss Terry formerly employed so unscrupulously in the scene of the presents and of the elopement that she made the audience positively howl with anguish. She now plays these scenes with infinite mercy and art, the effect, though less hysterical, being deeper, whilst the balance of the second act is for the first time properly adjusted. The third act should be seen by all those who know Ellen Terry only by her efforts to extract a precarious sustenance for her reputation from Shakespear: it will teach them what an artist we have thrown to our national theatrical Minotaur. When I think of the originality and modernity of the talent she revealed twenty years ago, and of its remorseless waste ever since in 'supporting' an actor who prefers The Iron Chest to Ibsen, my regard for Sir Henry Irving cannot blind me to the fact that it would have been better for us twenty-five years ago to have tied him up in a sack with every existing copy of the works of Shakespear, and dropped him into the crater of the nearest volcano. It really serves him right that his Vicar is far surpassed by Mr Hermann Vezin's. I do not forget that there never was a more beautiful, a more dignified, a more polished, a more cultivated, a more perfectly mannered Vicar than Sir Henry Irving's. He annihilated Thornhill, and scored off everybody else, by sheer force of behaviour. When, on receiving that letter that looked like a notice of distraint for rent, he said, with memorable charm of diction, 'The law never enters the poor man's house save as an oppressor,' it was difficult to refrain from jumping on the stage and saying, 'Heaven bless you, sir, why dont you go to London and start a proprietary chapel? You would be an enormous success there.' There is nothing of this about the Vezin Vicar. To Farmer Flamborough he may be a fine gentleman; but to Thornhill he is a very simple one. To the innkeeper he is a prodigy of learning; but out in the world, looking for his daughter, his strength lies only in the pathos of his anxious perseverance. He scores off nobody except in his quaint theological disputation with the Presbyterian; but he makes Thornhill ashamed by not scoring off him. It is the appeal of his humanity and not the beauty of his style that carries him through; and his idolatry of his daughter is unselfish and fatherly, just as her affection for him is at last touched with a motherly instinct which his unworldly helplessness rouses in her. Handling the part skilfully and sincerely from this point of view, Mr Hermann Vezin brings the play back to life on the boards where Sir Henry Irving, by making it the occasion of an exhibition of extraordinary refinement of execution and personality, very nearly killed it as a drama. In the third act, by appealing to our admiration and artistic appreciation instead of to our belief and human sympathy, Sir Henry Irving made Olivia an orphan. In the famous passage where the Vicar tries to reprove his daughter, and is choked by the surge of his affection for her, he reproved Olivia like a saint and then embraced her like a lover. With Mr Vezin the reproof is a pitiful stammering failure: its break-down is neither an 'effect' nor a surprise: it is foreseen as inevitable from the first, and comes as Nature's ordained relief when the sympathy is strained to bursting point. Mr Vezin's entry in this scene is very pathetic. His face is the face of a man who has been disappointed to the very heart every day for months; and his hungry look round, half longing, half anticipating another disappointment, gives just the right cue for his attitude towards Thornhill, to whom he says, 'I forget you,' not in conscious dignity and judgment, but as if he meant, 'Have I, who forget *myself*, any heart to remember *you* whilst my daughter is missing?' When a good scene is taken in this way, the very accessories become eloquent, like the decent poverty of Mr Vezin's brown overcoat. Sir Henry Irving, not satisfied to be so plain a person as the Vicar of Wakefield, gave us something much finer and more distinguished, the beauty of which had to stand as a substitute for the pathos of those parts of the play which it destroyed. Mr Vezin takes his part for better for worse, and fits himself faithfully into it. The result can only be appreciated by those whose memory is good enough to compare the effect of the third act in 1885 and today. Also, to weigh Olivia with the Vicar right against Olivia with the Vicar wrong. I purposely force the comparison between the two treatments because it is a typical one. The history of the Lyceum, with its twenty years' steady cultivation of the actor as a personal force, and its utter neglect of the drama, is the history of the English stage during that period. Those twenty years have raised the social status of the theatrical profession, and culminated in the official recognition of our chief actor as the peer of the President of the Royal Academy, and the figure-heads of the other arts. And now I, being a dramatist and not an actor, want to know when the drama is to have its turn. I do not suggest that G.B.S. should condescend to become K.C.B.; but I do confidently affirm that if the actors think they can do without the drama, they are most prodigiously mistaken. The huge relief with which I found myself turning from Olivia as an effective exhibition of the extraordinary accomplishments of Sir Henry Irving to Olivia as a naturally acted story has opened my eyes to the extent to which I have been sinking the true dramatic critic in the connoisseur in virtuosity, and forgetting what they were doing at the Lyceum in the contemplation of how they were doing it. Henceforth I shall harden my heart as Wagner hardened his heart against Italian singing, and hold diction, deportment, sentiment, personality, and character as dust in the balance against the play and the credibility of its representation.

The rest of the company, not supporting, but supported *by* Mr Vezin and Miss Terry—thereby reverting to the true artistic relation between the principal parts and the minor ones—appear to great advantage. Only, one misses Mr Terriss as Thornhill, since Mr Cooper cannot remake himself so completely as to give much point to Olivia's line, once so effective, 'As you stand there flicking your boot, you look the very picture of vain indifference.' Mr Norman Forbes does not resume his old part of Moses, which is now played by Mr Martin Harvey. Mr Macklin as Burchell and Mr Sam Johnson as Farmer Flamborough, Master Stewart Dawson and Miss Valli Valli as Dick and Bill, and Miss Julia Arthur as Sophia, all fall admirably into their places. Miss Maud Milton is a notably good Mrs Primrose: her share in the scene of the pistols, which attains a most moving effect, could not have been better. Miss Edith Craig makes a resplendent Bohemian Girl of the gipsy, the effect being very nearly operatic. Miss Craig may have studied her part from the life; but if so, I should be glad to know where, so that I may instantly ride off to have my fortune told by the original.

The new play at the Olympic is one of those melodramas which produce no illusion, but which, played with well-known incidents and situations according to certain rules, are now watched by adept playgoers with the same interest that a football match creates. The game is rather exciting in the third act, and tolerable in the others. Its success, if it does succeed, will be due mainly to the acting of Miss Cicely Richards, who pulls it through with great ability, seconded effectively by Mr Cockburn. Miss Esme Beringer's impersonation of the heroine, though altogether artificial, is clever; and Mr Courtenay Thorpe manages to play with some distinction as the father. Mr Abingdon is a comic American interviewer; but the part is beneath criticism. Besides, Mr Abingdon has no command of the American language. The manageress, Mrs Charles Sugden, is competent and intelligent as the lady villain.

The Prodigal Father, at the Strand, is a lively piece, without any other particular merit. It restores Miss Florence Gerard to the London stage after a long absence. She was, I think, unwise to begin with such a piece as the curtain-raiser entitled A Merry Christmas, which depends on that fastidious elegance of style which is so soon unlearnt in America and the Colonies; but in The Prodigal Father she was more than equal to the occasion. In fact, the whole cast, which included Miss May Palfrey, Miss Lulu Valli, Messrs Harry Paulton, Charles Collette, and Charles Weir—a strong combination—is more or less under-parted.

Shakespear in Manchester

ANTONY AND CLEOPATRA. *Shakespearean revival by* Mr Louis Calvert *at the Queen's Theatre, Manchester.*

[20 *March* 1897]

SHAKESPEAR is so much the word-musician that mere practical intelligence, no matter how well prompted by dramatic instinct, cannot enable anybody to understand his works or arrive at a right execution of them without the guidance of a fine ear. At the great emotional climaxes we find passages which are Rossinian in their reliance on symmetry of melody and impressiveness of march to redeem poverty of meaning. In fact, we have got so far beyond Shakespear as a man of ideas that there is by this time hardly a famous passage in his works that is considered fine on any other ground than that it sounds beautifully, and awakens in us the emotion that originally expressed itself by its beauty. Strip it of that beauty of sound by prosaic paraphrase, and you have nothing left but a platitude that even an American professor of ethics would blush to offer to his disciples. Wreck that beauty by a harsh, jarring utterance, and you will make your audience wince as if you were singing Mozart out of tune. Ignore it by 'avoiding sing-song'—that is, ingeniously breaking the verse up so as to make it sound like prose, as the professional elocutionist prides himself on doing—and you are landed in a stilted, monstrous jargon that has not even the prosaic merit of being intelligible. Let me give one example: Cleopatra's outburst at the death of Antony:

> Oh withered is the garland of the war,
> The soldier's pole is fallen: young boys and girls
> Are level now with men: the odds is gone,
> And there is nothing left remarkable
> Beneath the visiting moon.

This is not good sense—not even good grammar. If you ask what does it all mean, the reply must be that it means just what its utterer feels. The chaos of its thought is a reflection of her mind, in which one can vaguely discern a wild illusion that all human distinction perishes with the gigantic distinction between Antony and the rest of the world. Now it is only in music, verbal or other, that the feeling which plunges thought into confusion can be artistically expressed. Any attempt to deliver such music prosaically would be as absurd as an attempt to speak an oratorio of Handel's, repetitions and all. The right way to declaim Shakespear is the sing-song way. Mere metric accuracy is nothing. There must be beauty of tone, expressive inflection, and infinite variety of *nuance* to sustain the fascination of the infinite monotony of the chanting.

Miss Janet Achurch, now playing Cleopatra in Manchester, has a magnificent voice, and is as full of ideas as to vocal effects as to everything else on the stage. The march of the verse and the strenuousness of the rhetoric stimulate her great artistic susceptibility powerfully: she is determined that Cleopatra shall have rings on her fingers and bells on her toes, and that she shall have music wherever she goes. Of the hardihood of ear with which she carries out her original and often audacious conceptions of Shakespearean music I am too utterly unnerved to give any adequate description. The lacerating discord of her wailings is in my tormented ears as I write, reconciling me to the grave. It is as if she had been excited by the Hallelujah Chorus to dance on the keyboard of a great organ with all the stops pulled out. I cannot—dare not—dwell on it. I admit that when she is using the rich middle of her voice in a quite normal and unstudied way, intent only on the feeling of the passage, the effect leaves nothing to be desired; but the moment she raises the pitch to carry out some deeply planned vocal masterstroke, or is driven by Shakespear himself to attempt a purely musical execution of a passage for which no other sort of execution is possible, then—well then, hold on tightly to the elbows of your stall, and bear it like a man. And when the feat is accompanied, as it sometimes is, by bold experiments in facial expression which all the passions of Cleopatra, complicated by seventy-times-sevenfold demoniacal possession, could but faintly account for, the eye has to share the anguish of the ear instead of consoling it with Miss Achurch's beauty. I have only seen the performance once; and I would not unsee it again if I could; but none the less I am a broken man after it. I may retain always an impression that I have actually looked on Cleopatra enthroned dead in her regal robes, with her hand on Antony's, and her awful eyes inhibiting the victorious Cæsar. I grant that this 'resolution' of the discord is grand and memorable; but oh! how infernal the discord was whilst it was still unresolved! That is the word that sums up the objection to Miss Achurch's Cleopatra in point of sound: it is discordant.

I need not say that at some striking points Miss Achurch's performance shews the same exceptional inventiveness and judgment in acting as her Ibsen achievements did, and that her energy is quite on the grand scale of the play. But even if we waive the whole musical question—and that means waiving the better half of Shakespear—she would still not be Cleopatra. Cleopatra says that the man who has seen her 'hath seen some majesty, and should know.' One conceives her as a trained professional queen, able to put on at will the deliberate artificial dignity which belongs to the technique of court life. She may keep it for state occasions, like the unaffected Catherine of Russia, or always retain it, like Louis XIV, in whom affectation was nature; but that she should have no command of it—that she should rely in modern republican fashion on her personal force, with a frank contempt for ceremony and artificiality, as Miss Achurch does, is to spurn her own part. And then, her beauty is not the beauty of Cleopatra. I do not mean merely that she is not 'with Phœbus' amorous pinches black,' or brown, bean-eyed, and pickaxe-faced. She is not even the English (or Anglo-Jewish) Cleopatra, the serpent of old Thames. She is of the broad-browed, column-necked, Germanic type—the Wagner heroine type—which in England, where it must be considered as the true racial heroic type, has given us two of our most remarkable histrionic geniuses in Miss Achurch herself and our dramatic singer, Miss Marie Brema, both distinguished by great voices, busy brains, commanding physical energy, and untameable impetuosity and originality. Now this type has its limitations, one of them being that it has not the genius of worthlessness, and so cannot present it on the stage otherwise than as comic depravity or masterful wickedness. Adversity makes it superhuman, not subhuman, as it makes Cleopatra. When Miss Achurch comes on one of the weak, treacherous, affected streaks in Cleopatra, she suddenly drops from an Egyptian warrior queen into a naughty English *petite bourgeoise*, who carries off a little greediness and a little voluptuousness by a very unheroic sort of prettiness. That is, she treats it as a stroke of comedy; and as she is not a comedian, the stroke of comedy becomes in her hands a bit of fun. When the bourgeoise turns into a wild cat, and literally snarls and growls menacingly at the bearer of the news of Antony's marriage with Octavia, she is at least more Cleopatra; but when she masters herself, as Miss Achurch does, not in gipsy fashion, but by a heroic-grandiose act of self-mastery, quite foreign to the nature of the 'triple turned wanton' (as Mr Calvert bowdlerizes it) of Shakespear, she is presently perplexed by fresh strokes of comedy—

> He 's very knowing.
> I do perceive 't: there 's nothing in her yet:
> The fellow has good judgment.

At which what can she do but relapse farcically into the bourgeoise again, since it is not on the heroic side of her to feel elegantly self-satisfied whilst she is saying mean and silly things, as the true Cleopatra does? Miss Achurch's finest feat in this scene was the terrible look she gave the messenger when he said, in dispraise of Octavia, 'And I do think she 's thirty' —Cleopatra being of course much more. Only, as

Miss Achurch had taken good care not to look more, the point was a little lost on Manchester. Later on she is again quite in her heroic element (and out of Cleopatra's) in making Antony fight by sea. Her 'I have sixty sails, Cæsar none better,' and her overbearing of the counsels of Enobarbus and Canidius to fight by land are effective, but effective in the way of a Boadicea, worth ten guzzling Antonys. There is no suggestion of the petulant folly of the spoiled beauty who has not imagination enough to know that she will be frightened when the fighting begins. Consequently when the audience, already puzzled as to how to take Cleopatra, learns that she has run away from the battle, and afterwards that she has sold Antony to Cæsar, it does not know what to think. The fact is, Miss Achurch steals Antony's thunder and Shakespear's thunder and Ibsen's thunder and her own thunder so that she may ride the whirlwind for the evening; and though this *Walkürenritt* is intense and imposing, in spite of the discords, the lapses into farce, and the failure in comedy and characterization—though once or twice a really memorable effect is reached—yet there is not a stroke of Cleopatra in it; and I submit that to bring an ardent Shakespearean like myself all the way to Manchester to see Antony and Cleopatra with Cleopatra left out, even with Brynhild-cum-Nora Helmer substituted, is very different from bringing down soft-hearted persons like Mr Clement Scott and Mr William Archer, who have allowed Miss Achurch to make Ibsen-and-Wagner pie of our poor Bard's historical masterpiece without a word of protest.

And yet all that I have said about Miss Achurch's Cleopatra cannot convey half the truth to those who have not seen Mr Louis Calvert's Antony. It is on record that Antony's cooks put a fresh boar on the spit every hour, so that he should never have to wait long for his dinner. Mr Calvert looks as if he not only had the boars put on the spit, but ate them. He is inexcusably fat: Mr Bourchier is a sylph by comparison. You will conclude, perhaps, that his fulness of habit makes him ridiculous as a lover. But not at all. It is only your rhetorical tragedian whose effectiveness depends on the oblatitude of his waistcoat. Mr Calvert is a comedian—brimming over with genuine humane comedy. His one really fine tragic effect is the burst of laughter at the irony of fate with which, as he lies dying, he learns that the news of Cleopatra's death, on the receipt of which he mortally wounded himself, is only one of her theatrical, sympathy-catching lies. As a lover, he leaves his Cleopatra far behind. His features are so pleasant, his manner so easy, his humor so genial and tolerant, and his portliness so frank and unashamed, that no good-natured woman could resist him; and so the topsiturvitude of the performance culminates in the plainest evidence that Antony is the seducer of Cleopatra instead of Cleopatra of Antony. Only at one moment was Antony's girth awkward. When Eros, who was a slim and rather bony young man, fell on his sword, the audience applauded sympathetically. But when Antony in turn set about the Happy Despatch, the consequences suggested to the imagination were so awful that shrieks of horror arose in the pit; and it was a relief when Antony was borne off by four stalwart soldiers, whose sinews cracked audibly as they heaved him up from the floor.

Here, then, we have Cleopatra tragic in her comedy, and Antony comedic in his tragedy. We have Cleopatra heroically incapable of flattery or flirtation, and

Antony with a wealth of blarney in every twinkle of his eye and every fold of his chin. We have, to boot, certain irrelevant but striking projections of Miss Achurch's genius, and a couple of very remarkable stage pictures invented by the late Charles Calvert. But in so far as we have Antony and Cleopatra, we have it partly through the genius of the author, who imposes his conception on us through the dialogue in spite of everything that can be done to contradict him, and partly through the efforts of the secondary performers.

Of these Mr George F. Black, who plays Octavius Cæsar, speaks blank verse rightly, if a little roughly, and can find his way to the feeling of the line by its cadence. Mr Mollison—who played Henry IV here to Mr Tree's Falstaff—is Enobarbus, and spouts the description of the barge with all the honors. The minor parts are handled with the spirit and intelligence that can always be had by a manager who really wants them. A few of the actors are certainly very bad; but they suffer rather from an insane excess of inspiration than from apathy. Charmian and Iras (Miss Ada Mellon and Miss Maria Fauvet) produce an effect out of all proportion to their scanty lines by the conviction and loyalty with which they support Miss Achurch; and I do not see why Cleopatra should ungratefully take Iras's miraculous death as a matter of course by omitting the lines beginning 'Have I the aspic in my lips,' nor why Charmian should be robbed of her fine reply to the Roman's 'Charmian, is this well done?' 'It is well done, and fitted for a princess descended of so many royal kings.' No doubt the Cleopatras of the palmy days objected to anyone but themselves dying effectively, and so such cuts became customary; but the objection does not apply to the scene as arranged in Manchester. Modern managers should never forget that if they take care of the minor actors the leading ones will take care of themselves.

May I venture to suggest to Dr Henry Watson that his incidental music, otherwise irreproachable, is in a few places much too heavily scored to be effectively spoken through? Even in the *entr'actes* the brass might be spared in view of the brevity of the intervals and the almost continuous strain for three hours on the ears of the audience. If the music be revived later as a concert suite, the wind can easily be restored.

Considering that the performance requires an efficient orchestra and chorus, plenty of supernumeraries, ten or eleven distinct scenes, and a cast of twenty-four persons, including two leading parts of the first magnitude; that the highest price charged for admission is three shillings; and that the run is limited to eight weeks, the production must be counted a triumph of management. There is not the slightest reason to suppose that any London manager could have made a revival of Antony and Cleopatra more interesting. Certainly none of them would have planned that unforgettable statue death for Cleopatra, for which, I suppose, all Miss Achurch's sins against Shakespear will be forgiven her. I begin to have hopes of a great metropolitan vogue for that lady now, since she has at last done something that is thoroughly wrong from beginning to end.

Meredith on Comedy

AN ESSAY ON COMEDY. *By* George Meredith. *Westminster: Archibald Constable and Co.* 1897

[27 *March* 1897]

TWENTY years ago Mr George Meredith delivered a lecture at the London Institution on Comedy and the Uses of the Comic Spirit. It was afterwards published in the New Quarterly Magazine, and now reappears as a brown buckram book, obtainable at the inconsiderable price (considering the quality) of five shillings. It is an excellent, even superfine, essay, by perhaps the highest living English authority on its subject. And Mr Meredith is quite conscious of his eminence. Speaking of the masters of the comedic spirit (if I call it, as he does, the Comic Spirit, this darkened generation will suppose me to refer to the animal spirits of tomfools and merryandrews), he says, 'Look there for your unchallengeable upper class.' He should know; for he certainly belongs to it. At the first page I recognize the true connoisseur, and know that I have only to turn it to come to the great name of Molière, who has hardly been mentioned in London during the last twenty years by the dramatic critics, except as representing a quaint habit of the Comédie Française. That being so, why republish an essay on comedy now? Who cares for comedy today? —who knows what it is?—how many readers of Mr Meredith's perfectly straightforward and accurate account of the wisest and most exquisite of the arts will see anything in the book but a brilliant sally of table talk about old plays: to be enjoyed, without practical application, as one of the rockets in the grand firework display of contemporary *belles-lettres*?

However, since the thing is done, and the book out, I take leave to say that Mr Meredith knows more about plays than about playgoers. 'The English public,' he says, 'have the basis of the comic in them: an esteem for common sense.' This flattering illusion does not dupe Mr Meredith completely; for I notice that he adds 'taking them generally.' But if it were to be my last word on earth I must tell Mr Meredith to his face that whether you take them generally or particularly—whether in the lump, or sectionally as playgoers, churchgoers, voters, and what not—they are everywhere united and made strong by the bond of their common nonsense, their invincible determination to tell and be told lies about everything, and their power of dealing acquisitively and successfully with facts whilst keeping them, like disaffected slaves, rigidly in their proper place: that is, outside the moral consciousness. The Englishman is the most successful man in the world simply because he values success—meaning money and social precedence—more than anything else, especially more than fine art, his attitude towards which, culture-affectation apart, is one of half diffident, half contemptuous curiosity, and of course more than clear-headedness, spiritual insight, truth, justice, and so forth. It is precisely this unscrupulousness and singleness of purpose that constitutes the Englishman's pre-eminent 'common sense'; and this sort of common sense, I submit to Mr Meredith, is not only not 'the basis of the comic,' but actually makes comedy impossible, because it would not seem like common sense at all if it were not self-satisfiedly unconscious of its moral and intellectual bluntness, whereas the function of comedy is to dispel such unconsciousness by turning the searchlight of the keenest moral and intellectual analysis right on to it. Now the Frenchman, the Irishman, the American, the ancient Greek, is disabled from this true British common sense by intellectual virtuosity, leading to a love of accurate and complete consciousness of things—of intellectual mastery of them. This produces a positive enjoyment of disillusion (the most dreaded and hated of calamities in England), and consequently a love of comedy (the fine art of disillusion) deep enough to make huge sacrifices of dearly idealized institutions to it. Thus, in France, Molière was allowed to destroy the Marquises. In England he could not have shaken even such titles as the accidental sheriff's knighthood of the late Sir Augustus Harris. And yet the Englishman thinks himself much more independent, level-headed, and genuinely republican than the Frenchman—not without good superficial reasons; for nations with the genius of comedy often carry all the snobbish ambitions and idealist enthusiasms of the Englishman to an extreme which the Englishman himself laughs at. But they sacrifice them to comedy, to which the Englishman sacrifices nothing; so that, in the upshot, aristocracies, thrones, and churches go by the board at the attack of comedy among our devotedly conventional, loyal, and fanatical next-door neighbors; whilst we, having absolutely no disinterested regard for such institutions, draw a few of their sharpest teeth, and then maintain them determinedly as part of the machinery of worldly success.

The Englishman prides himself on this anti-comedic common sense of his as at least eminently practical. As a matter of fact, it is just as often as not most pigheadedly unpractical. For example, electric telegraphy, telephony, and traction are invented, and establish themselves as necessities of civilized life. The unpractical foreigner recognizes the fact, and takes the obvious step of putting up poles in his streets to carry wires. This expedient never occurs to the Briton. He wastes leagues of wire and does unheard-of damage to property by tying his wires and posts to such chimney stacks as he can beguile householders into letting him have access to. Finally, when it comes to electric traction, and the housetops are out of the question, he suddenly comes out in the novel character of an amateur in urban picturesqueness, and declares that the necessary cable apparatus would spoil the appearance of our streets. The streets of Nuremberg, the heights of Fiesole, may not be perceptibly the worse for these contrivances; but the beauty of Tottenham Court Road is too sacred to be so profaned: to its loveliness the strained bus-horse and his offal are the only accessories endurable by the beauty-loving Cockney eye. This is your common-sense Englishman. His helplessness in the face of electricity is typical of his helplessness in the face of everything else that lies outside the set of habits he calls his opinions and capacities. In the theatre he is the same. It is not common sense to laugh at your own prejudices: it is common sense to feel insulted when anyone else laughs at them. Besides, the Englishman is a serious person: that is, he is firmly persuaded that his prejudices and stupidities are the vital material of civilization, and that it is only by holding on to their moral prestige with the stiffest resolution that the world is saved from flying back into savagery and gorilladom, which he always conceives, in spite of natural history, as a condition of lawlessness and promiscuity, instead of, as it actually is, the extremity, long since grown unbearable, of his own notions of law and order, morality, and conventional respectability. Thus he is a moralist, an ascetic, a Christian, a truth-teller and a plain dealer by profession and by conviction; and it is wholly against this conviction that, judged by his own canons, he finds himself in practice a great rogue, a liar, an unconscionable pirate, a grinder of the face of the poor, and a libertine. Mr Meredith points out daintily that the cure for this self-treasonable confusion and darkness is Comedy, whose spirit overhead will 'look humanely malign and cast an oblique light on them, followed by volleys of silvery laughter.' Yes, Mr Meredith; but suppose the patients have 'common sense' enough not to want to be cured! Suppose they realize the immense commercial advantage of keeping their ideal life and their practical business life in two separate conscience-tight compartments, which nothing but 'the Comic Spirit' can knock into one! Suppose, therefore, they dread the Comic Spirit more than anything else in the world, shrinking from its 'illumination,' and considering its 'silvery laughter' in execrable taste! Surely in doing so they are only carrying out the common-sense view, in which an encouragement and enjoyment of comedy must appear as silly and suicidal and 'unEnglish' as the conduct of the man who sets fire to his own house for the sake of seeing the flying sparks, the red glow in the sky, the fantastic shadows on the walls, the excitement of the crowd, the gleaming charge of the engines, and the dismay of the neighbors. No doubt the day will come when we shall deliberately burn a London street every day to keep our city up to date in health and handsomeness, with no more misgiving as to our common sense than we now have when sending our clothes to the laundry every week. When that day comes, perhaps comedy will be popular too; for, after all, the function of comedy, as Mr Meredith after twenty years' further consideration is perhaps by this time ripe to admit, is nothing less than the destruction of old-established morals. Unfortunately, today such iconoclasm can be tolerated by our playgoing citizens only as a counsel of despair and pessimism. They can find a dreadful joy in it when it is done seriously, or even grimly and terribly as they understand Ibsen to be doing it; but that it should be done with levity, with silvery laughter like the crackling of thorns under a pot, is too scandalously wicked, too cynical, too heartlessly shocking to be borne. Consequently our plays must either be exploitations of old-established morals or tragic challengings of the order of Nature. Reductions to absurdity, however logical; banterings, however kindly; irony, however delicate; merriment, however silvery, are out of the question in matters of morality, except among men with a natural appetite for comedy which must be satisfied at all costs and hazards: that is to say, *not* among the English playgoing public, which positively dislikes comedy.

No doubt it is patriotically indulgent of Mr Meredith to say that 'Our English school has not clearly imagined society,' and that 'of the mind hovering above congregated men and women it has imagined nothing.' But is he quite sure that the audiences of our English school do not know too much about society and 'congregated men and women' to encourage any exposures from 'the vigilant Comic,' with its 'thoughtful laughter,' its 'oblique illumination,' and the rest of it? May it not occur to the purchasers of half-guinea stalls that it is bad enough to have to put up with the pryings of Factory Inspectors,

Public Analysts, County Council Inspectors, Chartered Accountants and the like, without admitting this Comic Spirit to look into still more delicate matters? Is it clear that the Comic Spirit would break into silvery laughter if it saw all that the nineteenth century has to shew it beneath the veneer? There is Ibsen, for instance: he is not lacking, one judges, in the Comic Spirit; yet his laughter does not sound very silvery, does it? No: if this were an age for comedies, Mr Meredith would have been asked for one before this. How would a comedy from him be relished, I wonder, by the people who wanted to have the revisers of the Authorized Version of the Bible prosecuted for blasphemy because they corrected as many of its mistranslations as they dared, and who reviled Froude for not suppressing Carlyle's diary and writing a fictitious biography of him, instead of letting out the truth? Comedy, indeed! I drop the subject with a hollow laugh.

The recasting of A Pierrot's Life at the *matinées* at the Prince of Wales Theatre greatly increases and solidifies the attraction of the piece. Felicia Mallet now plays Pierrot; but we can still hang on the upturned nose of the irresistible Litini, who reappears as Fifine. Litini was certainly a charming Pierrot; but the delicate, subtle charm was an intensely feminine one, and only incorporated itself dreamily with the drama in the tender shyness of the first act and the pathos of the last. Litini as a vulgar drunkard and gambler was as fantastically impossible as an angel at a horse-race. Felicia Mallet is much more credible, much more realistic, and therefore much more intelligible—also much less slim, and not quite so youthful. Litini was like a dissolute La Sylphide: Miss

Mallet is frankly and heartily like a scion of the very smallest bourgeoisie sowing his wild oats. She is a good observer, a smart executant, and a vigorous and sympathetic actress, apparently quite indifferent to romantic charm, and intent only on the dramatic interest, realistic illusion, and comic force of her work. And she avoids the conventional gesture-code of academic Italian pantomime, depending on popularly graphic methods throughout. The result is that the piece is now much fuller of incident, much more exciting in the second act (hitherto the weak point) and much more vivid than before. Other changes have helped to bring this about. Jacquinet, no longer ridiculously condemned to clothe a Parisian three-card-trick man in the attire of the fashionable lover in L'Enfant Prodigue, appears in his proper guise with such success that it is difficult to believe that he is the same person. Miss Ellas Dee is a much prettier Louisette, as prettiness is reckoned in London, than her predecessor, whom she also surpasses in grace and variety of expression. Litini is a brilliant Filine—the brevity of the part is regretted for the first time; and Rossi, though he is no better than before, probably would be if he had left any room for improvement. The band is excellent, and the music clever and effective, though it has none of those topical allusions which are so popular here—strangely popular, considering that the public invariably misses nine out of ten of them (who, for instance, has noticed that *entr'acte* in Saucy Sally in which the bassoon plays all manner of rollicking nautical airs as florid counterpoints to Tom Bowling?). Altogether the 'play without words' is now at its best. One must be a critic to understand the blessedness of going to the theatre without having to listen to slipshod dialogue and affectedly fashionable or nasally stagey voices. Merely to see plastic figures and expressive looks and gestures is a delicious novelty to me; but I believe some of the public rather resent having to pay full price for a play without words, exactly as they resent having to pay for a doctor's advice without getting a bottle of nasty medicine along with it. Some of these unhappy persons may be observed waiting all through the performance for the speaking to begin, and retiring at last with loud expressions of disappointment at having been sold by the management. For my part, I delight in these wordless plays, though I am conscious of the difficulty of making any but the most threadbare themes intelligible to the public without words. In my youth the difficulty could have been got over by taking some story that everyone knew; but nowadays nobody knows any stories. If you put the Sleeping Beauty on the stage in dumb show, the only thing you could depend on the whole house knowing about her would be her private name and address, her salary, her engagements for next year, her favorite pastimes, and the name of her pet dog.

Mr Pinero on Turning Forty

THE PHYSICIAN. *A new play of modern life in four acts. By* Henry Arthur Jones. *Criterion Theatre,* 25 *March* 1897.

THE PRINCESS AND THE BUTTERFLY, OF THE FANTASTICS. *An original comedy in five acts. By* Arthur W. Pinero. *St James's Theatre,* 29 *March* 1897.

[3 *April* 1897]

WHEN I was a fastidious youth, my elders, ever eager to confer bad advice on me and to word it with disgusting homeliness, used to tell me never to throw away dirty water until I got in clean. To which I would reply that as I had only one bucket, the thing was impossible. So until I grew middle-aged and sordid, I acted on the philosophy of Bunyan's couplet:

> A man there was, tho' some did count him mad,
> The more he cast away, the more he had.

Indeed, in the matter of ideals, faiths, convictions and the like, I was of opinion that Nature abhorred a vacuum, and that you might empty your bucket boldly with the fullest assurance that you would find it fuller than ever before you had time to set it down again. But herein I youthfully deceived myself. I grew up to find the genteel world full of persons with empty buckets. Now The Physician is a man with an empty bucket. 'By God!' he says (he doesnt believe in God), 'I dont believe theres in any London slum, or jail, or workhouse, a poor wretch with such a horrible despair in his heart as I have today. I tell you Ive caught the disease of our time, of our society, of our civilization—middle age, disillusionment. My youth's gone. My beliefs are gone. I enjoy nothing. I believe in nothing. Belief! Thats the placebo I want. That would cure me. My work means nothing to me. Success means nothing to me. I cure people with a grin and a sneer. I keep on asking myself, "To what end? To what end?"'

O dear! Have we not had enough of this hypochondriasis from our immortal bard in verse which—we have it on his own authority—'not marble, nor the gilded monuments of princes, shall outlive'? It is curable by Mr Meredith's prescription—the tonic of comedy; and when I see a comedian of Mr Wyndham's skill and a dramatist of Mr Jones's mother-wit entering into a physicianly conspiracy to trade in the disease it is their business to treat, I abandon all remorse, flatly refuse to see any 'sympathetic' drama in a mere shaking of the head at life, and vow that at least one of Dr Carey's audience shall tell him that there is nothing in the world more pitiably absurd than the man who goes about telling his friends that life is not worth living, when they know perfectly well that if he meant it he could stop living much more easily than go on eating. Even the incorrigible Hamlet admitted this, and made his excuse for not resorting to the bare bodkin; but Dr Carey, who says 'I never saw a man's soul,' has not Hamlet's excuse. His superstitions are much cruder: they do not rise above those of an African witch-finder or Sioux medicine-man. He pretends to 'cure' diseases—Mother Carey is much like Mother Seigel in this respect—and holds up a test-tube, whispering, 'I fancy I'm on the track of the cancer microbe: I'm not sure I havent got my gentleman here.' At which abject depth of nineteenth-century magicianism he makes us esteem Dr Diafoirus and the Apothecary in Romeo and Juliet as, in comparison, dazzling lights of science.

And now, as if it were not bad enough to have Mr Jones in this state of mind, we have Mr Pinero, who was born, as I learn from a recent biographic work of reference, in 1855, quite unable to get away from the same tragic preoccupation with the horrors of middle age. He has launched at us a play in five acts—two and a half of them hideously superfluous—all about being over forty. The heroine is forty, and can talk about nothing else. The hero is over forty, and is blind to every other fact in the universe. Having this topic of conversation in common, they get engaged in order that they may save one another from being seduced by the attraction of youth into foolish marriages. They then fall in love, she with a fiery youth of twenty-eight, he with a meteoric girl of eighteen. Up to the last moment I confess I had sufficient confidence in Mr Pinero's saving sense of humor to believe that he would give the verdict against himself, and admit that the meteoric girl was too young for the hero (twenty-seven years' discrepancy) and the heroine too old for the fiery youth (thirteen years' discrepancy). But no: he gravely decided that the heart that loves never ages; and now perhaps he will write us another drama, limited strictly to three acts, with, as heroine, the meteoric girl at forty with her husband at sixty-seven, and, as hero, the fiery youth at forty-nine with his wife at sixty-two.

Mr Henry Arthur Jones is reconciled to his own fate, though he cannot bear to see it overtake a woman. Hear Lady Val in his play! 'I smell autumn; I scent it from afar. I ask myself how many years shall I have a man for my devoted slave. . . . Oh, my God, Lewin [she is an Atheist], it never can be worth while for a woman to live one moment after she has ceased to be loved.' This, I admit, is as bad as Mr Pinero: the speech is actually paraphrased by Mrs St Roche in the St James's play. But mark the next sentence: 'And you men have the laugh of us. Age doesnt wither you or stale your insolent, victorious, self-satisfied, smirking, commonplace durability! Oh, you brutes, I hate you all, because youre warranted to wash and wear for fifty years.' Observe, *fifty* years, not forty. I turn again to my book of reference, and find, as I expected, that Mr Jones was born in 1851. I discover also that I myself was born in 1856. And this is '97. Well, my own opinion is that sixty is the prime of life for a man. Cheer up, Mr Pinero: courage,

Henry Arthur! 'What though the grey do something mingle with our younger brown' (excuse my quoting Shakespear), the world is as young as ever. Go look at the people in Oxford Street: they are always the same age.

As regards any conscious philosophy of life, I am bound to say that there is not so much (if any) difference between Mr Jones and Mr Pinero as the very wide differences between them in other respects would lead us to suppose. The moment their dramatic inventiveness flags, and they reach the sentimentally reflective interval between genuine creation and the breaking off work until next day, they fall back on the two great Shakespearean grievances—namely, that we cannot live for ever and that life is not worth living. And then they strike up the old tunes—'Out, out, brief candle!' 'Vanitas vanitatum,' 'To what end?' and so on. But in their fertile, live moments they are as unlike as two men can be in the same profession. At such time Mr Pinero has no views at all. Our novelists, especially those of the Thackeray–Trollope period, have created a fictitious world for him; and it is about this world that he makes up stage stories for us. If he observes life, he does so as a gentleman observes the picturesqueness of a gipsy. He presents his figures coolly, clearly, and just as the originals like to conceive themselves—for instance, his ladies and gentlemen are not real ladies and gentlemen, but ladies and gentlemen as they themselves (mostly modelling themselves on fiction) aim at being; and so Bayswater and Kensington have a sense of being understood by Mr Pinero. Mr Jones, on the other hand, works passionately from the real. By throwing himself sympathetically into his figures he gives them the stir of life; but he also often raises their energy to the intensity of his own, and confuses their feelings with the revolt of his own against them. Above all, by forcing to the utmost their aspect as they really are as against their pose, he makes their originals protest violently that he cannot draw them —a protest formerly made, on exactly the same grounds, against Dickens. For example, Lady Val in The Physician is a study of a sort of clever fashionable woman now current; but it is safe to say that no clever fashionable woman, nor any admirer of clever fashionable women, will ever admit the truth or good taste of the likeness. And yet she is very carefully studied from life, and only departs from it flatteringly in respect of a certain energy of vision and intensity of conscience that belong to Mr Jones and not in the least to herself.

Compare with Lady Val the Princess Pannonia in Mr Pinero's play. You will be struck instantly with the comparative gentlemanliness of Mr Pinero. He seems to say, 'Dear lady, do not be alarmed: I will shew just enough of your weaknesses to make you interesting; but otherwise I shall take you at your own valuation and make the most of you. I shall not forget that you are a Princess from the land of novels. My Friend Jones, who would have made an excellent Dissenting clergyman, has a vulgar habit of bringing persons indiscriminately to the bar of his convictions as to what is needful for the life and welfare of the real world. You need apprehend no such liberties from me. I have no convictions, no views, no general ideas of any kind: I am simply a dramatic artist, only too glad to accept a point of view from which you are delightful. At the same time, I am not insensible to the great and tragic issues that meet us wherever we turn. For instance, it is hardly possible to reach the age of forty without etc. etc. etc.' And accordingly you have a cool, tasteful, polished fancy picture which reflects the self-consciousness of Princesses and the illusions of their imitators much more accurately than if Mr Jones had painted it.

The two plays present an extraordinary contrast in point of dramatic craft. It is no exaggeration to say that within two minutes from the rising of the curtain Mr Jones has go tighter hold of his audience and further on with his play than Mr Pinero within two hours. During those two hours, The Princess marks time complacently on the interest, the pathos, the suggestiveness, the awful significance of turning forty. The Princess has done it; Sir George Lamorant has done it; Mrs St Roche has done it; so has her husband. Lady Chichele, Lady Ringstead, and Mrs Sabiston have all done it. And they have all to meditate on it like Hamlet meditating on suicide; only, since soliloquies are out of fashion, nearly twenty persons have to be introduced to listen to them. The resultant exhibition of High Life Above Stairs is no doubt delightful to the people who had rather read the fashionable intelligence than my articles. To me not even the delight of playing Peeping Tom whilst Princess Pannonia was getting out of bed and flattering me with a vain hope that the next item would be her bath could reconcile me to two hours of it. If the women had worn some tolerable cap-and-apron uniform I could have borne it better; but those dreadful dresses, mostly out of character and out of complexion—I counted nine failures to four successes—upset my temper, which was not restored by a witless caricature of Mr Max Beerbohm (would he had written it himself!), or by the spectacle of gilded youth playing with toys whilst Sir George Lamorant put on a fool's cap and warned them that they would all be forty-five presently, or even by the final tableau, unspeakably sad to the British mind, of the host and hostess retiring for the night to separate apartments instead of tucking themselves respectably and domestically into the same feather bed. Yet who shall say that there is no comedy in the spectacle of Mr Pinero moralizing, and the public taking his reflections seriously? He is much more depressing when he makes a gentleman throw a glass of water at another gentleman in a drawing-room, thereby binding the other gentleman in honor to attack his assailant in the street with a walking stick, whereupon the twain go to France to fight a duel for all the world as if they were at the Surrey Theatre. However, when this is over the worst is over. Mr Pinero gets to business at about ten o'clock, and the play begins in the middle of the third act—a good, old-fashioned, well-seasoned bit of sentimental drawing room fiction, daintily put together, and brightening at the end into a really light-hearted and amusing act of artificial comedy. So, though it is true that the man who goes to the St James's Theatre now at 7.45 will wish he had never been born, none the less will the man who goes at 9.30 spend a very pleasant evening.

The two authors have not been equally fortunate in respect of casting. Half Mr Jones's play—the women's half—is obliterated in performance. His Edana is a sterling, convinced girl-enthusiast. 'Her face,' says the Doctor, 'glowed like a live coal.' This sort of characterization cannot be effected on the stage by dialogue. Enthusiasts are magnetic, not by what they say, or even what they do, but by how they say and do it. Mr Jones could write 'yes' and 'no'; but it rested with the actress whether the affirmation and denial should be that of an enthusiast or not. Edana at the Criterion is played by Miss Mary Moore. Now Miss Moore is a dainty light comedian; and her intelligence, and a certain power of expressing grief rather touchingly and prettily, enable her to take painful parts on occasion without making herself ridiculous. But they do not enable her to play an enthusiast. Consequently her Edana is a simple substitution of what she can do for what she is required to do. The play is not only weakened by this—all plays get weakened somewhere when they are performed—it is dangerously confused, because Edana, instead of being a stronger character than Lady Val, and therefore conceivably able to draw the physician away from her, is just the sort of person who would stand no chance against her with such a man. To make matters worse, Lady Val is played by Miss Marion Terry, who is in every particular, from her heels to her hairpins, exactly what Lady Val could not be, her qualities being even more fatal to the part than her faults. A more hopeless pair of misfits has never befallen an author. On the other hand, Mr Jones has been exceptionally fortunate in his men. Mr Alfred Bishop's parson and Mr J. G. Taylor's Stephen Gurdon are perfect. Mr. Thalberg does what is wanted to set the piece going on the rising of the curtain with marked ability. The easy parts—which include some racy village studies—are well played. Mr Leslie Kenyon, as Brooker, has the tact that is all the part requires; and the Physician is played with the greatest ease by Mr Wyndham himself, who will no doubt draw all Harley Street to learn what a consulting room manner can be in the hands of an artist. The performance as a whole is exceptionally fine, the size of the theatre admitting of a delicacy of handling without which Mr Jones's work loses half its sincerity.

In The Princess matters are better balanced. There is a fearful waste of power: out of twenty-nine performers, of whom half are accustomed to play important parts in London, hardly six have anything to do that could not be sufficiently well done by nobodies. Mr Pinero seems to affirm his supremacy by being extravagant in his demands for the sake of extravagance; and Mr Alexander plays up to him with an equally high hand by being no less extravagant in his compliances. So the piece is at all events not underplayed; and it has crowned the reputation of Miss Fay Davis, whose success, the most sensational achieved at the St James's Theatre since that of Mrs Patrick Campbell as Paula Tanqueray, is a success of cultivated skill and self-mastery on the artist's part, and not one of the mere accidents of the stage. Miss Neilson, ever fair and fortunate, puts a pleasant face on a long and uninteresting part, all about the horrors of having reached forty without losing 'the aroma of a stale girlhood.' The Princess is ladylike and highly literary. When, in the familiar dilemma of the woman of forty with an inexperienced lover, she is forced to prevent his retiring in abashed despair by explaining to him that her terrifying fluster over his more personal advances only means that she likes them and wants some more, she choicely words it, 'I would not have it otherwise.' And his ardor is volcanic enough to survive even that. The lover's part falls to Mr H. B. Irving, who is gaining steadily in distinction of style and strength of feeling. Mr Alexander has little to do beyond what he has done often before—make himself interesting enough to conceal the emptiness of his part. He laments his forty-five years as mercifully as such a thing may be done; and he secures toleration for the silly episodes of the fool's cap and the quarrel with Maxime. Mr Esmond makes the most of a comic scrap of character; and Miss Rose Leclercq is duly exploited in the conventional manner as Lady Ringstead. Miss Patty Bell's Lady Chichele is not bad: the rest I must pass over from sheer exhaustion.

Madame Sans-Gêne

MADAME SANS-GÊNE. *Comedy in a prologue and* 3 *acts. By* MM. Sardou *and* Moreau. *Translated by* J. Comyns Carr. *Lyceum Theatre,* 10 *April* 1897.

[17 *April* 1897]

It is rather a nice point whether Miss Ellen Terry should be forgiven for sailing the Lyceum ship into the shallows of Sardoodledom for the sake of Madame Sans-Gêne. But hardly any controversy has arisen on this point: everyone seems content to discuss how Miss Ellen Terry can bring herself to impersonate so vulgar a character. And the verdict is that she has surmounted the difficulty wonderfully. In that verdict I can take no part, because I do not admit the existence of the difficulty. Madame Sans-Gêne is *not* a vulgar person; and Miss Ellen Terry knows it. No doubt most people will not agree with Miss Ellen Terry. But if most people could see everything that Miss Ellen Terry sees, they would all be Ellen Terries instead of what they are.

I know that it will not be conceded to me without a struggle that a washerwoman who spits on her iron and tells her employees to 'stir their stumps' is not vulgar. Let me, therefore, ask those persons of unquestioned fashion who have taken to bicycling, what they do when they find their pneumatic tyres collapsing ten miles from anywhere, and wish to ascertain, before undertaking the heavy labor of looking for a puncture, whether the valve is not leaking. The workman's way of doing this is no trade secret. He puts a film of moisture on the end of the valve, and watches whether that film is converted into a bubble by an escape of air. And he gets the moisture exactly where Madame Sans-Gêne gets the moisture for her flat iron. It may be that the washerwoman of the future, as soon as a trebling of her wages and a halving of her hours of labor enable her to indulge in a little fastidiousness, will hang a scent bottle with a spray diffuser at her chatelaine, though even then I doubt if the fashionable cyclist will prefer the resources of civilization to those of nature when nobody is looking. But by that time the washerwoman will no doubt smoke cigarets, as to which habit of tobacco smoking, in what form soever it be practised, I will say nothing more than that the people who indulge in it, whether male or female, have clearly no right to complain of the manners of people who spit on flat irons. Indeed I will go further, and declare that a civilization which enjoins the deliberate stiffening of its shirts with white mud and the hotpressing thereof in order that men may look in the evening like silhouettes cut out of mourning paper, has more to learn than to teach in the way of good manners (that is, good sense) from Madame Sans-Gêne.

As to 'stir your stumps,' that is precisely what an ideal duchess would say if she had to bustle a laundry, and had tact and geniality enough to make a success of it. It is true that she might as easily say, 'More diligence, ladies, please'; but she would not say it, because ideal duchesses do not deliberately say stupid and underbred things. Indeed our military officers, whose authority in matters of social propriety nobody will dispute, are apt to push the Sans-Gêne style to extremes in smartening the movements of Volunteers and others in reviews and inspections, to say nothing of the emergencies of actual warfare.

Concerning Madame Sans-Gêne's use of slang, which she carries to the extent of remarking, when there is a question of her husband being compelled by the Emperor to divorce her and marry a more aristocratic but slenderer woman, 'You like em crumby, dont you?', I can only say that her practice is in accord with that of the finest masters of language. I have known and conversed with men whose command of English, and sense of beauty and fitness in the use of it, had made them famous. They all revelled in any sort of language that was genuinely vernacular, racy, and graphic. They were just as capable as Madame Sans-Gêne of calling a nose a snout or a certain sort of figure crumby; and between such literary solemnities as 'magistrate' or 'policeman' and the slang 'beak' or the good English 'copper' they would not have hesitated for a moment on familiar occasions. And they would have been outraged in the last degree had they been represented as talking of 'bereavements,' 'melancholy occasions,' or any of the scores of pretentious insincerities, affectations and literary flourishes of tombstone, rostrum, shop-catalogue, foreign-policy-leading-article English which Miss Terry could pass off without a word of remonstrance as high-class conversation.

It is further objected that Miss Terry drops into the dialect of Whitechapel, or rather a sort of generalized country dialect with some Whitechapel tricks picked up and grafted on to it. Here I am coming on dangerous ground; for it is plain that criticism must sooner or later speak out fiercely about that hideous vulgarity of stage speech from which the Lyceum has long been almost our only refuge. It seems to me that actors and actresses never dream nowadays of learning to speak. What they do is this. Since in their raw native state they are usually quite out of the question as plausible representatives of those galaxies of rank and fashion, the *dramatis personae* of our smart plays, and having no idea that the simple remedy is to learn the alphabet over again and learn it correctly, they take great pains to parrot a detestable convention of 'smart' talking, supposed to represent refined speech by themselves and that huge majority of their audiences which knows no better, but actually a caricature of the affectations of the parvenu and the 'outsider.' Hence the common complaint among the better sort of gentlefolk that an evening at the theatre leaves an uncomfortable, almost outraged sensation of having been entrapped, like the Vicar of Wakefield, to a dinner-party at which the lords and ladies are really footmen and lady's maids 'shewing off.' The vulgarity of this convention is innocent compared to its unbearable monotony, fatal to that individuality without which no actor can interest an audience. All countries and districts send us parliamentary speakers who have cultivated the qualities of their native dialect and corrected its faults whilst aiming at something like a standard purity and clearness of speech. Take Mr Gladstone for instance. For his purposes as an orator he has studied his speech as carefully and with as great powers of application as any actor. But he has never lost, and never wanted to lose, certain features of his speech which stamp him as a North-countryman. When Mr T. P. O'Connor delivers a speech, he does not inflict on us the vulgarities of Beggar's Bush; but he preserves for us all the music of Galway, though he does not say 'Yis' for 'Yes' like a Galway peasant any more than he says 'Now' (Nah-oo) for 'No' like a would-be smart London actor. It is so with all good speakers off the stage. Among good speakers the Irishman speaks like an Irishman, the Scotsman like a Scotsman, the American like an American, and so on. It should be so on the stage also, both in classical plays and representations of modern society, though of course it is the actor's business to assume dialects and drop or change them at will in character parts, and to be something of a virtuoso in speech in all parts. A very moderate degree of accomplishment in this direction would make an end of stage smart speech, which, like the got-up Oxford mince and drawl of a foolish curate, is the mark of a snob. Indeed, the brutal truth is that the English theatre is at present suffering severely from an epidemic of second-rate snobbery. From that, at least, we are spared whilst Miss Ellen Terry and Sir Henry Irving are on the stage.

It is natural for those who think this snobbishness a really fine and genuine accomplishment to conclude that everybody must lust after it, and, consequently, that Madame Sans-Gêne's neglect to acquire it in spite of her opportunities as Duchess of Dantzig is incredible. Now far be it from me to deny that Sardou's assumption that the Duchess has not learnt to make a curtsey or to put on a low-necked dress must be taken frankly as an impossible pretext for a bit of clowning which may or may not be worth its cost in verisimilitude. But, apart from this inessential episode, the idea that Catherine, being happily Madame Sans-Gêne, should deliberately manufacture herself into a commonplace Court lady—a person with about as much political influence or genuine intimacy with ministers and princes as an upper housemaid in Downing Street—is to assume that she would gain by the exchange, and that her ideals and ambitions are those of an average solicitor's wife.

Here, then, you have the secret of Madame Sans-Gêne and Miss Terry's apparent condescension to a 'vulgar' part. There are a few people in the world with sufficient vitality and strength of character to get to close quarters with uncommon people quite independently of the drill which qualifies common people (whatever their rank) to figure in the retinue which is indispensable to the state of kings and minis-sters. And there are a few actresses who are able to interpret such exceptional people because they are exceptional themselves. Miss Terry is such an exceptional actress; and there the whole wonder of the business begins and ends. Granted this one rare qualification, the mere execution is nothing. The part does not take Miss Terry anywhere near the limit of her powers: on the contrary, it embarrasses her occasionally by its crudity. Réjane was also well within her best as Catherine; so that a comparison of the two artists is like comparing two athletes throwing the hammer ten feet. Miss Terry's difficulties are greater, because she has to make shift with a translation instead of the original text, and because her support, especially in the scenes with Lefebvre, is not so helpful as that enjoyed by Réjane. Also she coaxed the clowning scene through better than Réjane; and her retort upon the Queen of Naples, though it was perfectly genial and simple and laundresslike, set me wondering why we have never heard her deliver Marie Stuart's retort upon Elizabeth in Schiller's play, a speculation which Réjane certainly never suggested to me, and which I admit is not to the point. But, if there is to be any comparison, it must, as I have said, take us outside Madame Sans-Gêne, into which both actresses put as much acting as it will hold.

Sardou's Napoleon is rather better than Madame Tussaud's, and that is all that can be said for it. It is easy to take any familiar stage figure, make him up as Napoleon, put into his mouth a few allusions to the time when he was a poor young artillery officer in Paris and to Friedland or Jena, place at his elbow a Sherlock Holmes called Fouché and so forth, just as in another dress, and with Friedland changed to Pharsalia, you would have a stage Julius Cæsar; but if at the end of the play the personage so dressed up has felt nothing and seen nothing and done nothing that might not have been as appropriately felt, seen, and done by his valet, then the fact that the hero is called Emperor is no more important than the fact that the theatre, in nine cases out of ten, is called the Theatre Royal. On the other hand, if you get as your hero a prince of whom nobody ever heard before—say Hamlet—and make him genuinely distinguished, then he becomes as well known to us as Marcus Aurelius. Sardou's Napoleon belongs to the first variety. He is nothing but the jealous husband of a thousand fashionable dramas, talking Buonapartiana. Sir Henry Irving seizes the opportunity to shew what can be done with an empty part by an old stage hand. The result is that he produces the illusion of the Emperor behind the part: one takes it for granted that his abstinence from any adequately Napoleonic deeds and utterances is a matter of pure forbearance on his part. It is an amusingly crafty bit of business, and reminds one pleasantly of the days before Shakespear was let loose on Sir Henry Irving's talent.

Mr Comyns Carr's translation is much too literary. Catherine does not speak like a woman of the people except when she is helping herself out with ready-made locutions in the manner of Sancho Panza. After a long speech consisting of a bundle of such locutions padded with forced mistakes in grammar, she will say, 'That was my object,' or some similarly impossible piece of Ciceronian eloquence. It is a pity; for there never was a play more in need of an unerring sense of the vernacular and plenty of humorous adroitness in its use.

John Gabriel Borkman

JOHN GABRIEL BORKMAN. *A play in four acts. By* Henrik Ibsen. *English version by* William Archer. *Opening performance by the New Century Theatre at the Strand Theatre,* 3 *May* 1897.

[8 *May* 1897]

THE first performance of John Gabriel Borkman, the latest masterpiece of the acknowledged chief of European dramatic art, has taken place in London under the usual shabby circumstances. For the first scene in the gloomy Borkman house, a faded, soiled, dusty wreck of some gay French salon, originally designed, perhaps, for Offenbach's Favart, was fitted with an incongruous Norwegian stove, a painted staircase, and a couple of chairs which were no doubt white and gold when they first figured in Tom Taylor's Plot and Passion or some other relic of the days before Mr Bancroft revolutionized stage furniture, but have apparently languished ever since, unsold and unsaleable, among secondhand keys, framed lithographs of the Prince Consort, casual fenders and stair-rods, and other spoils of the broker. Still, this scene at least was describable, and even stimulative—to irony. In Act II, the gallery in which Borkman prowls for eight years like a wolf was no gallery at all, but a square box ugly to loathsomeness, and too destructive to the imagination and descriptive faculty to incur the penalty of criticism. In Act III (requiring, it will be remembered, the shifting landscape from Parsifal), two new cloths specially painted, and good enough to produce a tolerable illusion of snowy pinewood and midnight mountain with proper accessories, were made ridiculous by a bare acre of wooden floor and only one set of wings for the two. When I looked at that, and thought of the eminence of the author and the greatness of his work, I felt ashamed. What Sir Henry Irving and Mr George Alexander and Mr Wilson Barrett feel about it I do not know—on the whole, perhaps, not altogether displeased to see Ibsen belittled. For my part, I beg the New Century Theatre, when the next Ibsen play is ready for mounting, to apply to me for assistance. If I have a ten-pound note, they shall have it: if not, I can at least lend them a couple of decent chairs. I cannot think that Mr Massingham, Mr Sutro, and Mr William Archer would have grudged a few such contributions from their humble cots on this occasion if they had not hoped that a display of the most sordid poverty would have shamed the public as it shamed me. Unfortunately their moral lesson is more likely to discredit Ibsen than to fill the New Century coffers. They have spent either too little or too much. When Dr Furnivall performed Browning's Luria in the lecture theatre at University College with a couple of curtains, a chair borrowed from the board-room, and the actors in their ordinary evening dress, the absence of scenery was as completely forgotten as if we had all been in the Globe in Shakespear's time. But between that and an adequate scenic equipment there is no middle course. It is highly honorable to the pioneers of the drama that they are poor; but in art, what poverty can only do unhandsomely and stingily it should not do at all. Besides, to be quite frank, I simply do not believe that the New Century Theatre could not have afforded at least a better couple of chairs.

I regret to say that the shortcomings of the scenery were not mitigated by imaginative and ingenious stage management. Mr Vernon's stage management is very actor-like: that is to say, it is directed, not to secure the maximum of illusion for the play, but the maximum of fairness in distributing good places on the stage to the members of the cast. Had he been selfish enough, as some actor-managers are accused of being, to manage the stage so as to secure the maximum of prominence for himself, the effect would probably have justified him, since he plays Borkman. But his sense of equity is evidently stronger than his vanity; for he takes less than his share of conspicuity, repeatedly standing patiently with his back to the audience to be declaimed at down the stage by Miss Robins or Miss Ward, or whoever else he deems entitled to a turn. Alas! these conceptions of fairness, honorable as they are to Mr Vernon's manhood, are far too simply quantitative for artistic purposes. The business of the stage manager of John Gabriel Borkman is chiefly to make the most of the title part; and if the actor of that part is too modest to do that for himself, some one else should stage-manage. Mr Vernon perhaps pleased the company, because he certainly did contrive that every one of them should have the centre of the stage to himself or herself whenever they had a chance of self-assertion; but as this act of green-room justice was placed before the naturalness of the representation, the actors did not gain by it, whilst the play suffered greatly.

Mr Vernon, I suspect, was also hampered by a rather old-fashioned technical conception of the play as a tragedy. Now the traditional stage management of tragedy ignores realism—even the moderate degree of realism traditional in comedy. It lends itself to people talking at each other rhetorically from opposite sides of the stage, taking long sweeping walks up to their 'points,' striking attitudes in the focus of the public vision with an artificiality which, instead of being concealed, is not only disclosed but insisted on, and being affected in all their joints by emotions which a fine comedian conveys by the faintest possible inflexion of tone or eyebrow. John Gabriel Borkman is no doubt technically a tragedy because it ends with the death of the leading personage in it. But to stage-manage or act it rhetorically as such is like drawing a Dance of Death in the style of Caracci or Giulio Romano. Clearly the required style is the homely-imaginative, the realistic-fateful—in a word, the Gothic. I am aware that to demand Gothic art from stage managers dominated by the notion that their business is to adapt the exigences of stage etiquette to the tragic and comic categories of our pseudo-classical dramatic tradition is to give them an order which they can but dimly understand and cannot execute at all; but Mr Vernon is no mere routineer: he is a man of ideas. After all, Sir Henry Irving (in his Bells style), M. Lugné Poë, Mr Richard Mansfield, and Mr Charles Charrington have hit this mark (whilst missing the pseudo-classic one) nearly enough to shew that it is by no means unattainable. Failing the services of these geniuses, I beg the conventional stage-manager to treat Ibsen as comedy. That will not get the business right; but it will be better than the tragedy plan.

As to the acting of the play, it was fairly good, as acting goes in London now, whenever the performers were at all in their depth; and it was at least lugubriously well intentioned when they were out of it. Unfortunately they were very often out of it. If they had been anti-Ibsenites they would have marked their resentment of and impatience with the passages they did not understand by an irritable listlessness, designed to make the worst of the play as far as that could be done without making the worst of themselves. But the Ibsenite actor marks the speeches which are beyond him by a sudden access of pathetic sentimentality and an intense consciousness of Ibsen's greatness. No doubt this devotional plan lets the earnestness of the representation down less than the sceptical one; yet its effect is as false as false can be; and I am sorry to say that it is gradually establishing a funereally unreal tradition which is likely to end in making Ibsen the most portentous of stage bores. Take, for example, Ella Rentheim. Here you have a part which up to a certain point almost plays itself—a sympathetic old maid with a broken heart. Nineteen-twentieths of her might be transferred to the stage of the Princess's tomorrow and be welcomed there tearfully by the audiences which delight in Two Little Vagabonds and East Lynne. Her desire to adopt

Erhart is plainsailing sentimentalism: her reproach to Borkman for the crime of killing the 'love life' in her and himself for the sake of his ambition is, as a *coup de théâtre*, quite within the range of playwrights who rank considerably below Mr Pinero. All this is presented intelligently by Miss Robins—at moments even touchingly and beautifully. But the moment the dialogue crosses the line which separates the Ibsen sphere from the ordinary sphere her utterance rings false at once. Here is an example—the most striking in the play:

ELLA [*In strong inward emotion*]. Pity! Ha ha! I have never known pity since you deserted me. I was incapable of feeling it. If a poor starved child came into my kitchen, shivering and crying, and begging a morsel of food, I let the servants look to it. I never felt any desire to take the child to myself, to warm it at my own hearth, to have the pleasure of seeing it eat and be satisfied. And yet I wasnt like that when I was young: *that* I remember clearly. It is you that have created an empty, barren desert within me —and without me too!

What is there is this speech that might not occur in any popular novel or drama of sentiment written since Queen Anne's death? If Miss Millward were to introduce it into Black-Ey'd Susan, the Adelphi pit would accept it with moist eyes and without the faintest suspicion of Ibsen. But Ella Rentheim does not stop there. 'You have cheated me of a mother's joy and happiness in life,' she continues, 'and of a mother's sorrows and tears as well. And perhaps that is the heaviest part of the loss to me. It may be that a mother's sorrows and tears were what I needed most.' Now here the Adelphi pit would be puzzled; for here Ibsen speaks as the Great Man—one whose moral consciousness far transcends the common huckstering conception of life as a trade in happiness in which sorrows and tears represent the bad bargains and joys and happiness the good ones. And here Miss Robins suddenly betrays that she is an Ibsenite without being an Ibsenist. The genuine and touching tone of self-pity suddenly turns into a perceptibly artificial snivel (forgive the rudeness of the word); and the sentence, which is the most moving in the play provided it comes out simply and truthfully, is declaimed as a sentimental paradox which has no sort of reality or conviction for the actress. In this failure Miss Robins was entirely consistent with her own successes. As the woman in revolt against the intolerable slavery and injustice of ideal 'womanliness' (Karin and Martha in Pillars of Society) or against the man treating her merely as his sexual prey (Mariana in the recital of her mother's fate) her success has had no bounds except those set by the commercial disadvantages at which the performances were undertaken. As the impetuous, imaginative New Woman in her first youth, free, unscrupulous through ignorance, demanding of life that it shall be 'thrilling,' and terribly dangerous to impressionable Master Builders who have put on life's chains without learning its lessons, she has succeeded heart and soul, rather by being the character than by understanding it. In representing poignant nervous phenomena in their purely physical aspect, as in Alan's Wife, and Mrs Lessingham, she has set up the infection of agony in the theatre with lacerating intensity by the vividness of her reproduction of its symptoms. But in sympathetic parts properly so called, where wisdom of heart, and sense of identity and common cause with others—in short, the parts we shall probably call religious as soon as we begin to gain some glimmering of what religion means—Miss

Robins is only sympathetic as a flute is sympathetic: that is, she has a pretty tone, and can be played on with an affectation of sentiment; but there is no reality, no sincerity in it. And so Ella Rentheim, so far as she is sympathetic, eludes her. The fact is, Miss Robins is too young and too ferociously individualistic to play her. Ella's grievances come out well enough, also her romance, and some of those kindly amenities of hers—notably her amiable farewell to Erhart; but of the woman who understands that she has been robbed of her due of tears and sorrow, of the woman who sees that the crazy expedition through the snow with Borkman is as well worth trying as a hopeless return to the fireside, there is no trace, nothing but a few indications that Miss Robins would have very little patience with such wisdom if she met it in real life.

Mr Vernon's Borkman was not ill acted; only, as it was not Ibsen's Borkman, but the very reverse and negation of him, the better Mr Vernon acted the worse it was for the play. He was a thoroughly disillusioned elderly man of business, patient and sensible rather than kindly, and with the sort of strength that a man derives from the experience that teaches him his limits. I think Mr Vernon must have studied him in the north of Ireland, where that type reaches perfection. Ibsen's Borkman, on the contrary, is a man of the most energetic imagination, whose illusions feed on his misfortunes, and whose conception of his own power grows hyperbolical and Napoleonic in his solitude and impotence. Mr Vernon's excursion into the snow was the aberration of a respectable banker in whose brain a vessel had suddenly burst: the true Borkman meets the fate of a vehement dreamer who has for thirteen years been deprived of that daily contact with reality and responsibility without which genius inevitably produces unearthliness and insanity. Mr Vernon was as earthly and sane as a man need be until he went for his walk in the snow, and a Borkman who is that is necessarily a trifle dull. Even Mr Welch, though his scene in the second act was a triumph, made a fundamental mistake in the third, where Foldal, who has just been knocked down and nearly run over by the sleigh in which his daughter is being practically abducted by Erhart and Mrs Wilton, goes into ecstasies of delight at what he supposes to be her good fortune in riding off in a silver-mounted carriage to finish her musical education under distinguished auspices. The whole point of this scene, at once penetratingly tragic and irresistibly laughable, lies in the sincerity of Foldal's glee and Borkman's sardonic chuckling over it. But Mr Welch unexpectedly sacrificed the scene to a stage effect which has been done to death by Mr Harry Nicholls and even Mr Arthur Roberts. He played the heartbroken old man pretending to laugh—a descendant of the clown who jokes in the arena whilst his child is dying at home—and so wrecked what would otherwise have been the best piece of character work of the afternoon. Mr Martin Harvey, as Erhart, was clever enough to seize the main idea of the part—the impulse towards happiness—but not experienced enough to know that the actor's business is not to supply an idea with a sounding board, but with a credible, simple, and natural human being to utter it when its time comes and not before. He shewed, as we all knew he would shew, considerable stage talent and more than ordinary dramatic intelligence; but in the first act he was not the embarrassed young gentleman of Ibsen, but rather the 'soaring human boy' imagined by Mr Chadband; and later on this attitude of his very nearly produced a serious jar at a critical point in the representation.

Miss Geneviève Ward played Gunhild. The character is a very difficult one, since the violently stagey manifestations of maternal feeling prescribed for the actress by Ibsen indicate a tragic strenuousness of passion which is not suggested by the rest of the dialogue. Miss Ward did not quite convince me that she had found the temperament appropriate to both. The truth is, her tragic style, derived from Ristori, was not made for Ibsen. On the other hand, her conversational style, admirably natural and quite free from the Mesopotamian solemnity with which some of her colleagues delivered the words of the Master, was genuinely dramatic, and reminded me of her excellent performance, years ago with Mr Vernon, as Lona Hessel. Mrs Tree was clever and altogether successful as Mrs Wilton; and Miss Dora Barton's Frida was perfect. But then these two parts are comparatively easy. Miss Caldwell tried hard to modify her well-known representation of a farcical slavey into a passable Ibsenite parlormaid, and succeeded fairly except in the little scene which begins the third act.

On the whole, a rather disappointing performance of a play which cannot be read without forming expectations which are perhaps unreasonable, but are certainly inevitable.

Ibsen Triumphant

[22 *May* 1897]

CAN it possibly be true that The Hobby Horse was produced so recently as 1886? More amazing still, was this the comedy—comedy, mark you—which suggested to me just such hopes of Mr Pinero's future as others built upon The Profligate and The Second Mrs Tanqueray, both of which I contemned as relapses into drawing room melodrama. Going back to it now after an interval of ten years, I find it, not a comedy, but a provincial farce in three acts, decrepit in stage convention, and only capable of appearing fresh to those who, like myself, can wrench themselves back, by force of memory, to the point of view of a period when revivals of London Assurance were still possible. What makes the puerilities of the play more exasperating nowadays is that it is clear, on a survey of the original production and the present revival, that Mr Pinero was not driven into them by any serious deficiency in the executive talent at his disposal. In Mrs Kendal and Mr Hare he had two comedians for whose combined services an unfortunate modern dramatic author might well sacrifice half his percentage. Yet the part of Spencer Jermyn is made so easy that one may well ask the people who rave about Mr Hare's performance as a masterpiece of art what they suppose really difficult acting to be. And imagine Mrs Kendal condemned to make London laugh by pretending to treat a grown-up stepson as a little boy, arranging his hair, telling him not to be afraid, that she will not punish him, and so forth! One gasps at these things nowadays. They may be pardonable in the part of Shattock, who, as comic relief—for even comedy in England must have comic relief—is not expected to do or say anything credible or possible; but here they were thrust into the part of the heroine, enacted by the most accomplished actress in London. What sort of barbarians were we in the days when we took this sort of thing as a matter of course, and made merry over it?

And yet I was right about The Hobby Horse. It has character, humor, observation, genuine comedy, and literary workmanship in it as unmistakeably as The Benefit of the Doubt has them. What is the matter with the play is the distortion and debasement of all its qualities to suit the childishness and vulgarity of the theatre of ten years ago. It will be asked scornfully whether the theatre of today is any better—whether The Red Robe, for instance, is half as good as The Hobby Horse? Before answering that, let me compare The Hobby Horse with The Princess and the Butterfly! Could Mr Pinero venture nowadays to present to the St James's audience, as comedy, the humors of Mr Shattock and the scene between Lady Jermyn and her stepson? You may reply that the author who has given us the duel in The Princess and the Butterfly is capable of anything; but I would have you observe that the duel is a mere makeshift in the plot of The Princess, whereas the follies of The Hobby Horse are presented as flowers of comedy, and —please attend to this—are actually very good of their kind. That such a kind should have been the best of its day—nay, that the play should have suffered in 1886 because its comedy was rather too subtle for the taste of that time—is a staggering thing to think of. But I am prepared to go further as to our improvement by embracing even the comparison with The

Red Robe in support of my case. The nineteenth-century novel, with all its faults, has maintained itself immeasurably above the nineteenth-century drama. Take the women novelists alone, from Charlotte Brontë to Sarah Grand, and think of them, if you can, in any sort of relation except that of a superior species to the dramatists of their day. I unhesitatingly say that no novelist could, even if there were any reason for it, approach the writing of a novel with his mind warped, his hands shackled, and his imagination stultified by the conditions which Mr Pinero accepted, and even gloried in accepting, when he wrote The Hobby Horse. The state of public taste which turns from the first-rate comedies of the eighties to dramatizations of the third-rate novels of the nineties is emphatically a progressive state. These cloak-and-sword dramas, at their worst—if we have reached their worst, which is perhaps too much to hope—are only bad stories badly told: if they were good stories well told, there would be no more objection to them on my part than there is at present on that of the simple people for whom they are not too bad. But the sort of play they are supplanting, whether good or bad, was a wrong sort: the more craftily it was done the more hopelessly wrong it was. The dramatists who had mastered it despised the novelists, and said, 'You may sneer at our craft, but let us see you do it yourselves.' Just the sort of retort a card-sharper might make on a cardinal.

I need hardly go on to explain that Ibsen is at the back of this sudden explosion of disgusted intolerance on my part for a style of entertainment which I suffered gladly enough in the days of the Hare–Kendal management. On Monday last I sat without a murmur in a stuffy theatre on a summer afternoon from three to nearly half-past six, spellbound by Ibsen; but the price I paid for it was to find myself stricken with mortal impatience and boredom the next time I attempted to sit out the pre-Ibsenite drama for five minutes. Where shall I find an epithet magnificent enough for The Wild Duck! To sit there getting deeper and deeper into that Ekdal home, and getting deeper and deeper into your own life all the time, until you forget that you are in a theatre; to look on with horror and pity at a profound tragedy, shaking with laughter all the time at an irresistible comedy; to go out, not from a diversion, but from an experience deeper than real life ever brings to most men, or often brings to any man: that is what The Wild Duck was like last Monday at the Globe. It is idle to attempt to describe it; and as to giving an analysis of the play, I did that seven years ago, and decline now to give myself an antiquated air by treating as a novelty a masterpiece that all Europe delights in. Besides, the play is as simple as Little Red Ridinghood to anyone who comes to it fresh from life instead of stale from the theatre.

And now, what have our 'passing craze' theorists to say to the latest nine-days' wonder, the tremendous effect this ultra-Ibsen play has just produced eight years after the craze set in? As for me, what I have to say is simply, 'I told you so.'

We have by this time seen several productions of A Doll's House, three of Rosmersholm, and two of The Wild Duck. The first performances of A Doll's House (Mr Charrington's at the Novelty) and of Rosmersholm (Miss Florence Farr's at the Vaudeville) gave the actors such an overwhelming advantage as the first revealers to London of a much greater dramatist than Shakespear, that even the vehemently anti-Ibsenite critics lost all power of discrimination, and flattered the performers as frantically as they abused the plays. But since then the performers have had to struggle against the unreasonable expectations thus created; and the effect of the plays has been sternly proportionate to the intelligence and skill brought to bear on them. We have learnt that an Ibsen performance in the hands of Lugné Poë or Mr Charrington is a perfectly different thing from one in which there is individual talent but practically no stage management. M. Lugné Poë established his reputation at once and easily, because he was under no suspicion of depending on the genius of a particular actress: his Rosmersholm with Marthe Mellot as Rebecca had the magic atmosphere which is the sign of the true manager as unmistakeably as his Master Builder with Suzanne Auclaire as Hilda. But Mr Charrington, like Mr Kendal and Mr Bancroft, has a wife; and the difference made by Miss Janet Achurch's acting has always been much more obvious than that made by her husband's management to a public which has lost all tradition of what stage management really is, apart from lavish expenditure on scenery and furniture. But for that his production of Voss's Alexandra would have established his reputation as the best stage manager of true modern drama in London—indeed the only one, in the sense in which I am now using the words: the sense, that is, of a producer of poetically realistic illusion. Now, however, we have him at last with Miss Janet Achurch out of the bill. The result is conclusive. The same insight which enables Mr Charrington, in acting Relling, to point the moral of the play in half a dozen strokes, has also enabled him to order the whole representation in such a fashion that there is not a moment of bewilderment during the development of a dramatic action subtle enough in its motives to have left even highly trained and attentive readers of the play quite addled as to what it is all about. The dialogue, which in any other hands would have been cut to ribbons, is given without the slightest regard to the clock; and not even the striking of six produces the stampede that would set in after a quarter-past five if the play were a 'popular' one. That is a real triumph of management. It may be said that it is a triumph of Ibsen's genius; but of what use is Ibsen's genius if the manager has not the genius to believe in it?

The acting, for a scratch company, was uncommonly good: there was mettle in it, as there usually is where there is good leadership. Mr Laurence Irving, who played Relling to Mr Abingdon's Hjalmar Ekdal at the first production of the play by Mr Grein, handed over Relling to Mr Charrington, and played Hjalmar himself. In all dramatic literature, as far as I know it, there is no other such part for a comedian; and I do not believe any actor capable of repeating the lines intelligibly could possibly fail in it. To say therefore that Mr Irving did not fail is to give him no praise at all: to say that he quite succeeded would be to proclaim him the greatest comedian in London. He was very amusing, and played with cleverness and sometimes with considerable finesse. But though he did not overact any particular passage, he overdid the part a little as a whole by making Hjalmar grotesque. His appearance proclaimed his weakness at once: the conceited ass was recognizable at a glance. This was not right: Hjalmar should impose on us at first. The fact is, we all have to look much nearer home for the originals of Ibsen's characters than we imagine; and

Hjalmar Ekdals are so common nowadays that it is not they, but the other people, who look singular. Still, Mr Irving's performance was a remarkable achievement, and fairly entitles him to patronize his father as an old-fashioned actor who has positively never played a leading Ibsen part. Mr Courtenay Thorpe, as Gregers Werle, confirmed the success he made in A Doll's House as an Ibsen actor—that is, an actor of the highest class in modern drama; but considering the length of the play, he was too free in his use of repetitions and nervous stumblings to give an air of naturalness and spontaneity to his dialogue. Miss Kate Phillips, who made her Ibsen début as Gina, was quite as natural; and yet she never wasted an instant, and was clear, crisp, and punctual as clockwork without being in the least mechanical. I am on the side of smart execution: if there are two ways of being natural in speech on the stage, I suggest that Miss Phillips's way is better than the fluffy way. As to her impersonation of Gina, Nature prevented her from making it quite complete. Gina is as unique in drama as Hjalmar. All Shakespear's matrons rolled into one, from Volumnia to Mrs Quickly, would be as superficial and conventional in comparison with Gina as a classic sybil by Raphael with a Dutch cook by Rembrandt. That waddling housewife, with her practical sense and sympathy, and her sanely shameless insensibility to the claims of the ideal, or to any imaginative presentment of a case whatever, could only be done by Gina herself; and Gina certainly could not act. If Miss Phillips were to waddle, or counterfeit insensitiveness, or divest her speech of artistic character, the result would only be such a caricature as a child gives of its grandmother, or, worse still, something stage-Shakespearean, like her Audrey. She wisely made no attempt to denaturalize herself, but played the part sincerely and with the technical skill that marks her off, as it marks Mrs Kendal and her school off, from our later generation of agreeable amateurs who do not know the A B C of their business. Once, in the second act, she from mere habit and professional sympathy played with her face to a speech of Hjalmar's which Gina would have taken quite stolidly; but this was her only mistake. She got no laughs of the wrong sort in the wrong place; and the speech in which the worrited Gina bursts out with the quintessence of the whole comedy—'Thats what comes when crazy people go about making the claims of the what-d'yer-call-it'—went home right up to the hilt into our midriffs. Mr Welch's Ekdal left nothing to be said: it was faultless. Mr Charrington played Relling with great artistic distinction: nobody else got so completely free from conventional art or so convincingly behind the part and the play as he. The only failure of the cast was Molvik, who was well made up, but did not get beyond a crude pantomimic representation of sickness and drunkenness which nearly ruined the play at the most critically pathetic moment in the final act. Mr Outram was uninteresting as Werle: the part does not suit his age and style. Miss Ffolliott Paget was a capital Mrs Sörby.

Miss Winifred Fraser not only repeated her old triumph as Hedwig, but greatly added to it. The theatre could hardly have a more delicate talent at its service; and yet it seems to have no use for it. But Miss Fraser need not be discouraged. The British public is slow; but it is sure. By the time she is sixty it will discover that she is one of its best actresses; and then it will expect her to play Juliet until she dies of old age.

And this reminds me that I wandered away from The Hobby Horse without a word as to the acting of it. Mrs Kendal, always great in comedy, had an enchanting way of making Mrs Jermyn's silliness credible and attractive. Miss May Harvey is far too clever and too well acquainted with Mrs Kendal's methods to be at any great loss in replacing her; but she is no more specifically a comedian than Jane Hading is; and her decisive opportunity as an actress will evidently come in much more intense work. In technical skill she is far above the average of her generation—a generation, alas! of duffers—and I have no doubt that she will play a distinguished part in the theatrical history of the nineties and twenties. The lady who plays Miss Moxon cannot touch Mrs Beerbohm Tree's inimitable performance in that inglorious but amusing and lifelike part. On the other hand, Mr Fred Kerr has made the solicitor his own for ever. His acting is irresistibly funny, not because it is unscrupulously bad, as funny acting often is, but because it is perfectly in character and as good of its kind as can be. An actor of Mr Kerr's talent should not be allowed to waste himself on Miss Browns and Jedbury Juniors and such stuff. Mr Gilbert Hare has improved greatly, and is now as welcome for his own sake as he formerly was for his father's. Mr Groves of course does what can be done with the impossible but laughable Shattock; and the 'pushin' little cad' whom he denounces, though *persona muta* and unnamed in the bill, is richly endowed by Nature for his humble part.

Secret Service at the Adelphi, with a smart American cast, is pure regulation melodrama. The fact that it is brightly and imaginatively done in the American style, instead of stupidly and only half literally in the

Strand style, has imposed ludicrously on the English critics; but the article is the old article, only more aggressively machine-made than our clumsy hands would have left it. It has a capital situation, in Mr Gillette's best style, at the end of the second act. But this, like all the other situations, takes a huge deal of leading up to, and leads to nothing itself, being so speedily forgotten that before half an hour has elapsed the heroine quite forgets that it has involved, apparently, an act of fratricide on the part of the hero. The hero, by the way, is a spy; and why the intelligent gentleman (the only sensible man in the piece) who objects to him should be execrated as a villain, whilst all the rest rally round their betrayer and want to shake his hand repeatedly, is more than I can quite understand. I cannot even plead for him that—

> His honor rooted in dishonor stood;
> And faith unfaithful kept him falsely true;

for he first spies on the South and then, at the critical moment, betrays the North for purely personal reasons. Altogether an unredeemed rascal. But Mr Gillette plays him with so manly an air that the audience does not stop to ask what it is applauding; and everybody seems delighted. I confess I was disappointed; for I am an admirer of Mr Gillette's Held by the Enemy, which seemed to me a new departure in melodrama and an excellent play into the bargain. His Secret Service is certainly not to be compared to it. A Miss Odette Tyler almost bewitched us into believing that the comic relief was funny, especially in the scene with the telegraph operator (Mr W. B. Smith, I presume—there are several operators in the bill), who acted excellently.

Messrs John Lart and Charles Dickinson's Court of Honor must be a most thrilling and moving drama to those who, unlike myself, can place themselves at its evangelico-romantic point of view. I particularly admired the resolution and professional skill with which Miss Calhoun fought her way through a part which would have crushed any actress of no more than ordinary leading-ladyship.

Mainly About Shakespear

OTHELLO. *Lyric Theatre, 22 May 1897.*
ANTONY AND CLEOPATRA. *Olympic Theatre, 24 May 1897.*
BELLE BELAIR. *A new play in four acts. By* R. R. Lumley. *Avenue Theatre, 19 May 1897.*

[29 *May* 1897]

IF only I were a moralist, like Shakespear, how I could improve the occasion of the fall of the once Independent Theatre! A fortnight ago that body, whose glory was its freedom from actor-managership and its repertory of plays which no commercial theatre would produce, was hanging the wreath on the tip-top of the Independent tower over its performance of The Wild Duck. This week it has offered us, as choice Independent fare, the thirty-year-old 'acting version' of Shakespear's Antony and Cleopatra, with which Miss Janet Achurch made a sensation the other day in Manchester. I ask the directors of the Independent Theatre what they mean by this? I ask it as a shareholder who put down his hard-earned money for the express purpose of providing a refuge from such exhibitions. I ask it as a member of the body politic, whose only hope of dramatic nutrition is in the strict specialization of these newly and painfully evolved little organs, the Independent and New Century Theatres. I ask it as a critic who has pledged himself for the integrity of the Independent Theatre as recklessly as Falstaff did for Pistol's honesty. Even Pistol was able to retort on Falstaff, 'Didst thou not share? Hadst thou not fifteen pence?' But I have not had fifteen pence: I have only had an afternoon of lacerating anguish, spent partly in contemplating Miss Achurch's overpowering experiments in rhetoric, and partly in wishing I had never been born.

If I speak intemperately on this matter, please to remember what I have endured throughout a quarter of a century of play-going. Years ago—how many does not matter—I went to the theatre one evening to see a play called The Two Roses, and was much struck therein by the acting of one Henry Irving, who created a modern realistic character named Digby Grant in a manner which, if applied to an Ibsen play now, would astonish us as much as Miss Achurch's Nora astonished us. When next I saw that remarkable actor, he had gone into a much older established branch of his business, and was trying his hand at Richelieu. He was new to the work; and I suffered horribly; the audience suffered horribly; and I hope (though I am a humane man, considering my profession) that the actor suffered horribly. For I knew what rhetoric ought to be, having tasted it in literature, music, and painting; and as to the stage, I had seen great Italians do it in the days when Duse, like Ibsen, had not arrived. After a long period of convalescence, I ventured again to the Lyceum, and saw Hamlet. There was a change, Richelieu had been incessantly excruciating: Hamlet had only moments of violent ineptitude separated by lengths of dulness: and though I yawned, I felt none the worse next morning. When some unaccountable impulse led me to the Lyceum again (I suspect it was to see Miss Ellen Terry), The Lady of Lyons was in the bill. Before Claude Melnotte had moved his wrist and chin twice, I saw that he had mastered the rhetorical style at last. His virtuosity of execution soon became extraordinary. His Charles I, for instance, became a miracle of the most elaborate class of this sort of acting. It was a hard-earned and well-deserved triumph; and by it his destiny was accomplished; the anti-Irvingites were confuted; the caricaturists were disconcerted; and the foreign actor could no longer gasp at us when we talked of Irving as a master of his art. But suppose he had foregone this victory! Suppose he had said, 'I can produce studies of modern life and character like Digby Grant. I can create weird supernatural figures like Vanderdecken (Vanderdecken, now forgotten, was a masterpiece), and all sorts of grotesques. But if I try this rhetorical art of making old-fashioned heroics impressive and even beautiful, I shall not only make a fool of myself as a beginner where I have hitherto shone as an adept, but—what is of deeper import to me and the world—I shall give up a fundamentally serious social function for a fundamentally nonsensical theatrical accomplishment.' What would have been the result of such a renunciation? We should have escaped Lyceum Shakespear; and we should have had the ablest manager of the day driven by life-or-death necessity to extract from contemporary literature the proper food for the modern side of his talent, and thus to create a new drama instead of galvanizing an old one and cutting himself off from all contact with the dramatic vitality of his time. And what an excellent thing that would have been both for us and for him!

Now what Sir Henry Irving has done, for good or evil, Miss Janet Achurch can do too. If she is tired of being 'an Ibsenite actress' and wants to be a modern Ristori, it is clear that the public will submit to her apprenticeship as humbly as they submitted to Sir Henry Irving's. Mr Grossmith may caricature her at his recitals; flippant critics may pass jests through the stalls or pittites with an ungovernable sense of the ludicrous burst into guffaws; the orchestra may writhe like a heap of trodden worms at each uplifting of her favorite tragic wail; but now, as at the Lyceum of old, the public as a whole is clearly at her mercy; for in art the strength of a chain is its strongest link; and once the power to strike a masterstroke is clearly felt, the public will wait for it patiently through all extremities of experimental blundering. But the result will repeat itself as surely as the process. Let Miss Achurch once learn to make the rhetorical drama plausible, and thenceforth she will never do anything else. Her interest in life and character will be supplanted by an interest in plastique and execution; and she will come to regard emotion simply as the best of lubricants and stimulants, caring nothing for its specific character so long as it is of a sufficiently obvious and facile sort to ensure a copious flow without the fatigue of thought. She will take to the one-part plays of Shakespear, Schiller, Giacometti, and Sardou, and be regarded as a classic person by the Corporation of Stratford-on-Avon. In short, she will become an English Sarah Bernhardt. The process is already far advanced. On Monday last she was sweeping about, clothed with red Rossettian hair and beauty to match; revelling in the power of her voice and the steam pressure of her energy; curving her wrists elegantly above Antony's head as if she were going to extract a globe of gold fish and two rabbits from behind his ear; and generally celebrating her choice between the rare and costly art of being beautifully natural in lifelike human acting, like Duse, and the comparatively common and cheap one of being theatrically beautiful in heroic stage exhibition. Alas for our lost leaders! Shakespear and success capture them all.

Othello at the Lyric was a much less trying experience. Antony and Cleopatra is an attempt at a serious drama. To say that there is plenty of bogus characterization in it—Enobarbus, for instance—is merely to say that it is by Shakespear. But the contrast between Cæsar and Antony is true human drama; and Cæsar himself is deeper than the usual Shakespearean stage king. Othello, on the other hand, is pure melodrama. There is not a touch of character in it that goes below the skin; and the fitful attempts to make Iago something better than a melodramatic villain only make a hopeless mess of him and his motives. To anyone capable of reading the play with an open mind as to its merits, it is obvious that Shakespear plunged through it so impetuously that he had it finished before he had made up his mind as to the character and motives of a single person in it. Probably it was not until he stumbled into the sentimental fit in which he introduced the willow song that he saw his way through without making Desdemona enough of the 'supersubtle Venetian' of Iago's description to strengthen the case for Othello's jealousy. That jealousy, by the way, is purely melodramatic jealousy. The real article is to be found later on in A Winter's Tale, where Leontes is an unmistakeable study of a jealous man from life. But when the worst has been said of Othello that can be provoked by its superficiality and staginess, it remains magnificent by the volume of its passion and the splendor of its word-music, which sweep the scenes up to a plane on which sense is drowned in sound. The words do not convey ideas: they are streaming ensigns and tossing branches to make the tempest of passion visible. In this passage, for instance:

> Like to the Pontic sea,
> Whose icy current and compulsive course
> Ne'er feels retiring ebb, but keeps due on
> To the Propontic and the Hellespont,
> E'en so my bloody thoughts, with violent pace,
> Shall ne'er look back, ne'er ebb to humble love
> Till that a capable and wide revenge
> Swallow them up,

if Othello cannot turn his voice into a thunder and surge of passion, he will achieve nothing but a ludicrously misplaced bit of geography. If in the last scene he cannot throw the darkness of night and the shadow of death over such lines as

> I know not where is that Promethean heat
> That can thy light relume,

he at once becomes a person who, on his way to commit a pettish murder, stops to philosophize foolishly about a candle end. The actor cannot help himself by studying his part acutely; for there is nothing to study in it. Tested by the brain, it is ridiculous: tested by the ear, it is sublime. He must have the orchestral quality in him; and as that is a matter largely of physical endowment, it follows that only an actor of certain physical endowments can play Othello. Let him be as crafty as he likes without that, he can no more get the effect than he can sound the bottom C on a violoncello. The note is not there, that is all; and he had better be content to play Iago, which is within the compass of any clever actor of normal endowments.

When I have said that Mr Wilson Barrett has not this special musical and vocal gift, I have said everything needful; for in this matter a miss is as good as a mile. It is of no use to *speak* 'Farewell the tranquil mind'; for the more intelligently and reasonably it is spoken the more absurd it is. It must affect us as 'Ora per sempre addio, sante memorie' affects us when sung by Tamagno. Mr Wilson Barrett is an unmusical speaker except when he is talking Manx. He chops and drives his phrases like a smart carpenter with a mallet and chisel, hitting all the prepositions and conjunctions an extra hard tap; and he has a positive genius for misquotation. For example:

> Of one that loved not wisely but well

and

> Drop tears down-faster than the Arabian trees,

both of which appear to me to bear away the palm from Miss Achurch's

> By the scandering of this pelleted storm.

It is a pity that he is not built to fit Othello; for he produces the play, as usual, very well. At the Lyceum everyone is bored to madness the moment Sir Henry Irving and Miss Terry leave the stage: at the Lyric, as aforetime at the Princess's, the play goes briskly from beginning to end; and there are always three or four successes in smaller parts sparkling round Mr

Barrett's big part. Thus Mr Wigney Percyval, the first Cassio I ever saw get over the difficulty of appearing a responsible officer and a possible successor for Othello with nothing but a drunken scene to do it in, divides the honors of the second act with Iago; and Mr Ambrose Manning is interesting and amusing all through as Roderigo. Mr Franklin McLeay, as Iago, makes him the hero of the performance. But the character defies all consistency. Shakespear, as usual, starts with a rough general notion of a certain type of individual, and then throws it over at the first temptation. Iago begins as a coarse blackguard, whose jovial bluntness passes as 'honesty,' and who is professionally a routine subaltern incapable of understanding why a mathematician gets promoted over his head. But the moment a stage effect can be made, or a fine speech brought off by making him refined, subtle, and dignified, he is set talking like Hamlet, and becomes a godsend to students of the 'problems' presented by our divine William's sham characters. Mr McLeay does all that an actor can do with him. He follows Shakespear faithfully on the rails and off them. He plays the jovial blackguard to Cassio and Roderigo and the philosopher and mentor to Othello just as the lines lead him, with perfect intelligibility and with so much point, distinction, and fascination that the audience loads him with compliments, and the critics all make up their minds to declare that he shews the finest insight into the many-sided and complex character of the prince of villains. As to Miss Maud Jeffries, I came to the conclusion when she sat up in bed and said, 'Why I should fear, I know not,' with pretty petulance, that she did not realize the situation a bit; but her voice was so pathetically charming and musical, and she is so beautiful a woman, that I hasten to confess that I never saw a Desdemona I liked better. Miss Frances Ivor, always at her best in Shakespear, should not on that account try to deliver the speech about 'lashing the rascal naked through the world' in the traditional Mrs Crummles manner. Emilia's really interesting speeches, which contain some of Shakespear's curious anticipations of modern ideas, were of course cut; but Miss Ivor, in what was left, proved her aptitude for Shakespearean work, of which I self-denyingly wish her all possible abundance.

Mr Barrett's best scene is that in which he reads the despatch brought by Lodovico. His worst—leaving out of account those torrential outbreaks of savagery for which he is too civilized—is the second act. The storm, the dread of shipwreck, the darkness, the fierce riot, the 'dreadful bell that frights the isle from its propriety,' are not only not suggested, but contradicted, by the scenery and management. We are shewn a delightful Mediterranean evening; the bell is as pretty as an operatic angelus; Othello comes in like a temperance lecturer; Desdemona does not appear; and the exclamation,

> Look, if my gentle love be not raised up—
> I'll make thee an example,

becomes a ludicrously schoolmasterly 'I'll make thee an example,' twice repeated. Here Mr Barrett makes the Moor priggish instead of simple, as Shakespear meant him to be in the moments when he meant anything beyond making effective stage points. Another mistake in management is the business of the portrait in the third act, which is of little value to Othello, and interrupts Iago's speeches in a flagrantly obvious manner.

Belle Belair at the Avenue is a primitive and not very robust specimen of modern comedy, pleasantly held up by a cast which includes Mrs John Wood, Mr Weedon Grossmith, Mr Martin Harvey, and Miss Irene Vanbrugh. The title part was probably meant for Miss Ada Rehan rather than for Mrs John Wood; but Mrs John Wood can translate all sorts of parts into Mrs John Wood parts; so it does not greatly matter. Miss Louise Moodie, Mr Farquharson, and Mr Beauchamp are also in the cast; so if the piece fails it will not be from underplaying.

Robertson Redivivus

AN IRISH GENTLEMAN. *A play in three acts. By* David Christie Murray *and* John L. Shine. *Globe Theatre,* 9 *June* 1897.

FOR THE HONOUR OF THE FAMILY. *Anonymous adaptation of* Emile Augier's *Mariage d'Olympe. Comedy Theatre,* 10 *June* 1897.

CASTE. *By* T. W. Robertson. *Revival. Court Theatre,* 10 *June* 1897.

[19 *June* 1897]

THE revival of Caste at the Court Theatre is the revival of an epoch-making play after thirty years. A very little epoch and a very little play, certainly, but none the less interesting on that account to mortal critics whose own epochs, after full deductions for nonage and dotage, do not outlast more than two such plays. The Robertsonian movement caught me as a boy; the Ibsen movement caught me as a man; and the next one will catch me as a fossil.

It happens that I did not see Mr. Hare's revival of Caste at the Carrick, nor was I at his leave-taking at the Lyceum before his trip to America; so that until last week I had not seen Caste since the old times when the Hare–Kendal management was still in futurity, and the Bancrofts had not left Tottenham Court Road. During that interval a great many things have happened, some of which have changed our minds and morals more than many of the famous Revolutions and Reformations of the historians. For instance, there was supernatural religion then; and eminent physicists, biologists, and their disciples were 'infidels.' There was a population question then; and what men and women knew about one another was either a family secret or the recollection of a harvest of wild oats. There was no social question—only a 'social evil'; and the educated classes knew the working classes through novels written by men who had gathered their notions of the subject either from a squalid familiarity with general servants in Pentonville kitchens, or from no familiarity at all with the agricultural laborer and the retinues of the country house and west end mansion. Today the 'infidels' are bishops and church-wardens, without change of view on their part. There is no population question; and the young lions and lionesses of Chronicle and Star, Keynote and Pseudonym, without suspicion of debauchery, seem to know as much of erotic psychology as the most liberally educated Periclean Athenians. The real working classes loom hugely in middle-class consciousness, and have pressed into their service the whole public energy of the time; so that now even a Conservative Government has nothing for the classes but 'doles,' extracted with difficulty from its preoccupation with instalments of Utopian Socialism. The extreme reluctance of Englishmen to mention these changes is the measure of their dread of a reaction to the older order which they still instinctively connect with strict applications of religion and respectability.

Since Caste has managed to survive all this, it need not be altogether despised by the young champions who are staring contemptuously at it, and asking what heed they can be expected to give to the opinions of critics who think such stuff worth five minutes' serious consideration. For my part, though I enjoy it more than I enjoyed The Notorious Mrs Ebbsmith, I do not defend it. I see now clearly enough that the eagerness with which it was swallowed long ago was the eagerness with which an ocean castaway, sucking his bootlaces in an agony of thirst in a sublime desert of salt water, would pounce on a spoonful of flat salutaris and think it nectar. After years of sham heroics and superhuman balderdash, Caste delighted everyone by its freshness, its nature, its humanity. You will shriek and snort, O scornful young men, at this monstrous assertion. 'Nature! Freshness!' you will exclaim. 'In Heaven's name [if you are not too modern to have heard of Heaven], where is there a touch of nature in Caste?' I reply, 'In the windows, in the doors, in the walls, in the carpet, in the ceiling, in the kettle, in the fireplace, in the ham, in the tea, in the bread and butter, in the bassinet, in the hats and sticks and clothes, in the familiar phrases, the quiet, unpumped, everyday utterance: in short, the commonplaces that are now spurned because they are commonplaces, and were then inexpressibly welcome because they were the most unexpected of novelties.'

And yet I dare not submit even this excuse to a detailed examination. Charles Mathews was in the field long before Robertson and Mr Bancroft with the art of behaving like an ordinary gentleman in what looked like a real drawing room. The characters are very old stagers, very thinly 'humanized.' Captain Hawtrey may look natural now in the hands of Mr Fred Kerr; but he began by being a very near relation of the old stage 'swell,' who pulled his moustache, held a single eyeglass between his brow and cheek-bone, said 'Haw, haw' and 'By Jove,' and appeared in every harlequinade in a pair of white trousers which were blacked by the clown instead of his boots. Mr Henry Arthur Jones, defending his idealized early impressions as Berlioz defended the forgotten Dalayrac, pleads for Eccles as 'a great and vital tragi-comic figure.' But the fond plea cannot be allowed. Eccles is caricatured in the vein and by the methods which Dickens had made obvious; and the implied moral view of his case is the common Pharisaic one of his day. Eccles and Gerridge together epitomize mid-century Victorian shabby-genteel ignorance of the working classes. Polly is comic relief pure and simple; George and Esther have nothing but a milkcan to differentiate them from the heroes and heroines of a thousand sentimental dramas; and though Robertson happens to be quite right—contrary to the prevailing opinion among critics whose conception of the aristocracy is a theoretic one—in representing the 'Marquizzy' as insisting openly and jealously on her rank, and, in fact, having an impenitent and resolute flunkeyism as her class characteristic, yet it is quite evident that she is not an original study from life, but simply a ladyfication of the conventional haughty mother whom we lately saw revived in all her original vulgarity and absurdity at the Adelphi in Maddison Morton's All that Glitters is not Gold, and who was generally associated on the stage with the swell from whom Captain Hawtrey is evolved. Only, let it not be forgotten that in both there really is a humanization, as humanization was understood in the 'sixties: that is, a discovery of saving sympathetic qualities in personages hitherto deemed beyond redemption. Even theology had to be humanized then by the rejection of the old doctrine of eternal punishment. Hawtrey is a good fellow, which the earlier 'swell' never was; the Marquise is dignified and affectionate at heart, and is neither made ridiculous by a grotesque headdress nor embraced by the drunken Eccles; and neither of them is attended by a supercilious footman in plush whose head is finally punched powderless by Sam Gerridge. And if from these hints you cannot gather the real nature and limits of the tiny theatrical revolution of which Robertson was the hero, I must leave you in your perplexity for want of time and space for further exposition.

Of the performance I need say nothing. Caste is a task for amateurs: if its difficulties were doubled, the Court company could without effort play it twice as well as it need be played. Mr Hare's Eccles is the *tour de force* of a refined actor playing a coarse part; but it is all the more enjoyable for that. Of the staging I have one small criticism to offer. If George D'Alroy's drawing room is to be dated by a cluster of electric lights, Sam Gerridge must not come to tea in corduroy trousers, dirty shirt-sleeves, and a huge rule sticking out of his pocket. No 'mechanic' nowadays would dream of doing such a thing. A stockbroker in moleskins would not be a grosser solecism.

But if Robertson begins to wear a little, what is to be said of Augier? The version of his Mariage d'Olympe produced last week at the Comedy was ten times more obsolete than Caste, though Augier's was a solider talent than Robertson's. The Robertsonian 'humanity,' with its sloppy insistence on the soft place that is to be found in everybody—especially in the most hopelessly worthless people—was poor enough; but it was better than the invincible ignorance which could conscientiously produce such a tissue of arrant respectability-worshipping folly as Le Mariage d'Olympe. Augier was a true bourgeois: when he observed a human impulse that ran counter to the habits of his class, it never occurred to him that it opened a question as to their universal propriety. To him those habits were 'morality'; and what was counter to them was 'nostalgie de la boue.' Accordingly, the play is already a ridiculous inversion of moral order. Stupid and prejudiced old gentlemen are doubtless childish enough in their objection to rowdy daughters-in-law to wish occasionally that they would die; but they dont shoot them on principle; and the fact that Augier was driven to such a foolish solution is in itself a damning criticism of his play. But it is amusing and not uninteresting to watch Olympe nowadays, and note how completely her 'nostalgie de la boue' is justified as against the dull and sensual respectability of the father-in-law. In fact, the play now so plainly shews that it is better for a woman to be a liar and a rapscallion than a mere lady, that I should be inclined to denounce it as dangerously immoral if there were no further and better alternatives open to her.

Miss Eleanor Lane, a very capable American actress, played Olympe efficiently; and Mrs Rose Vernon-Paget made a distinct hit by giving a character sketch of the detrimental mother on which Granny Stephens at her best could not have improved. Mr Bell played the dashing man-about-town as such parts used to be played in the days of H. J. Byron; and Mrs Theodore Wright was particularly good as the wife of the Vindicator of Family Honor, who was better treated by Mr Gurney than he deserved.

An Irish Gentleman at the Globe is a typical product of our theatre. It has been evident for some time that we have in Mr J. L. Shine a comedian capable of restoring the popularity which Boucicault won for sketches of Irish character on the English stage. Accordingly, Mr Shine, who, like all experienced actors, knows just what will go down with the public, calls in Mr Christie Murray to act as penman, and manufactures a 'drama' with heroes, heroines, villains, Irish retainers, comic relief, incidental songs, and all needful accessories for the exploitation of his talent. And I have no doubt that Mr Shine and his backers were convinced that they had a fortune in the product, although they would have laughed to scorn a proposal to invest thirty shillings in an Ibsen production. They are wiser now. Fate was in her ironical mood on the first night. Neither Mr Shine nor any other of the stage Irishmen raised a smile: all the honors went to the Scotch villain (Mr J. B. Gordon) and to Miss Eva Moore, who was very charming and very English as the heroine.

Mr Hermann Vezin informs me that the 'view' of Prospero with which I credited him last week was less the result of his attitude towards Shakespear than of a startling bicycle accident which prevented him from having any views beyond a conviction of the extreme desirability of getting back as soon as possible to his bed, his doctor, and his nurse. I am happy to be able to add that he is out of their hands now, and none the worse for his mishap.

Ghosts at the Jubilee

GHOSTS. *By* Henrik Ibsen. *The Independent Theatre, Queen's Gate Hall, South Kensington,* 24, 25, *and* 26 *June* 1897.

[3 *July* 1897]

THE Jubilee and Ibsen's Ghosts! On the one hand the Queen and the Archbishop of Canterbury: on the other, Mrs Alving and Pastor Manders. Stupendous contrast! how far reflected in the private consciousness of those two august persons there is no means of ascertaining. For though of all the millions for the nourishment of whose loyalty the Queen must submit to be carried through the streets from time to time, not a man but is firmly persuaded that her opinions and convictions are exact facsimiles of his own, none the less she, having seen much of men and affairs, may quite possibly be a wise woman and worthy successor of Canute, and no mere butt for impertinent and senseless Jubilee odes such as their perpetrators dare not, for fear of intolerable domestic scorn and ridicule, address to their own wives or mothers. I am myself cut off by my profession from Jubilees; for loyalty in a critic is corruption. But if I am to avoid idolizing kings and queens in the ordinary human way, I must carefully realize them as fellow-creatures. And so, whilst the nation was burning war incense in a thousand cannons before the throne at Spithead, I was wondering, on my way home from Ghosts, how far life had brought to the Queen the lessons it brought to Mrs Alving. For Mrs Alving is not anybody in particular: she is a typical figure of the experienced, intelligent woman who, in passing from the first to the last quarter of the hour of history called the nineteenth century, has discovered how appallingly opportunities were wasted, morals perverted, and instincts corrupted, not only—sometimes not at all—by the vices she was taught to abhor in her youth, but by the virtues it was her pride and uprightness to maintain.

Suppose, then, the Queen were to turn upon us in the midst of our jubilation, and say, 'My Lords and Gentlemen: You have been good enough to describe at great length the changes made during the last sixty years in science, art, politics, dress, sport, locomotion, newspapers, and everything else that men chatter about. But you have not a word to say about the change that comes home most closely to me? I mean the change in the number, the character, and the intensity of the lies a woman must either believe or pretend to believe before she can graduate in polite society as a well-brought-up lady.' If Her Majesty could be persuaded to give a list of these lies, what a document it would be! Think of the young lady of seventy years ago, systematically and piously lied to by parents, governesses, clergymen, servants, everybody; and slapped, sent to bed, or locked up in the bedevilled and beghosted dark at every rebellion of her common sense and natural instinct against sham religion, sham propriety, sham decency, sham knowledge, and sham ignorance. Surely every shop-window picture of 'the girl Queen' of 1837 must tempt the Queen of 1897 to jump out of her carriage and write up under it, 'Please remember that there is not a woman earning twenty-four shillings a week as a clerk today who is not ten times better educated than this unfortunate girl was when the crown dropped on her head, and left her to reign by her mother wit and the advice of a parcel of men who to this day have not sense enough to manage a Jubilee, let alone an Empire, without offending everybody.' Depend on it, seventy-eight years cannot be lived through without finding out things that queens do not mention in Adelphi melodramas. Granted that the Queen's consort was not a Chamberlain Alving, and that too few of her wide, numerous and robust posterity have perished for even Ibsen to see in the dissoluteness of the ancestors of the First Gentleman in Europe any great menace to the longevity of their descendants; still nineteenth-century life, however it may stage-manage itself tragically and sensationally here, or settle itself happily and domestically there, is yet all of one piece; and it is possible to have better luck than Mrs Alving without missing all her conclusions.

Let us therefore guard ourselves against the gratuitous, but just now very common, assumption that the Queen, in her garnered wisdom and sorrow, is as silly as the noisiest of her subjects, who see in their ideal Queen the polar opposite of Mrs Alving, and who are so far right that the spirit of Ghosts is unquestionably the polar opposite of the spirit of the Jubilee. The Jubilee represents the nineteenth century proud of itself. Ghosts represents it loathing itself. And how it *can* loathe itself when it gets tired of its money! Think of Schopenhauer and Shelley, Lassalle and Karl Marx, Ruskin and Carlyle, Morris and Wagner and Ibsen. How fiercely they rent the bosom that bore them! How they detested all the orthodoxies, and respectabilities, and ideals we have just been jubilating! Of all their attacks, none is rasher or fiercer than Ghosts. And yet, like them all, it is perfectly unanswerable. Many generations have laughed at comedies like L'Etourdi, and repeated that hell is paved with good intentions; but never before have we had the well-brought-up, high-minded nineteenth-century lady and her excellent clergyman as the mischief-makers. With them the theme, though still in its essence comic, requires a god to laugh at it. To mortals who may die of such blundering it is tragic and ghastly.

The performance of Ghosts by the Independent Theatre Society left the two previous productions by the same society far behind. As in the case of The Wild Duck, all obscurity vanished; and Ibsen's clearness, his grip of his theme, and the rapidity, directness, and intensity of the action of the piece produced the effect they can always be depended on to produce in capable hands, such as Mr Charrington's (so far alone among those of Ibsenite stage-managers) have proved to be. Mrs Theodore Wright's Mrs Alving, originally an achievement quite beyond the culture of any other actress of her generation, is still hardly less peculiar to her. Mrs Wright's technique is not in the least that of the Ibsen school. Never for a moment would you suspect her of having seen Miss Janet Achurch or anyone remotely resembling her. She is unmistakeably a contemporary of Miss Ellen Terry. When I first saw her act she was playing Beatrice in Much Ado About Nothing, with a charm and intuition that I have not seen surpassed, and should not have seen equalled if I had never seen Miss Terry wasting her gifts on Shakespear. As it happened, Mrs Theodore Wright, perhaps because she was so fond of acting that the stage, where there is less opportunity for it than anywhere else in England, bored her intolerably, found her way behind the scenes of the revolutionary drama of the century at a time when the happy ending now in progress had not been reached, and played Shakespear and recited Shelley, Hood, and George Eliot before Karl Marx, Morris, Bradlaugh, and other volcanic makers of the difference between 1837 and 1897, as proudly as Talma played to his pit of kings. Her authors, it will be seen, were not so advanced as her audiences; but that could not be helped, as the progressive movement in England had not produced a dramatist; and nobody then dreamt of Norway, or knew that Ibsen had begun the drama of struggle and emancipation, and had declared that the really effective progressive forces of the moment were the revolt of the working classes against economic, and of the women against idealistic, slavery. Such a drama, of course, immediately found out that weak spot in the theatrical profession which Duse put her finger on the other day in Paris —the so-called stupidity of the actors and actresses. Stupidity, however, is hardly the word. Actors and actresses are clever enough on the side on which their profession cultivates them. What is the matter with them is the characteristic narrowness and ignorance of their newly conquered conventional respectability. They are now neither above the commonplaces of middle-class idealism, like the aristocrat and poet, nor below them, like the vagabond and Bohemian. The theatre has become very much what the Dissenting chapel used to be: there is not a manager in London who, in respect of liberality and enlightenment of opinion, familiarity and sympathy with current social questions, can be compared with the leaders of Noncomformity. Take Sir Henry Irving and Dr Clifford for example. The Dissenter is a couple of centuries ahead of the actor: indeed, the comparison seems absurd, so grotesquely is it to the disadvantage of the institution which still imagines itself the more cultured and less prejudiced of the two. And, but for Mr Henry Arthur Jones, the authors would cut as poor a figure from this point of view as the actors. Duse advises actors to read; but of what use is that? They *do* read—more than is good for them. They read the drama, and are eager students of criticism, though they would die rather than confess as much to a critic. (Whenever an actor tells me, as he invariably does, that he has not seen any notices of his performance, I always know that he has the Saturday Review in his pocket; but I respect the delicacy of an evasion which is as instinctive and involuntary as blushing.) When the drama loses its hold on life, and criticism is dragged down with it, the actor's main point of intellectual contact with the world is cut off; for he reads nothing else with serious attention. He then has to spin his culture out of his own imagination or that of the dramatist and critics, a facile but delusive process which leaves him nothing real to fall back on but his technical craft, which may make him a good workman, but nothing else.

If even technical craft became impossible at such a period—say through the long run and the still longer tour destroying the old training without replacing it by a new one—then the gaps in the actor's cultivation and the corresponding atrophied patches in his brain would call almost for a Mission for his Intellectual Reclamation. Something of this kind might have happened in our own time—I am not sure that a few cases of it did not actually happen—if Ibsen had not come to the rescue. At all events, things had gone so far that the reigning generation of actor-managers were totally incapable of understanding Ibsen: his plays were not even grammar and spelling to them, much less drama. That what they found there was the life of their own time; that its ideas had been seething round their theatres for years past; that they themselves, chivalrously 'holding up the banner of the ideal' in the fool's paradise of theatrical romance and sentiment, had served Ibsen, as they formerly served Goethe, as reductions-to-absurdity of that divorce of the imagined life from the real which is the main peril of an age in which everybody is provided with the means of substituting reading and romancing for real living: all this was quite outside their comprehension. To them the new phenomenon was literally 'the Ibsen craze,' a thing bound to disappear whilst they were rubbing their eyes to make sure that they saw the absurd monster clearly. But that was exactly Mrs Theodore Wright's opportunity. A lady who had talked over matters with Karl Marx was not to be frightened by Pastor Manders. She created Mrs Alving as easily, sympathetically, and intelligently as Miss Winifred Emery or Miss Kate Rorke will create the heroine of the next adaptation from the French drama of 1840 by Mr Grundy; and by that one step she walked over the heads of the whole profession, I cannot say into the first intellectual rank as an English actress, because no such rank then existed, but into a niche in the history of the English stage the prominence of which would, if they could foresee it, very considerably astonish those who think that making history is as easy as making knights. (The point of this venomous allusion will not be missed. It is nothing to be a knight-actor now that there are two of them. When will Sir Henry Irving bid for at least a tiny memorial inscription in the neighborhood of Mrs Theodore Wright's niche?)

The remarkable success of Mr Courtenay Thorpe

in Ibsen parts in London lately, and the rumors as to the sensation created by his Oswald Alving in America, gave a good deal of interest to his first appearance here in that part. He has certainly succeeded in it to his heart's content, though this time his very large share of the original sin of picturesqueness and romanticism broke out so strongly that he borrowed little from realism except its pathologic horrors. Since Miss Robins's memorable exploit in Alan's Wife we have had nothing so harrowing on the stage; and it should be noted, for guidance in future experiments in audience torture, that in both instances the limit of the victim's susceptibility was reached before the end of the second act, at which exhaustion produced callousness. Mrs Alving, who spared us by making the best of her sorrows instead of the worst of them, preserved our sympathy up to the last; but Oswald, who shewed no mercy, might have been burnt alive in the orphanage without a throb of compassion. Mr Leonard Outram improved prodigiously on his old impersonation of Pastor Manders. In 1891 he was still comparatively fresh from the apprenticeship as a rhetorical actor which served him so well when he played Valence to Miss Alma Murray's Colombe for the Browning Society; and his stiff and cautious performance probably meant nothing but cleverly concealed bewilderment. This time Mr Outram really achieved the character, though he would probably please a popular audience better by making more of that babyish side of him which excites the indulgent affection of Mrs Alving, and less of the moral cowardice and futility posing as virtue and optimism which brings down on him the contemptuous judgment of Ibsen himself. Miss Kingsley's attractions, made as familiar to us by the pencil of Mr Rothenstein as Miss Dorothy Dene's by that of Leighton, were excellently fitted to Regina; and Mr Norreys Connell, after a somewhat unpromising beginning, played Engstrand with much zest and humor.

Hamlet

[2 *October* 1897]

THE Forbes Robertson Hamlet at the Lyceum is, very unexpectedly at that address, really not at all unlike Shakespear's play of the same name. I am quite certain I saw Reynaldo in it for a moment; and possibly I may have seen Voltimand and Cornelius; but just as the time for their scene arrived, my eye fell on the word 'Fortinbras' in the program, which so amazed me that I hardly know what I saw for the next ten minutes. Ophelia, instead of being a strenuously earnest and self-possessed young lady giving a concert and recitation for all she was worth, was mad—actually mad. The story of the play was perfectly intelligible, and quite took the attention of the audience off the principal actor at moments. What is the Lyceum coming to? Is it for this that Sir Henry Irving has invented a whole series of original romantic dramas, and given the credit of them without a murmur to the immortal bard whose profundity (as exemplified in the remark that good and evil are mingled in our natures) he has just been pointing out to the inhabitants of Cardiff, and whose works have been no more to him than the word-quarry from which he has hewn and blasted the lines and titles of masterpieces which are really all his own? And now, when he has created by these means a reputation for

Shakespear, he no sooner turns his back for a moment on London than Mr Forbes Robertson competes with him on the boards of his own theatre by actually playing off against him the authentic Swan of Avon. Now if the result had been the utter exposure and collapse of that impostor, poetic justice must have proclaimed that it served Mr Forbes Robertson right. But alas! the wily William, by literary tricks which our simple Sir Henry has never quite understood, has played into Mr Forbes Robertson's hands so artfully that the scheme is a prodigious success. The effect of this success, coming after that of Mr Alexander's experiment with a Shakespearean version of As You Like It, makes it almost probable that we shall presently find managers vying with each other in offering the public as much of the original Shakespearean stuff as possible, instead of, as heretofore, doing their utmost to reassure us that everything that the most modern resources can do to relieve the irreducible minimum of tedium inseparable from even the most heavily cut acting version will be lavished on their revivals. It is true that Mr Beerbohm Tree still holds to the old scepticism, and calmly proposes to insult us by offering us Garrick's puerile and horribly caddish knockabout farce of Katharine and Petruchio for Shakespear's Taming of the Shrew; but Mr Tree, like all romantic actors, is incorrigible on the subject of Shakespear.

Mr Forbes Robertson is essentially a classical actor, the only one, with the exception of Mr Alexander, now established in London management. What I mean by classical is that he can present a dramatic hero as a man whose passions are those which have produced the philosophy, the poetry, the art, and the state-craft of the world, and not merely those which have produced its weddings, coroners' inquests, and executions. And that is just the sort of actor that Hamlet requires. A Hamlet who only understands his love for Ophelia, his grief for his father, his vindictive hatred of his uncle, his fear of ghosts, his impulse to snub Rosencrantz and Guildenstern, and the sportsman's excitement with which he lays the 'mousetrap' for Claudius, can, with sufficient force or virtuosity of execution, get a great reputation in the part, even though the very intensity of his obsession by these sentiments (which are common not only to all men but to many animals) shews that the characteristic side of Hamlet, the side that differentiates him from Fortinbras, is absolutely outside the actor's consciousness. Such a reputation is the actor's, not Hamlet's. Hamlet is not a man in whom 'common humanity' is raised by great vital energy to a heroic pitch, like Coriolanus or Othello. On the contrary, he is a man in whom the common personal passions are so superseded by wider and rarer interests, and so discouraged by a degree of critical self-consciousness which makes the practical efficiency of the instinctive man on the lower plane impossible to him, that he finds the duties dictated by conventional revenge and ambition as disagreeable a burden as commerce is to a poet. Even his instinctive sexual impulses offend his intellect; so that when he meets the woman who excites them he invites her to join him in a bitter and scornful criticism of their joint absurdity, demanding, 'What should such fellows as I do crawling between heaven and earth?' 'Why wouldst thou be a breeder of sinners?' and so forth, all of which is so completely beyond the poor girl that she naturally thinks him mad. And, indeed, there is a sense in which Hamlet is insane; for he trips over the mistake which lies on the threshold of intellectual self-consciousness: that of bringing life to utilitarian or hedonistic tests, thus treating it as a means instead of an end. Because Polonius is 'a foolish prating knave,' because Rosencrantz and Guildenstern are snobs, he kills them as remorselessly as he might kill a flea, shewing that he has no real belief in the superstitious reason which he gives for not killing himself, and in fact anticipating exactly the whole course of the intellectual history of Western Europe until Schopenhauer found the clue that Shakespear missed. But to call Hamlet mad because he did not anticipate Schopenhauer is like calling Marcellus mad because he did not refer the Ghost to the Psychical Society. It is in fact not possible for any actor to represent Hamlet as mad. He may (and generally does) combine some notion of his own of a man who is the creature of affectionate sentiment with the figure drawn by the lines of Shakespear; but the result is not a madman, but simply one of those monsters produced by the imaginary combination of two normal species, such as sphinxes, mermaids, or centaurs. And this is the invariable resource of the instinctive, imaginative, romantic actor. You will see him weeping bucketsful of tears over Ophelia, and treating the players, the gravedigger, Horatio, Rosencrantz, and Guildenstern as if they were mutes at his own funeral. But go and watch Mr Forbes Robertson's Hamlet seizing delightedly on every opportunity for a bit of philosophic discussion or artistic recreation to escape from the 'cursed spite' of revenge and love and other common troubles; see how he brightens up when the players come; how he tries to talk philosophy with Rosencrantz and Guildenstern the moment they come into the room; how he stops on his country walk with Horatio to lean over the churchyard wall and draw out the gravedigger whom he sees singing at his trade; how even his fits of excitement find expression in declaiming scraps of poetry; how the shock of Ophelia's death relieves itself in the fiercest intellectual contempt for Laertes's ranting, whilst an hour afterwards, when Laertes stabs him, he bears no malice for that at all, but embraces him gallantly and comradely; and how he dies as we forgive everything to Charles II for dying, and makes 'the rest is silence' a touchingly humorous apology for not being able to finish his business. See all that; and you have seen a true classical Hamlet. Nothing half so charming has been seen by this generation. It will bear seeing again and again.

And please observe that this is not a cold Hamlet. He is none of your logicians who reason their way through the world because they cannot feel their way through it: his intellect is the organ of his passion: his eternal self-criticism is as alive and thrilling as it can possibly be. The great soliloquy—no: I do NOT mean 'To be or not to be': I mean the dramatic one, 'O what a rogue and peasant slave am I!'—is as passionate in its scorn of brute passion as the most bull-necked affirmation or sentimental dilution of it could be. It comes out so without violence: Mr Forbes Robertson takes the part quite easily and spontaneously. There is none of that strange Lyceum intensity which comes from the perpetual struggle between Sir Henry Irving and Shakespear. The lines help Mr Forbes Robertson instead of getting in his way at every turn, because he wants to play Hamlet, and not to slip into his inky cloak a changeling of quite another race. We may miss the craft, the skill double-distilled by constant peril, the subtlety, the dark rays of heat generated by intense friction, the relentless parental tenacity and cunning with which Sir Henry nurses his own pet creations on Shakespearean food like a fox rearing its litter in the den of a lioness; but we get light, freedom, naturalness, credibility, and Shakespear. It is wonderful how easily everything comes right when you have the right man with the right mind for it—how the story tells itself, how the characters come to life, how even the failures in the cast cannot confuse you, though they may disappoint you. And Mr Forbes Robertson has certainly not escaped such failures, even in his own family. I strongly urge him to take a hint from Claudius and make a real ghost of Mr Ian Robertson at once; for there is no sort of use in going through that scene night after night with a Ghost so solidly, comfortably, and dogmatically alive as his brother. The voice is not a bad voice; but it is the voice of a man who does not believe in ghosts. Moreover, it is a hungry voice, not that of one who is past eating. There is an indescribable little complacent drop at the end of every line which no sooner calls up the image of purgatory by its words than by its smug elocution it convinces us that this particular penitent is cosily warming his shins and toasting his muffin at the flames instead of expiating his bad acting in the midst of them. His aspect and bearing are worse than his recitations. He beckons Hamlet away like a beadle summoning a timid candidate for the post of junior footman to the presence of the Lord Mayor. If I were Mr Forbes Robertson I would not stand that from any brother: I would cleave the general ear with horrid speech at him first. It is a pity; for the Ghost's part is one of the wonders of the play. And yet, until Mr Courtenay Thorpe divined it the other day, nobody seems to have had a glimpse of the reason why Shakespear would not trust anyone else with it, and played it himself. The weird music of that long speech which should be the spectral wail of a soul's bitter wrong crying from one world to another in the extremity of its torment, is invariably handed over to the most squaretoed member of the company, who makes it sound, not like Rossetti's Sister Helen, or even, to suggest a possible heavy treatment, like Mozart's statue-ghost, but like Chambers's Information for the People.

Still, I can understand Mr Ian Robertson, by sheer force of a certain quality of sententiousness in him, overbearing the management into casting him for the Ghost. What I cannot understand is why Miss Granville was cast for the Queen. It is like setting a fashionable modern mandolinist to play Haydn's sonatas. She does her best under the circumstances; but she would have been more fortunate had she been in a position to refuse the part.

On the other hand, several of the impersonations are conspicuously successful. Mrs Patrick Campbell's Ophelia is a surprise. The part is one which has hitherto seemed incapable of progress. From generation to generation actresses have, in the mad scene, exhausted their musical skill, their ingenuity in devising fantasias in the language of flowers, and their intensest powers of portraying anxiously earnest sanity. Mrs Patrick Campbell, with that complacent audacity of hers which is so exasperating when she is doing the wrong thing, this time does the right thing by making Ophelia really mad. The resentment of the audience at this outrage is hardly to be described. They long for the strenuous mental grasp and attentive coherence of Miss Lily Hanbury's conception of maiden lunacy; and this wandering, silly, vague Ophelia, who no sooner catches an emotional impulse than it drifts away from her again, emptying her voice of its tone in a way that makes one shiver, makes them horribly uncomfortable. But the effect on the play is conclusive. The shrinking discomfort of the King and Queen, the rankling grief of Laertes, are created by it at once; and the scene, instead of being a pretty interlude coming in just when a little relief from the inky cloak is welcome, touches us with a chill of the blood that gives it its right tragic power and dramatic significance. Playgoers naturally murmur when something that has always been pretty becomes painful; but the pain is good for them, good for the theatre, and good for the play. I doubt whether Mrs Patrick Campbell fully appreciates the dramatic value of her quite simple and original sketch—it is only a sketch—of the part; but in spite of the occasional triviality of its execution and the petulance with which it has been received, it seems to me to settle finally in her favor the question of her right to the very important place which Mr Forbes Robertson has assigned to her in his enterprises.

I did not see Mr Bernard Gould play Laertes: he was indisposed when I returned to town and hastened to the Lyceum; but he was replaced very creditably by Mr Frank Dyall. Mr Martin Harvey is the best Osric I have seen: he plays Osric from Osric's own point of view, which is, that Osric is a gallant and distinguished courtier, and not, as usual, from Hamlet's, which is that Osric is 'a waterfly.' Mr Harrison Hunter hits off the modest, honest Horatio capitally; and Mr Willes is so good a Gravedigger that I venture to suggest to him that he should carry his work a little further, and not virtually cease to concern himself with the play when he has spoken his last line and handed Hamlet the skull. Mr Cooper Cliffe is not exactly a subtle Claudius; but he looks as if he had stepped out of a picture by Madox Brown, and plays straightforwardly on his very successful appearance. Mr Barnes makes Polonius robust and elderly instead of aged and garrulous. He is good in the scenes where Polonius appears as a man of character and experience; but the senile exhibitions of courtierly tact do not match these, and so seem forced and farcical.

Mr Forbes Robertson's own performance has a continuous charm, interest, and variety which are the result not only of his well-known grace and accomplishment as an actor, but of a genuine delight—the rarest thing on our stage—in Shakespear's art, and a natural familiarity with the plane of his imagination. He does not superstitiously worship William: he enjoys him and understands his methods of expression. Instead of cutting every line that can possibly be spared, he retains every gem, in his own part or anyone else's, that he can make time for in a spiritedly brisk performance lasting three hours and a half with very short intervals. He does not utter half a line; then stop to act; then go on with another half line; and then stop to act again, with the clock running away with Shakespear's chances all the time. He plays as Shakespear should be played, on the line and to the line, with the utterance and acting simultaneous, inseparable and in fact identical. Not for a moment is he solemnly conscious of Shakespear's reputation or of Hamlet's momentousness in literary history: on the contrary, he delivers us from all these boredoms instead of heaping them on us. We forgive him the platitudes, so engagingly are they delivered. His novel and astonishingly effective and touching treatment of the final scene is an inspiration, from the fencing match onward. If only Fortinbras could also be inspired with sufficient force and brilliancy to rise to the warlike splendor of his helmet, and make straight for that throne like a man who intended to keep it against all comers, he would leave nothing to be desired. How many generations of Hamlets, all thirsting to outshine their competitors in effect and originality, have regarded Fortinbras, and the clue he gives to this kingly death for Hamlet, as a wildly unpresentable blunder of the poor foolish old Swan, than whom they all knew so much better! How sweetly they have died in that faith to slow music, like Little Nell in The Old Curiosity Shop! And now how completely Mr Forbes Robertson has bowled them all out by being clever enough to be simple.

By the way, talking of slow music, the sooner Mr Hamilton Clark's romantic Irving music is stopped, the better. Its effect in this Shakespearean version of the play is absurd. The four Offenbachian young women in tights should also be abolished, and the part of the player-queen given to a man. The courtiers should be taught how flatteringly courtiers listen when a king shews off his wisdom in wise speeches to his nephew. And that nice wooden beach on which the Ghost walks would be the better for a seaweedy looking cloth on it, with a handful of shrimps and a pennorth of silver sand.

Shakespear and Mr Barrie

THE TEMPEST. *Performance by the Elizabethan Stage Society at the Mansion House, 5 November 1897.*

THE LITTLE MINISTER. *A play in four acts. By* J. M. Barrie, *founded on his novel of that name. Haymarket Theatre, 6 November 1897.*

[13 *November* 1897]

IT was a curious experience to see The Tempest one night and The Little Minister the next. I should like to have taken Shakespear to the Haymarket play. How well he would have recognized it! For he also once had to take a popular novel; make a shallow, unnatural, indulgent, pleasant, popular drama of it; and hand it to the theatre with no hint of his feelings except the significant title As You Like It. And we have not even the wit to feel the snub, but go on complacently talking of the manufacture of Rosalinds and Orlandos (a sort of thing that ought really to be done in a jam factory) as 'delineation of character' and the like. One feels Shakespear's position most strongly in the plays written after he had outgrown his interest in the art of acting and given up the idea of educating the public. In Hamlet he is quite enthusiastic about naturalness in the business of the stage, and makes Hamlet hold forth about it quite Wagnerianly: in Cymbeline and The Tempest he troubles himself so little about it that he actually writes down the exasperating clownish interruptions he once denounced; brings on the god in the car; and, having indulged the public in matters which he no longer set any store by, took it out of them in poetry.

The poetry of The Tempest is so magical that it would make the scenery of a modern theatre ridiculous. The methods of the Elizabethan Stage Society (I do not commit myself to their identity with those of the Elizabethan stage) leave to the poet the work of conjuring up the isle 'full of noises, sounds and sweet airs.' And I do not see how this plan can be beaten. If Sir Henry Irving were to put the play on at the Lyceum next season (why not, by the way?), what could he do but multiply the expenditure enormously, and spoil the illusion? He would give us the screaming violin instead of the harmonious viol; 'characteristic' music scored for wood-wind and percussion by Mr German instead of Mr Dolmetsch's pipe and tabor; an expensive and absurd stage ship; and some windless, airless, changeless, soundless, electric-lit, wooden-floored mockeries of the haunts of Ariel. They would cost more; but would they be an improvement on the Mansion House arrangement? Mr Poel says frankly, 'See that singers' gallery up there! Well, let's pretend that it's the ship.' We agree; and the thing is done. But how could we agree to such a pretence with a stage ship? Before it we should say, 'Take that thing away: if our imagination is to create a ship, it must not be contradicted by something that apes a ship so vilely as to fill us with denial and repudiation of its imposture.' The singing gallery makes no attempt to impose on us: it disarms criticism by unaffected submission to the facts of the case, and throws itself honestly on our fancy, with instant success. In the same way a rag doll is fondly nursed by a child who can only stare at a waxen simulacrum of infancy. A superstitious person left to himself will see a ghost in every ray of moonlight on the wall and every old coat hanging on a nail; but make up a really careful, elaborate, plausible, picturesque, bloodcurdling ghost for him, and his cunning grin will proclaim that he sees through it at a glance. The reason is, not that a man can *always* imagine things more vividly than art can present them to him, but that it takes an altogether extraordinary degree of art to compete with the pictures which the imagination makes when it is stimulated by such potent forces as the maternal instinct, superstitious awe, or the poetry of Shakespear. The dialogue between Gonzalo and that 'bawling, blasphemous, incharitable dog' the boatswain, would turn the House of Lords into a ship: in less than ten words—'What care these roarers for the name of king?'—you see the white horses and the billowing green mountains playing football with crown and purple. But the Elizabethan method would not do for a play like The White Heather, excellent as it is of its kind. If Mr Poel, on the strength of the Drury Lane dialogue, were to leave us to imagine the singers' gallery to be the bicycling ring in Battersea Park, or Boulter's Lock, we should flatly decline to imagine anything at all. It requires the nicest judgment to know exactly how much help the imagination wants. There is no general rule, not even for any particular author. You can do best without scenery in The Tempest and A Midsummer Night's Dream, because the best scenery you can get will only destroy the illusion created by the poetry; but it does not at all follow that scenery will not improve a representation of Othello. Maeterlinck's plays, requiring a mystical inscenation in the style of Fernand Knopf, would be nearly as much spoiled by Elizabethan treatment as by Drury Lane treatment. Modern melodrama is so dependent on the most realistic scenery that a representation would suffer far less by the omission of the dialogue than of the scenery. This is why the manager who stages every play in the same way is a bad manager, even when he is an adept at his one way. A great deal of the distinction of the Lyceum productions is due to the fact that Sir Henry Irving, when the work in hand is at all within the limits of his sympathies, knows exactly how far to go in the matter of scenery. When he makes mistakes, they are almost always mistakes in stage management, by which he sacrifices the effect of some unappreciated passage of dialogue of which the charm has escaped him.

Though I was sufficiently close to the stage at The Tempest to hear, or imagine I heard, every word of the dialogue, yet it was plain that the actors were not eminent after-dinner speakers, and had consequently never received in that room the customary warning to speak to the second pillar on the right of the door, on pain of not being heard. Though they all spoke creditably, and some of them remarkably well, they took matters rather too easily, with the result that the quieter passages were inaudible to a considerable number of the spectators. I mention the matter because the Elizabethan Stage Society is hardly yet alive to the acoustic difficulties raised by the lofty halls it performs in. They are mostly troublesome places for a speaker; for if he shouts, his vowels make such a roaring din that his consonants are indistinguishable; and if he does not, his voice does not travel far enough. They are too resonant for noisy speakers and too vast for gentle ones. A clean, athletic articulation, kept up without any sentimental or indolent relaxations, is indispensable as a primary physical accomplishment for the Elizabethan actor who 'takes to the halls.'

The performance went without a hitch. Mr Dolmetsch looked after the music; and the costumes were worthy of the reputation which the Society has made for itself in this particular. Ariel, armless and winged in his first incarnation, was not exactly a tricksy sprite; for as the wing arrangement acted as a strait waistcoat, he had to be content with the effect he made as a living picture. This disability on his part was characteristic of the whole performance, which had to be taken in a somewhat low key and slow tempo, with a minimum of movement. If any attempt had been made at the impetuosity and liveliness for which the English experts of the sixteenth century were famous throughout Europe, it would have not only failed, but prevented the performers from attaining what they did attain, very creditably, by a more modest ambition.

To our host the Lord Mayor I take off my hat. When I think of the guzzling horrors I have seen in that room, and the insufferable oratory that has passed through my head from ear to ear on its way to the second pillar on the right of the door (which has the advantage of being stone deaf), I hail with sincere gratitude the first tenant of the Mansion House who had bidden me to an entertainment worthy of the first magistrate of a great city, instead of handing me over to an army of waiters to be dealt with as one 'whose god is his belly.'

The Little Minister is a much happier play than The Tempest. Mr Barrie has no impulse to throw his adaptation of a popular novel at the public head with a sarcastic title, because he has written the novel himself, and thoroughly enjoys it. Mr Barrie is a born storyteller; and he sees no further than his stories

—conceives any discrepancy between them and the world as a short-coming on the world's part, and is only too happy to be able to rearrange matters in a pleasanter way. The popular stage, which was a prison to Shakespear's genius, is a playground to Mr Barrie's. At all events he does the thing as if he liked it, and does it very well. He has apparently no eye for human character; but he has a keen sense of human qualities, and he produces highly popular assortments of them. He cheerfully assumes, as the public wish him to assume, that one endearing quality implies all endearing qualities, and one repulsive quality all repulsive qualities: the exceptions being comic characters, who are permitted to have 'weaknesses,' or stern and terrible souls who are at once understood to be saving up some enormous sentimentality for the end of the last act but one. Now if there is one lesson that real life teaches us more insistently than another, it is that we must not infer one quality from another, or even rely on the constancy of ascertained qualities under all circumstances. It is not only that a brave and good-humored man may be vain and fond of money; a lovable woman greedy, sensual, and mendacious; a saint vindictive; and a thief kindly; but these very terms are made untrustworthy by the facts that the man who is brave enough to venture on personal combat with a prizefighter or a tiger may be abjectly afraid of ghosts, mice, women, a dentist's forceps, public opinion, cholera epidemics, and a dozen other things that many timorous mortals face resignedly enough; the man who is stingy to miserliness with coin, and is the despair of waiters and cabmen, gives thousands (by cheque) to public institutions; the man who eats oysters by the hundred and legs of mutton by the dozen for wagers, is in many matters temperate, moderate, and even abstemious; and men and women alike, though they behave with the strictest conventional propriety when tempted by advances from people whom they do not happen to like, are by no means so austere with people whom they do like. In romance, all these 'inconsistencies' are corrected by replacing human nature by conventional assortments of qualities. When Shakespear objected to this regulation, and wrote All's Well in defiance of it, his play was not acted. When he succumbed, and gave us the required assortment 'as we like it,' he was enormously successful. Mr Barrie has no scruples about complying. He is one with the public in the matter, and makes a pretty character as a milliner makes a pretty bonnet, by 'matching' the materials. And why not, if everybody is pleased?

To that question I reply by indignantly refusing, as a contemporary of Master-Builder Solness, to be done out of my allowance of 'salutary self-torture.' People dont go to the theatre to be pleased: there are a hundred cheaper, less troublesome, more effective pleasures than an uncomfortable gallery can offer. We are led there by our appetite for drama, which is no more to be satisfied by sweetmeats than our appetite for dinner is to be satisfied with meringues and raspberry vinegar. One likes something solid; and that, I suppose, is why heroes and heroines with assorted qualities are only endurable when the author has sufficient tact and comic force to keep up an affectionate undercurrent of fun at their expense and his own. That was how Shakespear pulled his amiable fictions through; that is how Mr Carton does it; that is how Mr Barrie does it. Dickens, with his fundamental seriousness and social conscience always at war with his romantic instincts and idealism, and even with his unconquerable sense of humor, made desperate efforts to take his assorted heroines quite seriously by resolutely turning off the fun, with a result—Agnes Wickfield, Esther Summerson, and so forth—so utterly unbearable that they stand as a warning to all authors that it is dangerous to be serious unless you have something real to be serious about, even when you are a great genius. Happily, Mr Barrie is not serious about his little minister and his little minister's Babby. At most he is affectionate, which is quite a different thing. The twain are nine-tenths fun and the other tenth sentiment, which makes a very toothsome combination.

I should explain, however, that I took care not to read the novel before seeing the play; and I have not had time to read it since. But it is now clear to me that Mr Barrie has depended on the novel to make his hero and heroine known to the playgoer. Their parts consist of a string of amusing and sometimes touching trivialities; but it is easy to divine that the young minister's influence over his elders, and perhaps Babby's attraction for him, are more fully accounted for in the book. I should hope also that Rob Dow and the chief elder, who in the play are machine-made after a worn-out pattern, are more original and natural in the novel. Otherwise, I found the work self-sufficing.

As a success for the Haymarket Theatre the play has fulfilled and exceeded all expectation. It has every prospect of running into the next century. It is the first play produced under Mr Cyril Maude's own management that has given him a chance as an actor. It is quite characteristic of the idiotic topsyturviness of our stage that Mr Maude, who has a remarkable charm of quaintly naïve youthfulness, should have been immediately pitched upon—nay, have pitched on himself—as a born impersonator of old men. All he asked from the author was a snuff-box, a set of grease paints, and a part not younger than sixty-five to make him perfectly happy. There was Mr Grundy's Sowing the Wind, for instance: Mr Maude was never more pleased with himself than when, after spending the afternoon in pencilling impossible wrinkles all over his face, he was crustily taking snuff as the old man in that play. The spectacle used to exasperate me to such a degree that nothing restrained me from hurling the nearest opera-glass at those wrinkles but the fear that, as I am unfortunately an incorrigibly bad shot, I might lay Miss Emery low, or maim Mr Brandon Thomas for life. I do declare that of all the infuriating absurdities that human perversity has evolved, this painted-on 'character-acting' is the only one that entirely justifies man-slaughter. It was not that Mr Cyril Maude did it badly; on the contrary, he did it very cleverly indeed: it was that he ought to have been doing something else. The plague of the stage at present is the intolerable stereotyping of the lover: he is always the same sort of young man, with the same cast of features, the same crease down his new trousers, the same careful manners, the same air of behaving and dressing like a gentleman for the first time in his life and being overcome with the novelty and importance of it. Mr Maude was just the man to break this oppressive fashion; and instead of doing it, he amused himself with snuff, and crustiness, and wrinkles as aforesaid, perhaps for the sake of the novelty which gentility could not offer him. As the little minister he at last plays without disguise, and with complete success. He is naturally shy at shewing himself to the public for the first time; but the shyness becomes him in the part; and I dare say he will run Mr Forbes Robertson hard for the rest of the season as a much-admired man. Miss Winifred Emery, as Babby, has a rare time of it. She plays with the part like a child, and amuses herself and the audience unboundedly. Her sudden assumption of Red-Robe dignity for a few minutes in the fourth act constitutes what I think may be described safely as the worst bit of acting the world has yet seen from a performer of equal reputation, considering that it is supposed to represent the conduct of a girl just out of the schoolroom; but she soon relapses into an abandonment to fun compared to which Miss Rehan's most reckless attacks of that nature are sedate. Mr Kinghorne is, I think, the best of the elders; but Mr Brandon Thomas and Mrs Brooke are in great force. There was a good deal of curiosity among the women in the audience to see Mr Barrie, because of his evident belief that he was shewing a deep insight into feminine character by representing Babby as a woman whose deepest instinct was to find a man for her master. At the end, when her husband announced his intention of caning her if she deserved it, she flung her arms round his neck and exclaimed ecstatically that he was the man for her. The inference that, with such an experience of the sex, Mr Barrie's personality must be little short of godlike, led to a vociferous call for him when the curtain fell. In response, Mr Harrison appeared, and got as far as 'Mr Barrie is far too modest a man—' when he was interrupted by a wild shriek of laughter. I do not doubt that many amiable ladies may from time to time be afflicted with the fancy that there is something voluptuous in getting thrashed by a man.

In the classes where the majority of married women get that fancy gratified with excessive liberality, it is not so persistent as Mr Barrie might think. I seriously suggest to him that the samples of his notion of 'womanliness' given by Babby are nothing but silly travesties of that desire to find an entirely trustworthy leader which is common to men and women.

Sir A. C. Mackenzie's overture was drowned by the conversation, which was energetically led by the composer and Sir George Lewis. But I caught some scraps of refreshingly workmanlike polyphony; and the *mélodrame* at the beginning of the garden scene was charming.

Hamlet Revisited

[18 *December* 1897]

PUBLIC feeling has been much harrowed this week by the accounts from America of the 144 hours' bicycle race; but what are the horrors of such an exhibition compared to those of the hundred-nights run of Hamlet! On Monday last I went, in my private capacity, to witness the last lap but five of the Lyceum trial of endurance. The performers had passed through the stage of acute mania, and were for the most part sleep-walking in a sort of dazed blank-verse dream. Mr Barnes raved of some New England maiden named Affection Poo; the subtle distinctions made by Mrs Patrick Campbell between madness and sanity had blurred off into a placid idiocy turned to favor and to prettiness; Mr Forbes Robertson, his lightness of heart all gone, wandered into another play at the words 'Sleep? No more!' which he delivered as, 'Sleep no more.' Fortunately, before he could add 'Macbeth does murder sleep,' he relapsed into Hamlet and saved the situation. And yet some of the company seemed all the better for their unnatural exercise. The King was in uproarious spirits; and the Ghost, always comfortable, was now positively pampered, his indifference to the inconveniences of purgatory having developed into a bean-fed enjoyment of them. Fortinbras, as I judged, had sought consolation in religion: he was anxious concerning Hamlet's eternal welfare; but his general health seemed excellent. As Mr Gould did not play on the occasion of my first visit, I could not compare him with his former self; but his condition was sufficiently grave. His attitude was that of a castaway mariner who has no longer hope enough to scan the horizon for a sail; yet even in this extremity his unconquerable generosity of temperament had not deserted him. When his cue came, he would jump up and lend a hand with all his old alacrity and resolution. Naturally the players of the shorter parts had suffered least: Rosencrantz and Guildenstern were only beginning to enjoy themselves; and Bernardo (or was it Marcellus?) was still eagerly working up his part to concert pitch. But there could be no mistake as to the general effect. Mr Forbes Robertson's exhausting part had been growing longer and heavier on his hands; whilst the support of the others had been falling off; so that he was keeping up the charm of the representation almost single-handed just when the torturing fatigue and monotony of nightly repetition had made the task most difficult. To the public, no doubt, the justification of the effort is its success. There was no act which did not contain at least one scene finely and movingly played; indeed some of the troubled passages gained in verisimilitude by the tormented condition of the actor. But Hamlet is a very long play; and it only seems a short one when the high-mettled comedy with which it is interpenetrated from beginning to end leaps out with all the lightness and spring of its wonderful loftiness of temper. This was the secret of the delighted surprise with which the public, when the run began, found that Hamlet, far from being a funereally classical bore, was full of a celestial gaiety and fascination. It is this rare vein that gives out first when the exigences of theatrical commerce force an actor to abuse it. A sentimental Hamlet can go on for two years, or ten for the matter of that, without much essential depreciation of the performance; but the actor who sounds Hamlet from the lowest note to the top of his compass very soon finds that compass contracting at the top. On Monday night the first act, the third act, and the fifth act from the entrance of Laertes onward, had lost little more than they had gained as far as Mr Forbes Robertson was concerned; but the second act, and the colloquy with the gravedigger, which were the triumphs of the representation in its fresher stages, were pathetically dulled, with the result that it could no longer be said that the length of the play was forgotten.

The worst of the application of the long-run system to heroic plays is that, instead of killing the actor, it drives him to limit himself to such effects as he can repeat to infinity without committing suicide. The opposite system, in its extreme form of the old stock company playing two or three different pieces every night, led to the same evasion in a more offensive form. The recent correspondence in the Morning Post on The Stage as a Profession, to which I have myself luminously contributed, has produced the usual fallacious eulogies of the old stock company as a school of acting. You can no more prevent contributors to public correspondences falling into this twenty-times-exploded error than from declaring that duelling was a school of good manners, that the lash suppressed garotting, or any other of the gratuitous ignorances of the amateur sociologist. The truth is, it is just as impossible for a human being to study and perform a new part of any magnitude every day as to play Hamlet for a hundred consecutive nights. Nevertheless, if an actor is required to do these things, he will find some way out of the difficulty without refusing. The stock actor solved the problem by adopting a 'line': for example, if his 'line' was old age, he acquired a trick of doddering and speaking in a cracked voice: if juvenility, he swaggered and effervesced. With these accomplishments, eked out by a few rules of thumb as to wigs and face-painting, one deplorable step dance, and one still more deplorable 'combat,' he 'swallowed' every part given to him in a couple of hours, and regurgitated it in the evening over the footlights, always in the same manner, however finely the dramatist might have individualized it. His infamous incompetence at last swept him from the reputable theatres into the barns and booths; and it was then that he became canonized, in the imagination of a posterity that had never suffered from him, as the incarnation of the one quality in which he was quite damnably deficient: to wit, versatility. His great contribution to dramatic art was the knack of earning a living for fifty years on the stage without ever really acting, or either knowing or caring for the difference between the Comedy of Errors and Box and Cox.

A moment's consideration will shew that the results

of the long-run system at its worst are more bearable than the horrors of the past. Also, that even in point of giving the actor some chance of varying his work, the long-run system is superior, since the modern actor may at all events exhaust the possibilities of his part before it exhausts him, whereas the stock actor, having barely time to apply his bag of tricks to his daily task, never varies his treatment by a hair's breadth from one half century to another. The best system, of course, lies between these extremes. Take the case of the great Italian actors who have visited us, and whose acting is of an excellence apparently quite beyond the reach of our best English performers. We find them extremely chary of playing every night. They have a repertory containing plays which count as resting places for them. For example, Duse relieves Magda with Mirandolina just as our own Shakespearean star actors used to relieve Richard the Third and Othello with Charles Surface and Don Felix. But even with this mitigation no actor can possibly play leading parts of the first order six nights a week all the year round unless he underplays them, or routines them mechanically in the old stock manner, or faces a terrible risk of disablement by paralysis, or, finally, resorts to alcohol or morphia, with the usual penalties. What we want in order to get the best work is a repertory theatre with alternative casts. If, for instance, we could have Hamlet running at the Lyceum with Sir Henry Irving and Miss Ellen Terry on Thursdays and Saturdays, Mr Forbes Robertson and Mrs Patrick Campbell on Wednesdays and Fridays, and the other two days devoted to comedies in which all four could occasionally appear, with such comedians as Mr Charles Wyndham, Mr Weedon Grossmith, Mr Bourchier,

Mr Cyril Maude, and Mr Hawtrey, then we should have a theatre which we could invite serious people to attend without positively insulting them. I am aware that the precise combination which I have named is not altogether a probable one at present; but there is no reason why we should not at least turn our faces in that direction. The actor-manager system, which has hitherto meant the star system carried to its utmost possible extreme, has made the theatre so insufferable that, now that its monopoly has been broken up by the rise of the suburban theatres, there is a distinct weakening of the jealous and shameless individualism of the last twenty years, and a movement towards combination and co-operation.

By the way, is it quite prudent to start a public correspondence on the Stage as a Profession? Suppose someone were to tell the truth about it!

Tappertit on Cæsar

JULIUS CÆSAR. *Her Majesty's Theatre, 22 January* 1898.

[29 *January* 1898]

THE truce with Shakespear is over. It was only possible whilst Hamlet was on the stage. Hamlet is the tragedy of private life—nay, of individual bachelor-poet life. It belongs to a detached residence, a select library, an exclusive circle, to no occupation, to fathomless boredom, to impenitent mugwumpism, to the illusion that the futility of these things is the futility of existence, and its contemplation philosophy: in short, to the dream-fed gentlemanism of the age which Shakespear inaugurated in English literature: the age, that is, of the rising middle class bringing into power the ideas taught it by its servants in the kitchen, and its fathers in the shop—ideas now happily passing away as the onslaught of modern democracy offers to the kitchen-taught and home-bred the alternative of achieving a real superiority or going ignominiously under in the class conflict.

It is when we turn to Julius Cæsar, the most splendidly written political melodrama we possess, that we realize the apparently immortal author of Hamlet as a man, not for all time, but for an age only, and that, too, in all solidly wise and heroic aspects, the most despicable of all the ages in our history. It is impossible for even the most judicially minded critic to look without a revulsion of indignant contempt at this travestying of a great man as a silly braggart, whilst the pitiful gang of mischief-makers who destroyed him are lauded as statesmen and patriots. There is not a single sentence uttered by Shakespear's Julius Cæsar that is, I will not say worthy of him, but even worthy of an average Tammany boss. Brutus is nothing but a familiar type of English suburban preacher: politically he would hardly impress the Thames Conservancy Board. Cassius is a vehemently assertive nonentity. It is only when we come to Antony, unctuous voluptuary and self-seeking sentimental demagogue, that we find Shakespear in his depth; and in his depth, of course, he is superlative. Regarded as a crafty stage job, the play is a triumph: rhetoric, claptrap, effective gushes of emotion, all the devices of the popular playwright, are employed with a profusion of power that almost breaks their backs. No doubt there are slips and slovenliness of the kind that careful revisers eliminate; but they count for so little in the mass of accomplishment that it is safe to say that the dramatist's art can be carried no further on that plane. If Goethe, who understood Cæsar and the significance of his death—'the most senseless of deeds' he called it—had treated the subject, his conception of it would have been as superior to Shakespear's as St John's Gospel is to the Police News; but his treatment could not have been more magnificently successful. As far as sonority, imagery, wit, humor, energy of imagination, power over language, and a whimsically keen eye for idiosyncrasies can make a dramatist, Shakespear was the king of dramatists. Unfortunately, a man may have them all, and yet conceive high affairs of state exactly as Simon Tappertit did. In one of the scenes in Julius Cæsar a conceited poet bursts into the tent of Brutus and Cassius, and exhorts them not to quarrel with one another. If Shakespear had been able to present his play to the ghost of the great Julius, he would probably have had much the same reception. He certainly would have deserved it.

When it was announced that Mr Tree had resolved to give special prominence to the character of Cæsar in his acting version, the critics winked, and concluded simply that the actor-manager was going to play Antony and not Brutus. Therefore I had better say that Mr Tree must stand acquitted of any belittlement of the parts which compete so strongly with his own. Before going to Her Maesty's I was curious enough to block out for myself a division of the play into three acts; and I found that Mr Tree's division corresponded exactly with mine. Mr Waller's opportunities as Brutus, and Mr McLeay's as Cassius, are limited only by their own ability to take advantage of them; and Mr Louis Calvert figures as boldly in the public eye as he did in his own production of Antony and Cleopatra last year at Manchester. Indeed, Mr Calvert is the only member of the company who achieves an unequivocal success. The preference expressed in the play by Cæsar for fat men may, perhaps, excuse Mr Calvert for having again permitted himself to expand after his triumphant reduction of his girth for his last appearance in London. However, he acted none the worse: in fact, nobody else acted so skilfully or originally. The others, more heavily burdened, did their best, quite in the spirit of the man who had never played the fiddle, but had no doubt he could if he tried. Without oratory, without style, without specialized vocal training, without any practice worth mentioning, they assaulted the play with cheerful self-sufficiency, and gained great glory by the extent to which, as a masterpiece of the playwright's trade, it played itself. Some small successes were not lacking. Cæsar's nose was good: Calpurnia's bust was worthy of her: in such parts Garrick and Siddons could have achieved no more. Miss Evelyn Millard's Roman matron in the style of Richardson—Cato's daughter as Clarissa—was an unlooked-for novelty; but it cost a good deal of valuable time to get in the eighteenth century between the lines of the first B.C. By operatic convention—the least appropriate of all conventions—the boy Lucius was played by Mrs Tree, who sang Sullivan's ultra-nineteenth-century Orpheus with his Lute, modulations and all, to a pizzicato accompaniment supposed to be played on a lyre with eight open and unstoppable strings, a feat complexly and absurdly impossible. Mr Waller, as Brutus, failed in the first half of the play. His intention clearly was to represent Brutus as a man superior to fate and circumstance; but the effect he produced was one of insensibility. Nothing could have been more unfortunate; for it is through the sensibility of Brutus that the audience have to learn what they cannot learn from the phlegmatic pluck of Casca or the narrow vindictiveness of Cassius: that is, the terrible momentousness, the harrowing anxiety and dread, of the impending catastrophe. Mr Waller left that function to the thunderstorm. From the death of Cæsar onward he was better; and his appearance throughout was effective; but at best his sketch was a water-color one. Mr Franklyn McLeay carried off the honors of the evening by his deliberate staginess and imposing assumptiveness: that is, by as much of the grand style as our playgoers now understand; but in the last act he was monotonously violent, and died the death of an incorrigible poseur, not of a noble Roman. Mr Tree's memory failed him as usual; and a good deal of the technical part of his work was botched and haphazard, like all Shakespearean work nowadays; nevertheless, like Mr Calvert, he made the audience believe in the reality of the character before them. But it is impossible to praise his performance in detail. I cannot recall any single passage in the scene after the murder that was well done: in fact, he only secured an effective curtain by bringing Calpurnia on the stage to attitudinize over Cæsar's body. To say that the demagogic oration in the Forum produced its effect is nothing; for its effect is inevitable, and Mr Tree neither made the most of it nor handled it with any pretence of mastery or certainty. But he was not stupid, nor inane, nor Bard-of-Avon ridden; and he contrived to interest the audience in Antony instead of trading on their ready-made interest in Mr Beerbohm Tree. And for that many sins may be forgiven him nowadays, when the playgoer, on first nights at all events, goes to see the cast rather than the play.

What is missing in the performance, for want of the specific Shakespearean skill, is the Shakespearean music. When we come to those unrivalled grandiose passages in which Shakespear turns on the full organ, we want to hear the sixteen-foot pipes booming, or, failing them (as we often must, since so few actors are naturally equipped with them), the ennobled tone, and the tempo suddenly steadied with the majesty of deeper purpose. You have, too, those moments when the verse, instead of opening up the depths of sound, rises to its most brilliant clangor, and the lines ring like a thousand trumpets. If we cannot have these effects, or if we can only have genteel drawing room arrangements of them, we cannot have Shakespear; and that is what is mainly the matter at Her Majesty's: there are neither trumpets nor pedal pipes there. The conversation is metrical and emphatic in an elocutionary sort of way; but it makes no distinction between the arid prairies of blank verse which remind one of Henry VI at its crudest, and the places where the morass suddenly piles itself into a mighty mountain. Cassius in the first act has a twaddling forty-line speech, base in its matter and mean in its measure, followed immediately by the magnificent torrent of rhetoric, the first burst of true Shakespearean music in the play, beginning—

> Why, man, he doth bestride the narrow world
> Like a Colossus, and we petty men
> Walk under his huge legs and peep about
> To find ourselves dishonorable graves.

I failed to catch the slightest change of elevation or reinforcement of feeling when Mr McLeay passed from one to the other. His tone throughout was dry; and it never varied. By dint of energetic, incisive articulation, he drove his utterances harder home than the others; but the best lines seemed to him no more than the worst: there were no heights and depths, no contrast of black thunder-cloud and flaming lightning flash, no stirs and surprises. Yet he was not inferior in oratory to the rest. Mr Waller certainly cannot be reproached with dryness of tone; and his delivery of the speech in the Forum was perhaps the best piece of formal elocution we got; but he also kept at much the same level throughout, and did not at any moment attain to anything that could be called grandeur. Mr Tree, except for a conscientiously desperate effort to cry havoc and let slip the dogs of war in the robustious manner, with no better result than to all but extinguish his voice, very sensibly left oratory out of the question, and tried conversational sincerity, which answered so well that his delivery of 'This was the noblest Roman of them all' came off excellently.

The real hero of the revival is Mr Alma Tadema. The scenery and stage coloring deserve everything that has been said of them. But the illusion is wasted by want of discipline and want of thought behind the scenes. Every carpenter seems to make it a point of honor to set the cloths swinging in a way that makes Rome reel and the audience positively seasick. In Brutus's house the door is on the spectators' left: the knocks on it come from the right. The Roman soldiers take the field each man with his two javelins neatly packed up like a fishing-rod. After a battle, in which they are supposed to have made the famous Roman charge, hurling these javelins in and following them up sword in hand, they come back carrying the javelins still undisturbed in their rug-straps, in perfect trim for a walk-out with the nursery-maids of Philippi.

The same want of vigilance appears in the acting version. For example, though the tribunes Flavius and Marullus are replaced by two of the senators, the lines referring to them by name are not altered. But the oddest oversight is the retention in the tent scene of the obvious confusion of the original version of the play, in which the death of Portia was announced to Brutus by Messala, with the second version, into which the quarrel scene was written to strengthen the fourth act. In this version Brutus, already in possession of the news, reveals it to Cassius. The play has come down to us with the two alternative scenes strung together; so that Brutus's reception of Messala's news, following his own revelation of it to Cassius, is turned into a satire on Roman fortitude, the suggestion being that the secret of the calm with which a noble Roman received the most terrible tidings in public was that it had been carefully imparted to him in private beforehand. Mr Tree has not noticed this; and the two scenes are gravely played one after the other at Her Majesty's. This does not matter much to our playgoers, who never venture to use their common sense when Shakespear is in question; but it wastes time. Mr Tree may without hesitation cut out Pindarus and Messala, and go straight on from the bowl of wine to Brutus's question about Philippi.

The music, composed for the occasion by Mr Raymond Roze, made me glad that I had already taken care to acknowledge the value of Mr Roze's services to Mr Tree; for this time he has missed the Roman vein rather badly. To be a Frenchman was once no disqualification for the antique, because French musicians used to be brought up on Gluck as English ones were brought up on Handel. But Mr Roze composes as if Gluck had been supplanted wholly in his curriculum by Gounod and Bizet. If that prelude to the third act were an attempt to emulate the overtures to Alceste or Iphigenia I could have forgiven it. But to give us the soldiers' chorus from Faust, crotchet for crotchet and triplet for triplet, with nothing changed but the notes, was really too bad.

I am sorry I must postpone until next week all consideration of Mr Pinero's Trelawny of the Wells. The tragic circumstances under which I do are as follows. The manager of the Court Theatre, Mr Arthur Chudleigh, did not honor the Saturday Review with the customary invitation to the first performance. When a journal is thus slighted, it has no resource but to go to its telephone and frantically offer any terms to the box-offices for a seat for the first night. But on fashionable occasions the manager is always master of the situation: there are never any seats to be had except from himself. It was so on this occasion; and the Saturday Review was finally brought to its knees at the feet of the Sloane Square telephone. In response to a humble appeal, the instrument scornfully replied that 'three lines of adverse criticism were of no use to it.' Naturally my curiosity was excited to an extraordinary degree by the fact that the Court Theatre telephone, which knew all about Mr Pinero's comedy, should have such a low opinion of it as to be absolutely certain that it would deserve an unprecedentedly contemptuous treatment at my hands. I instantly purchased a place for the fourth performance, Charlotte Corday and Julius Cæsar occupying my time on the second and third nights; and I am now in a position to assure that telephone that its misgivings were strangely unwarranted, and that, if it will excuse my saying so, it does not know a good comedietta when it sees one. Reserving my reasons for next week, I offer Mr Pinero my apologies for a delay which is not my own fault. (Will the Mining Journal please copy, as Mr Pinero reads no other paper during the current fortnight?)

I find this article has already run to such a length that I must postpone consideration of Charlotte Corday also, merely remarking for the present that I wish the play was as attractive as the heroine.

Mr Pinero's Past

TRELAWNY OF THE WELLS. *An original comedietta in four acts. By* Arthur W. Pinero. *Court Theatre,* 20 *January* 1898.

[5 *February* 1898]

CHARLOTTE CORDAY. *A drama in four acts. Anonymous. Adelphi Theatre,* 21 *January* 1898.

MR PINERO has not got over it yet. That fatal turning-point in life, the fortieth birthday, still oppresses him. In The Princess and the Butterfly he unbosomed himself frankly, making his soul's trouble the open theme of his play. But this was taken in such extremely bad part by myself and others (gnawed by the same sorrow) that he became shy on the subject, and, I take it, began to cast about for some indirect means of returning to it. It seems to have occurred to him at last that by simply shewing on the stage the fashions of forty years ago, the crinoline, the flounced skirt, the garibaldi, the turban hat, the chenille net, the horse-hair sofa, the peg-top trouser, and the 'weeper' whisker, the chord of memory could be mutely struck without wounding my vanity. The delicacy of this mood inspires the whole play, which has touched me more than anything else Mr Pinero has ever written.

But first let me get these old fashions—or rather these middle-aged fashions: after all, one is not Methuselah—off my mind. It is significant of the difference between my temperament and Mr Pinero's, that when he, as a little boy, first heard Ever of thee I'm fondly dreaming, he wept; whereas, at the same tender age, I simply noted with scorn the obvious plagiarism from Cheer, Boys, Cheer.

To me the sixties waft ballads by Virginia Gabriel and airs from Il Trovatore; but Mr Pinero's selection is none the less right; for Virginia Gabriel belonged to Cavendish Square and not to Bagnigge Wells; and Il Trovatore is still alive, biding its time to break out again when M. Jean de Reszke also takes to fondly dreaming.

The costumes at the Court Theatre are a mixture of caricature and realism. Miss Hilda Spong, whose good looks attain most happily to the 1860 ideal (Miss Ellen Terry had not then been invented), is dressed exactly after Leech's broadest caricatures of crinolined English maidenhood; whereas Miss Irene Vanbrugh clings to the finer authority of Millais' masterly illustrations to Trollope. None of the men are properly dressed: the 'lounge coat' which we all wear unblushingly today as a jacket, with its corners sloped away in front, and its length behind involving no friction with the seats of our chairs, then clung nervously to the traditions of the full coat, and was longer, straighter, rectangular—cornerder and franker as to the shoulders than Mr Pinero has been able to persuade the tailors of the Court Theatre to make it today. I imagine, too, that Cockney dialect has changed a good deal since then. Somewhere in the eighties, Mr Andrew Tuer pointed out in the Pall Mall Gazette that the conventional representations in fiction of London pronunciation had ceased to bear any recognizable relation to the actual speech of the coster and the flower-girl; and Mr Anstey, in Punch, was the first author to give general literary currency to Mr Tuer's new phonetics. The lingo of Sam Weller had by that time passed away from London, though suggestions of it may be heard even today no further off than Hounslow. Sir Henry Irving can no longer be ridiculed, as he was in the seventies, for substituting pure vowel sounds for the customary colloquial diphthongs; for the man in the street, without at all aiming at the virtuosity of our chief actor, has himself independently introduced a novel series of pure vowels. Thus *i* has become *aw*, and *ow ah*. In spite of Sir Henry, *o* has not been turned into a true vowel; but it has become a very marked *ow*, whilst the English *a* is changed to a flagrant *i*. There is, somewhere in the old files of All the Year Round a Dickensian description of an illiterate lady giving a reading. Had she been represented as saying, 'The scene tikes plice dahn in the Mawl En' Rowd' (takes place down in the Mile End Road) Dickens would apparently not have understood the sentence, which no Londoner with ears can now mistake. On these grounds, I challenge the pronunciation of Avonia Bunn, in the person of Miss Pattie Browne, as an anachronism.

I feel sure that if Avonia had made *so* rhyme to *thou* in the sixties, she would have been understood to have alluded to the feminine pig. On this point, however, my personal authority is not conclusive, as I did not reach London until the middle of the seventies. In England everything is twenty years out of date before it gets printed; and it may be that the change had been in operation long before it was accurately observed. It has also to be considered that the old literary school never dreamt of using its eyes or ears, and would invent descriptions of sights and sounds with an academic self-sufficiency which led later on to its death from acute and incurable imposture. Its ghost still walks in our resurrectionary reviewing enterprises, with precipitous effects on the circulation.

It is not in the nature of things possible that Mr Pinero's first variation on the theme of The Princess should be successfully acted by a modern London company. If he had scoured the provinces and America for elderly actors, thirty years out of date, and, after raising their wildest hopes by a London engagement, met them at rehearsal with the brutal announcement that they were only wanted to burlesque themselves, the thing might doubtless have been done. But every line of the play proclaims the author incapable of such heartlessness. There are only two members of the 'theatrical-folk' section of the cast who carry much conviction; and these are the two Robertsonians, to whom success comes only with the then new order. Miss Irene Vanbrugh is quite the woman who was then the New Woman; and Mr Paul Arthur, a contemporary American, only needs to seize the distinction made by the Atlantic between 'comedy' and 'cawmedy' to hit off the historical moment of the author of Caste to perfection. And

Miss Spong's fairness, fortunately, is universal enough to fit all the centuries and all the decades. But when we come to Ferdinand Gadd, the leading juvenile of The Wells, we find Mr Gerald Du Maurier in a difficulty. At his age his only chance of doing anything with the part is to suggest Sir Henry Irving in embryo. But Mr Pinero has not written it that way: he has left Ferdinand Gadd in the old groove as completely as Mr Crummles was. The result is that the part falls between two stools. The Telfers also miss the mark. Mr Athol Forde, the English creator of Kroll in Rosmersholm, is cut off from the sixties by a mighty gulf. Mrs Telfer's criticism of stage queens as being 'considered merely as parts, not worth a tinker's oath,' is not founded on the real experience of Mrs Saker, whose career has run on lighter lines. My own age in the sixties was so tender that I cannot pretend to know with any nicety what the 'principal boy' of the pantomime was like in her petticoats as a private person at that period; but I have a strong suspicion that she tended to be older and occasionally stouter than the very latest thing in that line; and it is the ultra-latest thing that Miss Pattie Browne has studied for Avonia Bunn. On the whole I doubt whether the Court company knows a scrap more about the professional atmosphere of the old 'Wells' than the audience.

The 'non-theatrical folk' came off better, with one exception. I know that Mr Dion Boucicault as Sir William Gower can claim a long-established stage convention in favor of his method of portraying crusty senility. But I have grown out of all endurance of that convention. It is no more like a real old man than a worn-out billiard table is like a meadow; and it wastes and worries and perverts the talent of an actor perfectly capable of making a sincere study of the part. We would all, I believe, willingly push the stage old man into the grave upon whose brink he has been cackling and doddering as long as we can remember him. If my vengeance could pursue him beyond the tomb, it should not stop there. But so far, at least, he shall go if my malice can prevail against him. Miss Isabel Bateman is almost charming as Sir William's ancient sister, and would be quite so if she also were not touched by the tradition that old age, in comedy, should always be made ridiculous. Mr James Erskine is generally understood to be a Lordling, and, as such, a feeble amateur actor. I am bound to say, in defence of a trampled aristocracy, that he rose superior to the accident of birth, and acted his part as well as it could be acted. This, I observe, is explained away on the ground that he has only to be himself on the stage. I can only reply that the accomplishment of a feat so extremely difficult entitles him to count the explanation as a very high compliment. Mr Sam Sothern gives us a momentary glimpse of Lord Dundreary: I wonder what the younger generation thinks of it? Miss Irene Vanbrugh, in the title part, which is not, to tell the truth, a difficult one in the hands of the right person, vanquishes it easily and successfully, getting quite outside those comic relief lines within which her lot has been so often cast.

As to the play itself, its charm, as I have already hinted, lies in a certain delicacy which makes me loth to lay my critical fingers on it. The life that it reproduces had been already portrayed in the real sixties by Dickens in his sketch of the Crummles company, and by Anthony Trollope in his chronicles of Barsetshire. I cannot pretend to think that Mr Pinero, in reverting to that period, has really had to turn back the clock as far as his own sympathies and ideals are concerned. It seems to me that the world is to him still the world of Johnny Eames and Lily Dale, Vincent Crummles and Newman Noggs: his Paula Tanquerays and Mrs Ebbsmiths appearing as pure aberrations whose external differences he is able to observe as far as they can be observed without the inner clue, but whose point of view he has never found. That is why Mr Pinero, as a critic of the advanced guard in modern life, is unendurable to me. When I meet a musician of the old school, and talk Rossini and Bellini and Donizetti, Spohr and Mendelssohn and Meyerbeer with him, we get on excellently together; for the music that is so empty and wooden and vapid and mechanical to the young lions of Bayreuth, is full of sentiment, imagination, and dramatic force to us. But when he begins to deplore the 'passing craze' for Wagner, and to explain the horrors and errors of the Bayreuth school: its lack of melody, its perpetual 'recitative,' its tearing discords, its noisy orchestration overwhelming and ruining the human voice, I get up and flee. The unsympathetic discourse about Wagner may be wittier than the sympathetic discourse about Donizetti; but that does not make it any the more tolerable to me, the speaker having passed from a subject he understands to one that has virtually no existence for him. It is just so with Mr Pinero. When he plays me the tunes of 1860, I appreciate and sympathize. Every stroke touches me: I dwell on the dainty workmanship shewn in the third and fourth acts: I rejoice in being old enough to know the world of his dreams. But when he comes to 1890, then I thank my stars that he does not read the Saturday Review. Please remember that it is the spirit and not the letter of the date that I insist on. The Benefit of the Doubt is dressed in the fashions of today; but it might have been written by Trollope. Trelawny of the Wells confessedly belongs to the days of Lily Dale. And whenever Lily Dale and not Mrs Ebbsmith is in question, Mr Pinero may face with complete equanimity the risk of picking up the Saturday Review in mistake for the Mining Journal.

Very different are my sentiments towards the author of Charlotte Corday at the Adelphi, whoever he may be. He has missed a rare chance of giving our playgoers a lesson they richly deserve. Jean Paul Marat, 'people's friend' and altruist *par excellence*, was a man just after their own hearts—a man whose virtue consisted in burning indignation at the sufferings of others and an intense desire to see them balanced by an exemplary retaliation. That is to say, his morality was the morality of the melodrama, and of the gallery which applauds frantically when the hero knocks the villain down. It is only by coarsely falsifying Marat's character that he has been made into an Adelphi villain—nay, prevented from bringing down the house as an Adelphi hero, as he certainly would if the audience could be shewn the horrors that provoked him and the personal disinterestedness and sincerity with which he threw himself into a war of extermination against tyranny. Ibsen may have earned the right to prove by the example of such men as Marat that these virtues were the making of a scoundrel more mischievous than the most openly vicious aristocrat for whose head he clamored; but the common run of our playgoers will have none of Ibsen's morality, and as much of Marat's as our romantic dramatists can stuff them with. Charlotte Corday herself was simply a female Marat. She, too, hated tyranny and idealized her passionate instinct for bloody retaliation. There is the true tragic irony in Marat's death at her hand: it was not really murder: it was suicide—Marat slain by the spirit of Marat. No bad theme for a playwright capable of handling it!

What the Adelphi play must seem to anyone who understands this situation, I need not say. On its own conventional stage lines, it appears as a page of romantic history, exciting as the police intelligence is exciting, but not dramatic. Mr Kyrle Bellew's Marat is a made-up business, extremely disfiguring to himself, which could be done as well or better by any other actor in the very competent company. Mrs Brown Potter is everything that can be desired from the pictorial point of view (school of Delaroche); and her cleverness and diligence carry her successfully through all the theatrical business of the part. Miss Mabel Hackney and Mr Vibart gain some ground by their playing: the older hands do not lose any. But the play is of no real importance.

Beaumont and Fletcher

THE COXCOMB. *By* Beaumont *and* Fletcher. *Acted by the Elizabethan Stage Society in the Hall of the Inner Temple,* 10 *February* 1898.

THE DOVE-COT (JALOUSE). *From the French of* MM. Bisson *and* Leclerq. *The Duke of York's Theatre,* 12 *February* 1898.

[19 *February* 1898]

I CONFESS to a condescending tolerance for Beaumont and Fletcher. It was, to be sure, no merit of theirs that they were born late enough to come into the field enthusiastically conscious of their art in the full development to which Shakespear had brought it, instead of blundering upon its discovery like the earlier men. Still, merit or no merit, they were saved from the clumsy horseplay and butcherly rant of Marlowe as models of wit and eloquence, and from the resourceless tum-tum of his 'mighty line' as a standard for their verse. When one thinks of the donnish insolence and perpetual thick-skinned swagger of Chapman over his unique achievements in sublime balderdash, and the opacity that prevented Webster, the Tussaud laureate, from appreciating his own stupidity—when one thinks of the whole rabble of dehumanized specialists in elementary blank verse posing as the choice and master-spirits of an art that had produced the stories of Chaucer and the old mystery plays, and was even then pregnant with The Pilgrim's Progress, it is hard to keep one's critical blood cold enough to discriminate in favor of any Elizabethan whatever. Nothing short of a statue at Deptford to the benefactor of the human species who exterminated Marlowe, and the condemnation of Mr Swinburne to spend the rest of his life in selling photographs of it to American tourists, would meet the poetic justice of the case. We are not all, happily, victims of the literary aberration that led Charles Lamb to revive Elizabethanism as a modern cult. We forgive him his addiction to it as we forgive him his addiction to gin.

Unfortunately, Shakespear dropped into the middle of these ruffianly pedants; and since there was no other shop than theirs to serve his apprenticeship in, he had perforce to become an Elizabethan too. In such a school of falsehood, bloody-mindedness, bombast, and intellectual cheapness, his natural standard was inevitably dragged down, as we know to our cost; but the degree to which he dragged their standard up has saved them from oblivion. It makes one giddy to compare the execrable rottenness of the Jew of Malta with the humanity and poetry of the Merchant of Venice. Hamlet, Othello, and Iago are masterpieces beside Faustus, Bussy d'Amboise, and Bosola. After Shakespear, the dramatists were in the position of Spohr after Mozart. A ravishing secular art had been opened up to them, and was refining their senses and ennobling their romantic illusions and enthusiasms instead of merely stirring up their basest passions. Cultivated lovers of the beauties of Shakespear's art—true amateurs, in fact—took the place of the Marlovian crew. Such amateurs, let loose in a field newly reaped by a great master, have always been able to glean some dropped ears, and even to raise a brief aftermath. In this way the world has gained many charming and fanciful, though not really original, works of art—blank verse dramas after Shakespear, rhetorical frescoes after Raphael, fugues after Bach, operas after Mozart, symphonies after Beethoven, and so on. This, I take it, is the distinction between Marlowe and Company and the firm of Beaumont and Fletcher. The pair wrote a good deal that was pretty disgraceful; but at all events they had been educated out of the possibility of writing Titus Andronicus. They had no depth, no conviction, no religious or philosophic basis, no real power or seriousness—Shakespear himself was a poor master in such matters—but they were dainty romantic poets, and really humorous character-sketchers in Shakespear's popular style: that is, they neither knew nor cared anything about human psychology, but they could mimic the tricks and manners of their neighbors, especially the vulgarer ones, in a highly entertaining way.

The Coxcomb is not a bad sample of their art. Mr Poel has had to bowdlerize it in deference to the modesty of the barristers of the Inner Temple. For instance, Mercury's relations with Maria stop short of exacting her husband's crowning sacrifice to friendship; and when the three merry gentlemen make Riccardo too drunk to keep his appointment to elope with Viola, the purpose with which the four roysterers sally out into the street, much insisted on by Beaumont and Fletcher, is discreetly left to the guilty imagination of the more sophisticated spectators. With these exceptions the play was presented as fairly as could be expected.

The performance was one of the best the Elizabethan Stage Society has achieved. I confess that I anticipated failure in the part of Riccardo, who is not a human being, but an embodiment of the most delicate literary passion of Elizabethan romantic poetry. Miss Rehan, one felt, might have done something with it on the lines of her Viola in Twelfth Night; but then Miss Rehan was not available. The lady who was available did not allow her name to appear in the bill; and I have no idea who she is. But she certainly hit that part off to perfection, having, by a happy temperamental accident, the musical root of the poetic passion in her. Her performance was apparently quite original. There was no evidence in it of her ever having seen Miss Rehan act: if she suggested anybody, it was Calvé. Mr Sherbrooke's Mercury also was an excellent performance. The vivacity of his pantomime, and a trick of pronouncing his *d*'s and *t*'s foreign fashion, with the tongue against the teeth, raised some doubt as to whether he was quite as

English as his name; but his performance was none the worse. In delivering his asides he convinced me more than any of the rest that he had divined the method and style of the Elizabethan stage. I should like to say a special word about every one of the performers, but the program reminds me that there are no less than twenty-four of them; so I can only add hastily that Mr Poel himself played the Coxcomb; that Mr Paget Bowman spoke the prologue and played Valerio; that the Justice was impersonated by Mr J. H. Brewer, and not, as some supposed, by Sir Peter Edlin; that Miss Imogen Surrey played Viola and Miss Hepworth Valerio's mother; and that these and all the other parts, especially the tinker and his trull, and not forgetting Mr Leonard Howard's Alexander, come out quite vividly and intelligibly. I have no doubt some of the audience were bored; but the explanation of that is simple: they were the people who have no taste for Elizabethan drama. After all, you cannot plunge into these things absolutely without connoisseurship.

The most remarkable point in the adaptation of Jalouse at the Duke of York's Theatre is its recognition of the fact, often insisted on in these columns, that no English audience, however frivolous, can bear three acts of farcical comedy without weariness and demoralization. The Dove-cot is saved by the sentimentality of its second act. It almost invariably happens, when a play is altered to meet the views of the management, that nobody in the theatre is sharp enough to detect the contingent alterations which the main one involves. The Dove-cot is no exception to this rule. The adaptation is a jumble; but it serves its turn. It is very well acted. Miss Ellis Jeffreys, who captured the leading position for this sort of work during Mr Alexander's recent supplementary season at the Royalty, holds that position firmly. It is a kind of work in which manners make the actress: vulgarly played, it is detestable; elegantly played, it is delightful. Miss Jeffreys plays it elegantly. Miss Leonora Braham, no longer a Savoy prima donna, is the flamboyant Carlist. Mr Seymour Hicks, Mr James Welch, Mr William Wyes, Mr Sugden, and Miss Carlotta Addison are also in the cast, which is unusually strong and well chosen.

Shakespear's Merry Gentlemen

MUCH ADO ABOUT NOTHING. *St James's Theatre,* 16 *February* 1898.

[26 *February* 1898]

MUCH ADO is perhaps the most dangerous actor-manager trap in the whole Shakespearean repertory. It is not a safe play like The Merchant of Venice or As You Like It, nor a serious play like Hamlet. Its success depends on the way it is handled in performance; and that, again, depends on the actor-manager being enough of a critic to discriminate ruthlessly between the pretension of the author and his achievement.

The main pretension in Much Ado is that Benedick and Beatrice are exquisitely witty and amusing persons. They are, of course, nothing of the sort. Benedick's pleasantries might pass at a sing-song in a public-house parlor; but a gentleman rash enough to venture on them in even the very mildest £52-a-year suburban imitation of polite society today would assuredly never be invited again. From his first joke, 'Were you in doubt, sir, that you asked her?' to his last, 'There is no staff more reverend than one tipped with horn,' he is not a wit, but a blackguard. He is not Shakespear's only failure in that genre. It took the Bard a long time to grow out of the provincial conceit that made him so fond of exhibiting his accomplishments as a master of gallant badinage. The very thought of Biron, Mercutio, Gratiano, and Benedick must, I hope, have covered him with shame in his later years. Even Hamlet's airy compliments to Ophelia before the court would make a cabman blush. But at least Shakespear did not value himself on Hamlet's indecent jests as he evidently did on those of the four merry gentlemen of the earlier plays. When he at last got conviction of sin, and saw this sort of levity in its proper light, he made masterly amends by presenting the blackguard *as* a blackguard in the person of Lucio in Measure for Measure. Lucio, as a character study, is worth forty Benedicks and Birons. His obscenity is not only inoffensive, but irresistibly entertaining, because it is drawn with perfect skill, offered at its true value, and given its proper interest, without any complicity of the author in its lewdness. Lucio is much more of a gentleman than Benedick, because he keeps his coarse sallies for coarse people. Meeting one woman, he says humbly, 'Gentle and fair: your brother kindly greets you. Not to be weary with you, he's in prison.' Meeting another, he hails her sparkingly with 'How now? which of your hips has the more profound sciatica?' The one woman is a lay sister, the other a prostitute. Benedick or Mercutio would have cracked their low jokes on the lay sister, and been held up as gentlemen of rare wit and excellent discourse for it. Whenever they approach a woman or an old man, you shiver with apprehension as to what brutality they will come out with.

Precisely the same thing, in the tenderer degree of her sex, is true of Beatrice. In her character of professed wit she has only one subject, and that is the subject which a really witty woman never jests about, because it is too serious a matter to a woman to be made light of without indelicacy. Beatrice jests about it for the sake of the indelicacy. There is only one thing worse than the Elizabethan 'merry gentleman,' and that is the Elizabethan 'merry lady.'

Why is it then that we still want to see Benedick and Beatrice, and that our most eminent actors and actresses still want to play them? Before I answer that very simple question let me ask another. Why is it that Da Ponte's 'dramma giocosa,' entitled Don Giovanni, a loathsome story of a coarse, witless, worthless libertine, who kills an old man in a duel and is finally dragged down through a trapdoor to hell by his twaddling ghost, is still, after more than a century, as 'immortal' as Much Ado? Simply because Mozart clothed it with wonderful music, which turned the worthless words and thoughts of Da Ponte into a magical human drama of moods and transitions of feeling. That is what happened in a smaller way with Much Ado. Shakespear shews himself in it a commonplace librettist working on a stolen plot, but a great musician. No matter how poor, coarse, cheap, and obvious the thought may be, the mood is charming, and the music of the words expresses the mood. Paraphrase the encounters of Benedick and Beatrice in the style of a bluebook, carefully preserving every idea they present, and it will become apparent to the most infatuated Shakespearean that they contain at best nothing out of the common in thought or wit, and at worst a good deal of vulgar naughtiness. Paraphrase Goethe, Wagner, or Ibsen in the same way, and you will find original observation, subtle thought, wide comprehension, far-reaching intuition, and serious psychological study in them. Give Shakespear a fairer chance in the comparison by paraphrasing even his best and maturest work, and you will still get nothing more than the platitudes of proverbial philosophy, with a very occasional curiosity in the shape of a rudiment of some modern idea, not followed up. Not until the Shakespearean music is added by replacing the paraphrase with the original lines does the enchantment begin. Then you are in another world at once. When a flower-girl tells a coster to hold his jaw, for nobody is listening to him, and he retorts, 'Oh, youre there, are you, you beauty?' they reproduce the wit of Beatrice and Benedick exactly. But put it this way. 'I wonder that you will still be talking, Signior Benedick: nobody marks you.' 'What! my dear Lady Disdain, are you yet living?' You are miles away from costerland at once. When I tell you that Benedick and the coster are equally poor in thought, Beatrice and the flower-girl equally vulgar in repartee, you reply that I might as well tell you that a nightingale's love is no higher than a cat's. Which is exactly what I do tell you, though the nightingale is the better musician. You will admit, perhaps, that the love of the worst human singer in the world is accompanied by a higher degree of intellectual consciousness than that of the most ravishingly melodious nightingale. Well, in just the same way, there are plenty of quite second-rate writers who are abler thinkers and wits than William, though they are unable to weave his magic into the expression of their thoughts.

It is not easy to knock this into the public's head, because comparatively few of Shakespear's admirers are at all conscious that they are listening to music as they hear his phrases turn and his lines fall so fascinatingly and memorably; whilst we all, no matter how stupid we are, can understand his jokes and platitudes, and are flattered when we are told of the subtlety of the wit we have relished, and the profundity of the thought we have fathomed. Englishmen are specially susceptible to this sort of flattery, because intellectual subtlety is not their strong point. In dealing with them you must make them believe that you are appealing to their brains when you are really appealing to their senses and feelings. With Frenchmen the case is reversed: you must make them believe that you are appealing to their senses and feelings when you are really appealing to their brains. The Englishman, slave to every sentimental ideal and dupe of every sensuous art, will have it that his great national poet is a thinker. The Frenchman, enslaved and duped only by systems and calculations, insists on his hero being a sentimentalist and artist. That is why Shakespear is esteemed a master-mind in England, and wondered at as a clumsy barbarian in France.

However indiscriminate the public may be in its Shakespear worship, the actor and actress who are to make a success of Much Ado must know better. Let them once make the popular mistake of supposing that what they have to do is to bring out the wit of Benedick and Beatrice, and they are lost. Their business in the 'merry' passages is to cover poverty of thought and coarseness of innuendo by making the most of the grace and dignity of the diction. The sincere, genuinely dramatic passages will then take care of themselves. Alas! Mr Alexander and Miss Julia Neilson have made the plunge without waiting for my advice. Miss Neilson, throwing away all her grace and all her music, strives to play the merry lady by dint of conscientious gambolling. Instead of uttering her speeches as exquisitely as possible, she rattles through them, laying an impossible load of archness on every insignificant conjunction, and clipping all the important words until there is no measure or melody left in them. Not even the wedding scene can stop her: after an indignant attitude or two she redoubles her former skittishness. I can only implore her to give up all her deep-laid Beatricisms, to discard the movements of Miss Ellen Terry, the voice of Mrs Patrick Campbell, and the gaiety of Miss Kitty Loftus, and try the effect of Julia Neilson in all her grave grace taken quite seriously. Mr Alexander makes the same mistake, though, being more judicious than Miss Neilson, he does not carry it out so disastrously. His merry gentleman is patently a dutiful assumption from beginning to end. He smiles, rackets, and bounds up and down stairs like a quiet man who has just been rated by his wife for habitual dullness before company. It is all hopeless: the charm of Benedick cannot be realized by the spryness of the actor's legs, the flashing of his teeth, or the rattle of his laugh: nothing but the music of the words—above all, not their meaning—can save the part. I wish I could persuade Mr Alexander that if he were to play the part exactly as he played Guy Domville, it would at once become ten times more fascinating. He should at least take the revelation of Beatrice's supposed love for him with perfect seriousness. The more remorsefully sympathetic Benedick is when she comes to bid him to dinner after he has been gulled into believing she loves him, the more exquisitely ridiculous the scene becomes. It is the audience's turn to laugh then, not Benedick's.

Of all Sir Henry Irving's manifold treasons against Shakespear, the most audacious was his virtually cutting Dogberry out of Much Ado. Mr Alexander does not go so far; but he omits the fifth scene of the third act, upon which the whole effect of the later scenes depends, since it is from it that the audience really gets Dogberry's measure. Dogberry is a capital study of parochial character. Sincerely played, he always comes out as a very real and highly entertaining person. At the St James's, I grieve to say, he does not carry a moment's conviction: he is a mere mouthpiece for malapropisms, all of which he shouts at the gallery with intense consciousness of their absurdity, and with open anxiety lest they should pass unnoticed. Surely it is clear, if anything histrionic is clear, that Dogberry's first qualification must be a complete unconsciousness of himself as he appears to others.

Verges, even more dependent than Dogberry on that cut-out scene with Leonato, is almost annihilated by its excision; and it was hardly worth wasting Mr Esmond on the remainder.

When I have said that neither Benedick nor Beatrice have seen sufficiently through the weakness of Shakespear's merriments to concentrate themselves on the purely artistic qualities of their parts, and that Dogberry is nothing but an excuse for a few laughs, I have made a somewhat heavy deduction from my praises of the revival. But these matters are hardly beyond remedy: and the rest is excellent. Miss Fay Davis's perfect originality contrasts strongly with Miss Neilson's incorrigible imitativeness. Her physical grace is very remarkable; and she creates her part between its few lines, as Hero must if she is to fill up her due place in the drama. Mr Fred Terry is a most engaging Don Pedro; and Mr H. B. Irving is a striking Don John, though he is becoming too accomplished an actor to make shift with that single smile which is as well known at the St James's by this time as the one wig of Mr Pinero's hero was at 'The Wells.' Mr Vernon and Mr Beveridge are, of course, easily within their powers as Leonato and Antonio; and all the rest come off with credit— even Mr Loraine, who has not a trace of Claudio in him. The dresses are superb, and the scenery very handsome, though Italy contains so many palaces and chapels that are better than handsome that I liked the opening scenes best. If Mr Alexander will only make up his mind that the piece is irresistible as poetry, and hopeless as epigrammatic comedy, he need not fear for its success. But if he and Miss Neilson persist in depending on its attempts at wit and gallantry, then it remains to be seen whether the public's sense of duty or its boredom will get the upper hand.

I had intended to deal here with the O.U.D.S. and its performance of Romeo and Juliet; but Much Ado has carried me too far; so I must postpone Oxford until next week.

The Drama in Hoxton

[9 *April* 1898]

OF late, I am happy to say, the theatres have been so uneventful that I should have fallen quite out of the habit of my profession but for a certain vigorously democratic clergyman, who seized me and bore me off to the last night of the pantomime at 'the Brit.'

The Britannia Theatre is in Hoxton, not far from Shoreditch Church, a neighborhood in which the Saturday Review is comparatively little read. The manager, a lady, is the most famous of all London managers. Sir Henry Irving, compared to her, is a mushroom, just as his theatre, compared to hers, is a back drawing room. Over 4000 people pay nightly at her doors; and the spectacle of these thousands, serried in the vast pit and empyrean gallery, is so fascinating that the stranger who first beholds it can hardly turn away to look at the stage. Forty years ago Mrs Sara Lane built this theatre; and she has managed it ever since. It may be no such great matter to handle a single playhouse—your Irvings, Trees, Alexanders, Wyndhams, and other upstarts of yesterday can do that; but Mrs Lane is said to own the whole ward in which her theatre stands. Madame Sarah Bernhardt's diamonds fill a jewel-box: Mrs Lane's are reputed to fill sacks. When I had the honor of being presented to Mrs Lane, I thought of the occasion when the late Sir Augustus Harris, her only serious rival in managerial fame, had the honor of being presented to me. The inferiority of the man to the woman was manifest. Sir Augustus was, in comparison, an hysterical creature. Enterprise was with him a frenzy which killed him when it reached a climax of success. Mrs Lane thrives on enterprise and success, and is capable, self-contained, practical, vigilant, everything that a good general should be. A West End star is to her a person to whom she once gave so many pounds or shillings a week, and who is now, in glittering and splendid anxiety, begging for engagements, desperately wooing syndicates and potential backers, and living on Alnaschar dreams and old press notices which were unanimously favorable (if you excluded those which were obviously malignant personal attacks). Mrs Lane, well furnished with realities, has no use for dreams; and she knows syndicates and capitalists only as suspicious characters who want her money, not as courted deities with powers of life and death in their hands. The fortune of her productions means little to her: if the piece succeeds, so much the better: if not, the pantomime pays for all.

The clergyman's box, which was about as large as an average Metropolitan railway station, was approached from the stage itself; so that I had opportunities of criticizing both from before the curtain and behind it. I was struck by the absence of the worthless, heartless, incompetent people who seem to get employed with such facility—nay, sometimes apparently by preference—in West End theatres. The West End calculation for musical farce and pantomime appears to be that there is 'a silver mine' to be made by paying several pounds a week to people who are worth nothing, provided you engage enough of them. This is not Mrs Lane's plan. Mr Bigwood, the stage-manager, is a real stage-manager, to whom one can talk on unembarrassed human terms as one capable man to another, and not by any means an erratic art failure from Bedford Park and the Slade School, or one of those beachcombers of our metropolitan civilization who drift to the West End stage because its fringe of short-lived ventures provides congenital liars and impostors with unique opportunities of drawing a few months' or weeks' salary before their preoccupied and worried employers have leisure to realize that they have made a bad bargain. I had not the pleasure of making the prompter's acquaintance; but I should have been surprised to find him the only person in the theatre who could not read, though in the West End I should have expected to find that his principal qualification. I made my way under the stage to look at the working of the star-trap by which Mr Lupino was flung up through the boards like a stone from a volcano; and there, though I found eight men wasting their strength by overcoming a counterweight which, in an up-to-date French *théâtre de féerie*, is raised by one man with the help of a pulley, the carpenter-machinist in command was at once recognizable as a well-selected man. On the stage the results of the same instinctive sort of judgment were equally apparent. The display of beauty was sufficiently voluptuous; but there were no good-for-nothings: it was a company of men and women, recognizable as fellow-creatures, and not as accidentally pretty cretinous freaks. Even the low comedians were not blackguards, though they were certainly not fastidious, Hoxton being somewhat Rabelaisian in its ideas of broad humor. One scene, in which the horrors of sea-sickness were exploited with great freedom, made the four thousand sons and daughters of Shoreditch scream with laughter. At the climax, when four voyagers were struggling violently for a single bucket, I looked stealthily round the box, in which the Church, the Peerage, and the Higher Criticism were represented. All three were in convulsions. Compare this with our West End musical farces, in which the performers strive to make some inane scene 'go' by trying to suggest to the starving audience that there is something exquisitely loose and vicious beneath the dreary fatuity of the surface. Who would not rather look at and laugh at four men pretending to be sea-sick in a wildly comic way than see a row of young women singing a chorus about being 'Gaiety

Girls' with the deliberate intention of conveying to the audience that a Gaiety chorister's profession—their own profession—is only a mask for the sort of life which is represented in Piccadilly Circus and Leicester Square after midnight? I quite agree with my friend the clergyman that decent ladies and gentlemen who have given up West End musical farce in disgust will find themselves much happier at the Britannia pantomime.

I shall not venture on any searching artistic criticism of Will o' the Wisp, as the pantomime was called. If it were a West End piece, I should pitch into it without the slightest regard to the prestige and apparent opulence of the manager, not because I am incorruptible, but because I am not afraid of the mere shadow of success. I treat its substance, in the person of Mrs Lane, with careful respect. Shew me real capacity; and I bow lower to it than anybody. All I dare suggest to the Hoxtonians is that when they insist on an entertainment lasting from seven to close upon midnight, they have themselves to thank if the actors occasionally have to use all their ingenuity to spin out scenes of which a judicious playgoer would desire to have at least ten minutes less.

The enthusiasm of the pit on the last night, with no stalls to cut it off from the performers, was frantic. There was a great throwing of flowers and confectionery on the stage; and it would happen occasionally that an artist would overlook one of these tributes, and walk off, leaving it unnoticed on the boards. Then a shriek of tearing anxiety would arise, as if the performer were wandering blindfold into a furnace or over a precipice. Every factory girl in the house would lacerate the air with a mad scream of 'Pick it up, Topsy!' 'Pick it up, Voylit!' followed by a gasp of relief, several thousand strong, when Miss Topsy Sinden, or Miss Violet Durkin would return and annex the offering. I was agreeably astonished by Miss Topsy Sinden's dancing. Thitherto it had been my miserable fate to see her come on, late in the second act of some unspeakably dreary inanity at the West End, to interpolate a 'skirt dance,' and spin out the unendurable by the intolerable. On such occasions I have looked on her with cold hatred, wondering why the 'varieties' of a musical farce should not include a few items from the conventional 'assault-at-arms,' culminating in some stalwart sergeant, after the usual slicing of lemons, leaden bars, and silk handkerchiefs, cutting a skirt-dancer in two at one stroke. At the Britannia Miss Sinden really danced, acted, and turned out quite a charming person. I was not surprised; for the atmosphere was altogether more bracing than at the other end of the town. These poor playgoers to whom the expenditure of half a guinea for a front seat at a theatre is as outrageously and extravagantly impossible as the purchase of a deer forest in Mars is to a millionaire, have at least one excellent quality in the theatre. They are jealous *for* the dignity of the artist, not derisively covetous of his (or her) degradation. When a white statue which had stood for thirteen minutes in the middle of the stage turned out to be Mr Lupino, who forthwith put on a classic plasticity, and in a series of rapid poses claimed popular respect for 'the antique,' it was eagerly accorded; and his demon conflict with the powers of evil, involving a desperate broad-sword combat, and the most prodigious plunges into the earth and projections therefrom by volcanic traps as aforesaid, was conducted with all the tragic dignity of Richard III and received in the true Aristotelean spirit by the audience. The fairy queen, a comely prima donna who scorned all frivolity, was treated with entire respect and seriousness. Altogether, I seriously recommend those of my readers who find a pantomime once a year good for them, to go next year to the Britannia, and leave the West End to its boredoms and all the otherdoms that make it so expensively dreary.

Oh, these sentimental, second-sighted Scotchmen! Reader: would you like to see me idealized by a master hand? If you would, buy the Sunday Special of the 3rd instant, and study Mr Robert Buchanan's open letter to me. There you will find the ideal G. B. S. in 'the daring shamelessness of a powerful and fearless nudity.' This is the sort of thing that flatters a timid, sedentary literary man. Besides, it protects him: other people believe it all, and are afraid to hit the poor paper Titan. Far be it from me to say a word against so effective an advertisement; though when I consider its generosity I cannot but blush for having taken in so magnanimous an idealizer. Yet a great deal of it is very true: Mr Buchanan is altogether right, it seems to me, in identifying my views with his father's Owenism; only I claim that Comte's law of the three stages has been operating busily since Owen's time, and that modern Fabianism represents the positive stage of Owenism. I shall not plead against the highly complimentary charge of impudence in its proper sense of shamelessness. Shame is to the man who fights with his head what cowardice is to the man who fights with his hands: I have the same opinion of it as Bunyan put into the mouth of Faithful in the Valley of Humiliation. But I do not commit myself to Mr

Buchanan's account of my notions of practical reform. It is true that when I protest against our marriage laws, and Mr Buchanan seizes the occasion to observe that 'the idea of marriage, spiritually speaking, is absolutely beautiful and ennobling,' I feel very much as if a Chinese mandarin had met my humanitarian objection to starving criminals to death or cutting them into a thousand pieces, by blandly remarking that 'the idea of evil-doing leading to suffering is, spiritually speaking, absolutely beautiful and ennobling.' If Mr Buchanan is content to be forbidden to spiritually ennoble himself except under legal conditions so monstrous and immoral that no disinterestedly prudent and self-respecting person would accept them when free from amorous infatuation, then I am not. Mr Buchanan's notion that I assume that 'marriage is essentially and absolutely an immoral bargain between the sexes in so far as it conflicts with the aberrations and caprices of the human appetite,' is a wildly bad shot. What on earth has marriage to do with the aberrations and caprices of human appetite? People marry for companionship, not for debauchery. Why that wholesome companionship should be a means of making amiable and honest people the helpless prey of drunkards, criminals, pestiferous invalids, bullies, viragoes, lunatics, or even persons with whom, through no fault on either side, they find it impossible to live happily, I cannot for the life of me see; and if Mr Buchanan can, I invite him to give his reasons. Can any sane person deny that a contract 'for better, for worse' destroys all moral responsibility? And is it not a revolting and indecent thing that any indispensable social contract should compulsorily involve a clause, abhorrent to both parties if they have a scrap of honor in them, by which the persons of the parties are placed at each other's disposal by legal force? These abominations may not belong to 'the idea of marriage, spiritually speaking'; but they belong to the fact of marriage, practically speaking; and it is with this fact that I, as a Realist (Mr Buchanan's own quite correct expression), am concerned. If I were to get married myself, I should resort to some country where the marriage law is somewhat less than five centuries out of date; and as this seems to me as unreasonable a condition for the ordinary man as a trip to Bayreuth is to the ordinary gallery opera-goer, I do what I can to relieve him of it, and make married people as responsible for their good behavior to one another as business partners are. Hereupon Mr Buchanan discourses in the following terms:—'The Naked Man [me!] posing as a realist, cries, "away with sanctions! let us have no more of them"; but the man who is clothed and in his right mind knows that they are inevitable and accepts them.' Did anyone ever hear such nonsense? Do the Americans accept them? Do the French accept them? Would we accept them but for our national preference for hypocrisy eked out with collusive divorce cases? I have no objection to Mr Buchanan idealizing me; but when he takes to idealizing the English law at its stupidest, he oversteps my drawn line. I am none the less obliged to him for giving me an excuse for another assault on these patent beautifiers and ennoblers without which, it is assumed, we should all fall to universal rapine, though the danger of licence is plainly all the other way. I verily believe that if the percentage of happy marriages ever rises to, say, twenty-five, the existence of the human intellect will be threatened by the very excesses against which our marriage law is supposed to protect us.

Kate Terry

THE MASTER. *An original comedy in three acts. By* G. Stuart Ogilvie. *Globe Theatre,* 23 *April* 1898.

LORD AND LADY ALGY. *An original light comedy in three acts. By* R. C. Carton. *Comedy Theatre,* 21 *April* 1898.

[30 *April* 1898]

I MUST say Mr Stuart Ogilvie has an odd notion of how to write a part to suit a particular actor. Here is Mr Hare, one of the very few English actors one dare send a foreigner to see, excelling in the representation of all sorts and conditions of quick, clear, crisp, shrewd, prompt, sensible men. Enter to him Mr Ogilvie, with a part expressly designed to shew that all this is nothing but a pig-headed affectation, and that the true humanity beneath it is the customary maudlin, muzzy, brainless, hysterical sentimentality and excitability which is supposed to touch the heart of the British playgoer, and which, no doubt, does affect him to some extent when he induces in himself the necessary degree of susceptibility with a little alcohol. What a situation! And it would have been so easy to provide Mr Hare with a part shewing the worth and dignity of his own temperament! All through The Master Mr Ogilvie seems to be trying to prove to Mr Hare what a much finer and more genuine fellow he would have been if nature had made him a Charles Warner or a Henry Neville. Apart from the point being an extremely debateable one, it seems hardly quite polite to Mr Hare, who, after all, cannot help being himself. This comes of an author making no serious attempt to get the point of view of the character he professes to have dramatized —of simply conspiring with the stupid section of the pit to make an Aunt Sally of it. Half the play might be made plausible if The Master were played as a savage, iron-jawed, madly selfish old brute, but the other half is evidently laid out for Mr Hare's refinement and humanity of style. And then there is a revolting obviousness about the operations of destiny with a view to a happy ending. The old gentleman first puts his son out of the house, then puts out his daughter, and finally puts out his wife, whereupon the servants leave of their own accord. Immediately, with a punctuality and perfect expectedness which is about as dramatic as the response of a box of vestas to a penny in the slot, comes the winning of the Victoria Cross in India by the disinherited son, the heroic rescue of a band of entombed miners by the manly young husband for whose sake the daughter defies her father, and the sacrifice by the discarded wife of her whole fortune to save her oppressor from ruin. For a man of Mr Ogilvie's calibre I call this gross. It is not the fine art of the dramatist: it is the trade of the playwright, and not even a first-class job at that. For the life of me I cannot see why Mr Ogilvie should thus aim at rank commonness in his drama any more than at the rank illiteracy of expression which usually accompanies it, and which he saves his play from absolute intolerableness by avoiding. He may reply that the public like rank commonness. That may be, when it comes from the man to whom it is natural, and who, in doing it, is doing his best. But whether the public will like it from Mr Ogilvie remains to be seen. Miss Marie Corelli's novels may be more widely read within a month of their publication than Mr Meredith's used to be; but it does not at all follow that if Mr Meredith were deliberately to try to do Miss Corelli's work the result would be popular. The public does not like to see a man playing down; and I should insult Mr Ogilvie most fearfully if I were to assume that he was doing his best in The Master. When, after stooping to a baby, he took the final plunge with a band playing Soldiers of our Queen to a cheering crowd outside, I hid my face and heard no more.

The interest of the occasion was strongly helped out by the reappearance of Miss Kate Terry, an actress unknown, except as an assiduous playgoer, to the present generation. Miss Terry entered apologetically, frankly taking the position of an elderly lady who had come to look after her daughter, and tacitly promising to do her best not to be intrusive, nor to make any attempt at acting or anything of that sort, if the audience would only be a little indulgent with her. She sat down on a sofa, looking very nice and kindly; but the moment she had to say something to Mr Hare her old habits got the better of her, and the sentence was hardly out of her mouth before she recognized, as its cadence struck her ear, that she had acted it, and acted it uncommonly well. The shame of this discovery made her nervous; but the more nervous she was, the less she could help acting; and the less she could help acting, the more she put on the youth of the time when she had last acted—a fearful indiscretion. However, as the audience, far from taking it in bad part, evidently wanted more of it, Miss Terry, after a brief struggle, abandoned herself to her fate and went recklessly for her part. It was not much of a part; but she gave the audience no chance of finding that out. She apparently began, in point of skill and practice, just where she had left off years ago, without a trace of rust. Her first two or three speeches, though delicately distinct, had a certain privacy of pitch, I thought; but almost before I had noticed it, it vanished, as she recaptured the pitch of the theatre and the ear of the crowded audience. She has distinguished skill, infallible judgment, altogether extraordinary amenity of style, and withal a quite enchanting air of being a simple-minded motherly lady, who does not mean to be clever in the least, and never was behind the scenes in a theatre in her life. I sometimes dream that I am on a concert platform with a violin in my hands and an orchestra at my back, having in some inexplicable madness undertaken to play the Brahms Concerto before a full audience without knowing my G string from my chanterelle. Whoever has not dreamt this dream does not know what humility means. Trembling and desperate, I strike Joachim's attitude, and find, to my amazement, that the instrument responds instantly to my sense of the music, and that I am playing away like anything. Miss Terry's acting reminds me of my imaginary violin-playing: she seems utterly innocent of it, and yet there it is, all happening infallibly and delightfully. But, depend on it, she must know all about it; for how else does her daughter, Miss Mabel Terry, come to be so cunningly trained? She has walked on to the stage with a knowledge of her business, and a delicacy in its execution, to which most of our younger leading ladies seem no nearer than when they first blundered on to the boards in a maze of millinery and professional ignorance. Yes: the daughter gives the apparent naïveté of the mother away: if that art were an accident of Nature it could never be taught so perfectly. Indeed, there were plenty of little revelations of this kind for sharp eyes. I have already described how Miss Kate Terry's momentary nervousness at first threw her back to the acting of thirty years ago. In that moment one saw how much of the original Kate Terry her daughter had just been reproducing for us. Then Miss Terry recovered her self-possession and her own age; and here again one saw that she was by no means going to be the maidenly Kate Terry with a matronly face and figure, but virtually a new actress of matronly parts, unsurpassed in stage accomplishment, and with a certain charm of temperament that will supply our authors with something that they get neither from the dazzling cleverness of Mrs Kendal nor the conviction and comic force of Mrs Calvert, who alone can lay claim to anything approaching her technical powers. I do not feel sure that Miss Terry could play Mrs Alving in Ghosts as Mrs Theodore Wright plays it—if, indeed, she could bring herself to play it at all—but I am sure that her art will not fail her in any play, however difficult, that does not positively antagonize her sympathies.

Stage art, even of a highly cultivated and artificial kind, sits so naturally on the Terrys that I daresay we shall hear a great deal about the family charm and very little about the family skill. Even Miss Ellen Terry, whose keenness of intelligence is beyond all dissimulation, has often succeeded in making eminent critics believe that her stagecraft and nervous athleticism are mere efflorescences of her personal charm. But Miss Mabel Terry has no special enchantments to trade upon—only the inevitable charms of her age. She is not recognizably her aunt's niece. She is not majestically handsome and graceful like Miss Julia Neilson; nor voluptuously lovely like Miss Lily Hanbury; nor perilously bewitching like Mrs Patrick

Campbell. But she can speak beautifully, without the slightest trick or mannerism of any sort; and no moment of nervousness can disable her: the word gets rightly touched even when she can hardly hear it herself. She never makes a grimace, nor is there a trace of consciousness or exaggeration about her gestures. She played between her mother and Mr Hare without being technically outclassed. Most of our stage young ladies would have sustained the comparison like an understudy volunteered in a desperate emergency by the nearest amateur. If we are to write this down as the family charm, let us not forget that it is a charm which includes a good deal of industriously acquired skill. It ought to be called artistic conscience.

Mr Gilbert Hare is condemned to his usual premature grey hairs. If he ever gets a chance as Romeo, I am convinced that, from mere force of habit, the first thing he will say to Juliet will be, 'I have known your uncle close on fifty years. Your mother was a sweet, gentle lady, God bless her.' There is only five minutes—more's the pity—of Mr Kerr. His Major Hawkwood is a younger brother of Baron Croodle, whose second coming, by the way, ought to be at hand by this time. Mr Gillmore and Mr Cherry as the two heroes, and Mr Rock as the butler, leave nothing to be desired except less obvious parts for them. Mr Ross struck me as not quite plausible enough in his villainy for the favorite of so exacting a principal as The Master.

Lord and Lady Algy at the Comedy is an ignoble, but not unamusing, three-act farce. I should have nothing more to say about it had my eye not been caught by the astounding epithet 'wholesome' applied to it. I declare that it is the most immoral play I ever saw. Lord and Lady Algy are a middle-aged pair more completely and shamelessly void of self-respect than any other couple for whom the theatre has ventured to claim sympathy. They have one resource, one taste, one amusement, one interest, one ambition, one occupation, one accomplishment, and that is betting on the turf. The 'wholesomeness' consists of the woman's boast that though she flirts, she always 'runs straight'—as if it mattered a straw to any human being whether she ran straight or not. A lady who is a gambler, a loafer, and a sponge, is not likely to have any motive of the smallest moral value for refraining from adultery. There are people who are beneath lawbreaking as well as people who are above it, and Lord and Lady Algy are of that class. But the play is altogether too trivial and sportive to raise moral questions; and I laughed at its humors without scruple. Mr Henry Ford's jockey was the best bit of character in the performance. Mr Hawtrey, as the Duke of Marlborough at a fancy ball, harmlessly drunk, makes plenty of inoffensive fun; and he and Miss Compton have plenty of their popular and familiar business in the first and third acts. The other parts are really exasperating in view of the talent thrown away in them.

G. B. S. Vivisected

[14 *May* 1898]

EUREKA! I have found it out at last. I now understand the British drama and the British actor. It has come about in this way.

A few weeks ago one of my feet, which had borne me without complaining for forty years, struck work.

The spectacle of a dramatic critic hopping about the metropolis might have softened a heart of stone; but the managers, I regret to say, seized the opportunity to disable me by crowding a succession of first nights on me. After The Medicine Man at the Lyceum, the foot got into such a condition that it literally had to be looked into. I had no curiosity in the matter myself; but the administration of an anæsthetic made my views of no importance. It is to the anæsthetic that I owe the discovery which elicits my cry of Eureka!

The beginning of the anæsthesia threw no new light on the theatre. I was extinguished by the gas familiar to dentists' patients, and subsequently kept in a state of annihilation with ether. My last recollection is a sort of chuckle at being wideawake enough to know when the operator lifted my eyelid and tapped my eyeball to convince himself that he had made an end of me. It was not until I was allowed to recover that the process became publicly interesting. For then a very strange thing happened. *My character did not come back all at once.* Its artistic and sentimental side came first: its morality, its positive elements, its common sense, its incorrigible Protestant respectability, did not return for a long time after. For the first time in my life I tasted the bliss of having no morals to restrain me from lying, and no sense of reality to restrain me from romancing. I overflowed with what people call 'heart.' I acted and lied in the most touchingly sympathetic fashion; I felt prepared to receive unlimited kindness from everybody with the deepest, tenderest gratitude; and I was totally incapable of even conceiving the notion of rendering anyone a service myself. If only I could have stood up and talked distinctly as a man in perfect health and self-possession, I should have won the hearts of everybody present until they found me out later on. Even as it was, I was perfectly conscious of the value of my prostrate and half-delirious condition as a bait for sympathy; and I deliberately played for it in a manner which now makes me blush. I carefully composed effective little ravings, and repeated them, and then started again and let my voice die away, without an atom of shame. I called everybody by their Christian names, except one gentleman whose Christian name I did not know, and I called him 'dear old So-and-so.' Artistically, I was an immense success: morally, I simply had no existence.

At last they quietly extinguished the lights, and stole out of the chamber of the sweet invalid who was now sleeping like a child, but who, noticing that the last person to leave the room was a lady, softly breathed that lady's name in his dreams. Then the effect of the anæsthetic passed away more and more; and in less than an hour I was an honest taxpayer again, with my heart perfectly well in hand. And now comes the great question, Was that a gain or a loss? The problem comes home to me with special force at this moment, because I have just seriously distracted public attention from the American war by publishing my plays; and I have been overwhelmed as usual by complaints of my want of heart, my unnaturally clear intellectual consciousness, my cynicism, and all the rest of it. One of my female characters, who drinks whisky, and smokes cigars, and reads detective stories, and regards the fine arts, especially music, as an insufferable and unintelligible waste of time, has been declared by my friend Mr William Archer to be an exact and authentic portrait of myself, on no other grounds in the world except that she is a woman of business and not a creature of romantic impulse. In this 'nation of shopkeepers,' the critics no sooner meet a character on the stage with the smallest trace of business sagacity, or an author who makes the least allowance for the provident love of money and property as a guarantee of security, comfort, and independence, which is so powerful a factor in English society, than they immediately declare such a character totally inhuman and unnatural, and such an author a cynical crank. If I am the unfortunate author, they dispose of the character at once as a mere dramatization of my own personal eccentricities.

This, regarded as one of the humors of natural self-unconsciousness, is so farcically paradoxical and preposterous that I have always felt it to be too coarse for the exquisite high comedy of real life. And I have been right. The protests come only from what we call the artistic class, by which contemptuous expression (for such it is in England) we mean the men and women who love books and pictures, histories and operas, and shrink from business and public affairs so persistently that in the end their consciousness becomes absolutely fictitious, in which condition reality seems unreal to them, and the most commonplace characteristics of English life, when dramatized, produce on them the effect of a mere bizarrerie. When this effect is strong enough to give a serious jar to their artistic habits, they generally mistake the disagreeable sensation for a shock to their moral sense, it being one of their artistic conventions that it is possible to shirk real life, and yet possess moral sense.

Often as I have had to point this out, I had, until yesterday, yet to realize fully the difference between observing it in other people and experiencing it oneself. At last I can speak of it at first hand; and now

I understand it as I never understood it before. No longer shall I look at my sentimental, fiction-loving friends as Bismarck might look at a rather engaging South Sea chief; for I have actually changed personalities with them. What is more, I know how to reproduce the miracle at will as certainly as if I possessed the wishing-cap of Siegfried. My wishing-cap is a bag of ether. With that, I can first plunge into the darkness that existed before my birth and be simply nothing. Then I can come to life as an artist and a man of feeling—as everything that I have been reproached so bitterly for not being. I can prolong that condition indefinitely by taking a whiff or two of ether whenever I feel the chill of a moral or intellectual impulse. I can write plays in it; I can act in it; I can gush in it; I can borrow money to set myself up as an actor-manager in it; I can be pious and patriotic in it; I can melt touchingly over disease and death and murder and hunger and cold and poverty in it, turning all the woes of the world into artistic capital for myself; and finally I can come back to full consciousness and criticize myself as I was in it. The parable of Dr Jekyll and Mr Hyde will be fulfilled in me, with this difference, that it is Hyde who will be popular and petted, and Jekyll who will be rebuked for his callous, heartless cynicism. I have already ordered a set of cards inscribed 'G. B. S. . . . At Home . . . Tuesdays and Fridays under ether for sentimental, theatrical, and artistic purposes . . . Mondays and Saturdays normal for business engagements and public affairs.'

Here I must summarily break off. My doctor's investigation of my interior has disclosed the fact that for many years I have been converting the entire stock of energy extractable from my food (which I regret to say he disparages) into pure genius. Expecting to find bone and tissue, he has been almost wholly disappointed, and a pale, volatile moisture has hardly blurred the scalpel in the course of its excursions through my veins. He has therefore put it bluntly to me that I am already almost an angel, and that it rests with myself to complete the process summarily by writing any more articles before I have recovered from the effects of the operation and been renovated in the matter of bone and muscle. I have therefore pledged myself to send only the briefest line explaining why my article cannot appear this week. It is also essential, in order to keep up the sympathy which rages at my bedside, to make the very worst of my exhausted condition. Sad to say, there is enough of the ether clinging round me still to keep me doing this with a very perceptible zest.

I can no more.

Valedictory

[21 *May* 1898]

As I lie here, helpless and disabled, or, at best, nailed by one foot to the floor like a doomed Strasburg goose, a sense of injury grows on me. For nearly four years—to be precise, since New Year 1895—I have been the slave of the theatre. It has tethered me to the mile radius of foul and sooty air which has its centre in the Strand, as a goat is tethered in the little circle of cropped and trampled grass that makes the meadow ashamed. Every week it clamors for its tale of written words; so that I am like a man fighting a windmill: I have hardly time to stagger to my feet from the knock-down blow of one sail, when the next strikes me down. Now I ask, is it reasonable to expect me to spend my life in this way? For just consider my position. Do I receive any spontaneous recognition for the prodigies of skill and industry I lavish on an unworthy institution and a stupid public? Not a bit of it: half my time is spent in telling people what a clever man I am. It is no use merely doing clever things in England. The English do not know what to think until they are coached, laboriously and insistently for years, in the proper and becoming opinion. For ten years past, with an unprecedented pertinacity and obstination, I have been dinning into the public head that I am an extraordinarily witty, brilliant, and clever man. That is now part of the public opinion of England; and no power in heaven or on earth will ever change it. I may dodder and dote; I may pot-boil and platitudinize; I may become the butt and chopping-block of all the bright, original spirits of the rising generation; but my reputation shall not suffer: it is built up fast and solid, like Shakespear's, on an impregnable basis of dogmatic reiteration.

Unfortunately, the building process has been a most painful one to me, because I am congenitally an extremely modest man. Shyness is the form my vanity and self-consciousness take by nature. It is humiliating, too, after making the most dazzling displays of professional ability, to have to tell people how capital it all is. Besides, they get so tired of it, that finally, without dreaming of disputing the alleged brilliancy, they begin to detest it. I sometimes get quite frantic letters from people who feel that they cannot stand me any longer.

Then there are the managers. Are *they* grateful? No: they are simply forbearing. Instead of looking up to me as their guide, philosopher, and friend, they regard me merely as the author of a series of weekly outrages on their profession and their privacy. Worse than the managers are the Shakespeareans. When I began to write, William was a divinity and a bore. Now he is a fellow-creature; and his plays have reached an unprecedented pitch of popularity. And yet his worshippers overwhelm my name with insult.

These circumstances will not bear thinking of. I have never had time to think of them before; but now I have nothing else to do. When a man of normal habits is ill, everyone hastens to assure him that he is going to recover. When a vegetarian is ill (which fortunately very seldom happens), everyone assures him that he is going to die, and that they told him so, and that it serves him right. They implore him to take at least a little gravy, so as to give himself a chance of lasting out the night. They tell him awful stories of cases just like his own which ended fatally after indescribable torments; and when he tremblingly inquires whether the victims were not hardened meat-eaters, they tell him he must not talk, as it is not good for him. Ten times a day I am compelled to reflect on my past life, and on the limited prospect of three weeks or so of lingering moribundity which is held up to me as my probable future, with the intensity of a drowning man. And I can never justify to myself the spending of four years on dramatic criticism. I have sworn an oath to endure no more of it. Never again will I cross the threshold of a theatre. The subject is exhausted; and so am I.

Still, the gaiety of nations must not be eclipsed. The long string of beautiful ladies who are at present in the square without, awaiting, under the supervision of two gallant policemen, their turn at my bedside, must be reassured when they protest, as they will, that the light of their life will go out if my dramatic articles cease. To each of them I will present the flower left by her predecessor, and assure her that there are as good fish in the sea as ever came out of it. The younger generation is knocking at the door; and as I open it there steps spritely in the incomparable Max.

For the rest, let Max speak for himself. I am off duty for ever, and am going to sleep.

INDEX

Of plays, playwrights, and chief performers

PRINTED IN GREAT BRITAIN
AT THE UNIVERSITY PRESS, OXFORD
BY VIVIAN RIDLER
PRINTER TO THE UNIVERSITY